A Protestant Speaks His Mind

A Protestant
Speaks His Mind

by
ILION T. JONES

Philadelphia

THE WESTMINSTER PRESS

Library of Congress Catalog Card No. 60–5095

PRINTED IN THE UNITED STATES OF AMERICA

Contents

Preface

Tensions between Protestants and Roman Catholics in our country have been slowly building up for the last thirty years, or since Al Smith, a Roman Catholic, was a candidate for the presidency of the United States in 1928. They have been increasing in intensity for the last ten years, or since the World Council of Churches came into being in 1948. The appearance of that organization dramatically focused the attention of Protestants upon the possibility of all the churches of Christendom, including the Roman Catholic Church, uniting into one universal, or ecumenical, body. Immediately thereafter differences and similarities between Protestants and Roman Catholics began to be discussed in an increasing number of books and journals.

In 1948, another organization, Protestants and Other Americans United for Separation of Church and State (POAU), was created to center the attention of the American people upon the organized effort of the Roman Catholic hierarchy to break down the wall of separation between church and state in America and to make this country a Catholic state. The work of this organization has publicized the basic conflicts between the two religious bodies.

Within the last two years there has emerged on a national scale a campaign to nominate again a Roman Catholic as a candidate for the presidency. This campaign has turned loose a veritable flood of discussion of the Protestant–Roman Catholic problem in the newspapers, magazines, and other media of public com-

7

munication. Therefore, we can expect tensions between the two groups to reach a high pitch of intensity by 1960.

Another factor of unique social significance has recently appeared on the American scene, possibly as an outgrowth of the events just mentioned. Secular organizations are taking the lead in conducting public discussions in which the Protestant–Roman Catholic problem is being aired and publicized. In May, 1958, the first of a series of interfaith conferences in which this problem is to play an important role, was held under the auspices of the Fund for the Republic. In November, 1958, a three-day conference on Religion and the Face of America, in which aspects of this same problem were discussed, was held at Asilomar, California, under the direction of the Extension Department of the University of California, Berkeley. Interfaith conferences of this nature, which are expected to increase in number in the next few years, will center attention on this problem and make it necessary for Protestants to reconsider and reformulate their distinctive beliefs.

With the present American situation in mind, I have prepared this book for Protestants. My intentions are to provide them with historical, Biblical, theological, and factual information on which to make a comparison of the beliefs and practices of the two groups and of the political implications of the same. Specifically, my purposes are: to acquaint the average Protestant reader, ministerial and lay, with the nature of the issues between Protestantism and Roman Catholicism; to identify, clarify, and evaluate these issues; to submit information that is essential to a proper understanding and a well-rounded discussion of the subject; to stimulate the reader to further study and refer him to source material for that purpose; and to offer some suggestions as to the possible contributions Protestants can make to peaceable living together in our free American society.

ILION T. JONES

San Anselmo, California

Chapter I

The Irenic Movement

One of the estimable by-products of the ecumenical movement is the friendly, sympathetic attitudes being shown by Protestants and Roman Catholics toward each other and the conciliatory spirit in which they are discussing and comparing each other's beliefs. Until recently this has been mostly unofficial and unorganized. However, an organized movement known as the Irenic Movement has recently appeared in Europe. Small groups of members of Protestant, Roman Catholic, and Orthodox churches, dedicated to the task of preparing the way for a united church, meet together for friendly exchange of ideas in a spirit of understanding and love. The movement was briefly explained to American readers in an article entitled "The Third Hour: The Ecumenical Spirit and Christian Fellowship," by Maria Fuerth Sulzbach, in *Religion in Life,* Summer, 1955.

A corresponding American movement was launched at a luncheon in New York City in the fall of 1957 when the Fund for the Republic announced a new research project, "Religion in a Democratic Society." The expressed purposes of the project were to discover reasons for the tensions among the religious groups in the United States and to devise new bridges of understanding and harmony among Americans of all religious faiths. These purposes are to be sought through a series of conferences in which Protestant, Roman Catholic, and Jewish leaders gather around a table and talk their problems out. A report of the first of these conferences appeared in *The Christian Century,* May 28, 1958 (p. 638).

The report described the meeting as the " beginning of civil dialogue " between the three religious groups and stated that such dialogue is the best means of achieving " coexistence." So a new expression, " coexistence through civil dialogue," was coined at the meeting, an expression that will undoubtedly become the slogan for similar conferences throughout the country in the near future.[1]

In this connection mention should be made of one other American organization with a somewhat similar purpose but with different methods, which has been in operation for a number of years. This is the National Conference of Christians and Jews. This movement originated outside the organized churches, although it is participated in by individual members of Protestant, Jewish, and Roman Catholic churches.

The organization has devoted itself almost solely to the task of creating good will among the three constituent religious groups. To this end it has promoted the annual American Brotherhood Week on an interfaith basis, with representatives of the three religious groups participating. An effort is made during this week to induce people to sign the following commitment: " I pledge allegiance to the basic ideal of my country — fair play to all. I pledge unto my fellow Americans all the rights and dignities I desire for myself."

The participants in the movement try to create good will and oppose religious bigotry. All public mention of the main areas of conflict between the religious groups is scrupulously avoided, and none of the fundamental beliefs of the groups is ever questioned. Hence, it makes no attempt to reconcile differences of opinion or to find common ground or to bring about unity among the groups.

The organization has been growing rapidly, operates on a national scale, has the support of many wealthy patrons, and is quite influential especially in business and professional men's organizations throughout the country. Without doubt this group has played an important part in producing an irenic spirit among certain segments of the American religious population. But it has had no official connection with the ecumenical movement — has, in fact, operated on the edges of that movement.

Wholly apart from these formally organized movements, both Protestant and Catholic writers have, for a number of years, been engaged in an examination of each other's beliefs in a conciliatory spirit. This should be thought of as a phase of the Irenic Movement, although it has been purely voluntary and unorganized.

Some Protestants and Catholics are participating in these activities for the same purposes. Both are concerned about the divisions among Christians, and both are hoping that sympathetic understanding of each other's beliefs will ultimately result in a united Christendom. But the two groups do not mean the same thing when they use the term "united." Most Protestants are thinking of a common-denominator church attained by negotiation, compromise, and the give-and-take of democratic debate. Most Catholics are thinking of all other Christians reuniting with the Roman Catholic Church just as it is, without modification or alteration.

The purpose of this chapter is to make a study of this irenic phase of the ecumenical movement with a view to ascertaining the similarities and differences between Protestant and Roman Catholic purposes and motives and to discover what the prospects of the two groups' getting together are.

PROTESTANT ECUMENISM

Protestants are responsible for the beginning of the ecumenical movement and have been the dominating influence in every phase of its growth. The movement, developing slowly to begin with, but increasing in extent and influence rapidly in recent years, attained one of its major goals in the organization of the World Council of Churches in 1948. Ecumenicity among the churches parallels the effort of the nations to devise some form of unity in a world of diversity of cultures. What a United Nations is trying to achieve politically among the nations, a "United Churches" is trying to achieve religiously among the churches. Parenthetically, it may be said that to a larger degree than is ordinarily realized the success of the former depends upon the success of the latter.

The unnecessary and unbrotherly divisions among the churches of Christendom, their overemphasis upon secondary and peripheral matters, their wasteful competitive efforts and institutions, their lack of co-operation for common purposes and objectives, their failure to make a united impact upon secular institutions of the social order in which they function — these are some of the main reasons why the movement for a better unity among the churches has gained such momentum. There is little or no disagreement about the need and the desire for this unity, but only about the kind of unity that should be sought and that has any possibility of being attained in our religiously pluralistic America (and world).

1. *The Psychology of Protestant Ecumenism.* As the movement has developed, several deep-rooted emotions have developed alongside it within Protestants and have played a prominent role in it.

A giant guilt complex over the ancient and persistent divisions among Christians has grown up among Protestants. Sooner or later in every book written by a Protestant dealing with any phase of the church's life and work, the author's deep sense of guilt over these divisions is certain to be revealed. Divisions are condemned in the strongest language available and in the spirit of the ancient prophets pronouncing divine judgment upon the world. These divisions are declared to be scandalous, an offense to God, a betrayal of Christ, irreconcilable with the will of God, the church's besetting sin that is preventing it from performing its divine functions in the world.

This guilt complex has produced an agonizing yearning for unity that has all but become an obsession with many Protestants, so much so, that it has become an inner compulsion that is consuming all their time and energies and is their principal objective. They are in a great hurry to get the job of a united Christendom done. No time must be lost. They give the impression that unity must be achieved quickly and at all costs.

Concurrently a strong conviction has arisen among Protestants that a united church must and ultimately will include the Roman Catholic Church. Hence they are intent on finding — incited by an ardent desire to find — some way to persuade Rome to join the ecumenical movement. They doggedly persist in making overtures of one kind or another, directly or indirectly, to Rome. Repeatedly ignored or repelled, they have refused, like a rejected suitor, to accept " no " for an answer.

2. *Protestant Kindliness Toward Catholics.* These emotions just described have combined to generate among Protestants an immoderate kindliness toward Roman Catholics and all things connected with them and their church. This attitude is expressed in a variety of ways.

Protestants are taking advantage of every opportunity to list the things Catholicism and Protestantism have in common, to acknowledge their indebtedness to the Roman Church, to compliment it and its activities and policies, to understand its theological positions sympathetically, to introduce their fellow Protestants to Catholic practices, customs, and beliefs, and to avoid saying anything that Catholics would consider critical or that might conceivably injure their feelings. At the same time, they quickly take to task their fellow Protestants who write articles containing objective evaluations of Roman Catholic beliefs and practices.

A case in point is a paper entitled " The Marian Cult," written by Dr. John A. Mackay, at the time president of Princeton Seminary, for and adopted by the 1955 General Assembly of the now United Presbyterian Church. The paper was a dispassionate, objective, factual, and scholarly explanation and evaluation of the Roman Catholic teaching about the Virgin Mary. In the summer of 1955 both *Presbyterian Life* (June 11) and *The Christian Century* (June 29) reprinted the paper. In subsequent issues both magazines published letters of protest from Protestant readers about the article. The writers of these letters did not challenge the accuracy of the facts, or disagree with the truths in the article, but simply objected to the author's publicly criticizing Roman

Catholic beliefs. Yet the teaching of the Roman Church about the Virgin Mary is a matter of open record, has in fact been published, widely distributed, and commented on in newspapers and magazines for several years, especially since the Marian Year, 1954. A writer of one letter declared that the article was likely to " sabotage " current efforts to bring about a better understanding among Protestants and Catholics.[2] That is to say, a kindly attitude toward Catholics must take precedence over a discussion of facts.

A similar attitude is now manifested quite commonly in group conversations. If anyone in a Protestant group refers to Roman Catholic beliefs or practices with which he disagrees, someone else is likely to come to the instant defense of the Catholics and to protest against stirring up religious strife by airing such views. The one thing that provokes the quickest objection from many Protestants is the mention that some public official is a Roman Catholic and that this has some bearing upon his qualifications for office. These attitudes are especially common among Protestant young people. Even in Protestant educational institutions, including theological seminaries, some students and professors resent any references in classrooms, in public utterances, and in publications to the existence of a Roman Catholic–Protestant problem. In short, saying anything except something complimentary about Roman Catholics is becoming a taboo, being debarred by social usage, in certain Protestant circles.

A curious new method of comparing Protestantism and Roman Catholicism is appearing so often in Protestant books as to become noticeable. The principle seems to be that one should never criticize adversely anything in Catholicism without at the same time criticizing adversely something comparable in Protestantism. And often in the comparison Protestantism is made to appear worse than Catholicism. This is a negative irenicism, an irenicism in reverse, an impartial measuring out of blame to all groups alike.

In the midst of his treatment of the subject of church organization, Daniel Jenkins compares Protestant and Catholic practices thus:

> Clerical domination, expressed in the cult of the popular preacher or of the minister as the managing director of the church's affairs, is nearly as widespread in some Protestant churches as it is in Catholicism, with fewer safeguards against personal eccentricities and the arbitrary use of power. . . . [Some Protestant churches] suffer from an aggressive laicism which is at least as deadly as aggressive clericalism.[3]

When Walter M. Horton is dealing with Roman Catholic Mariology, he declares:

> If Catholics need to be made aware of the danger of idolatry in the veneration of the virgin and the saints, Protestants need to be made aware of the danger of reverting, through fear of idolatry, to a bare austere Old Testament piety, in which the joyful New Testament sense of " God with us " would be lost. . . . If there is idolatry in Catholic Mariology, there is a worse idolatry . . . at the root of Protestant sectarianism.[4]

In criticizing Paul Blanshard's books on Roman Catholicism, Robert McAfee Brown says:

> One wonders whether it would be worse to live in a country dominated by the Catholic mentality Blanshard describes or the Blanshard mentality he embodies. His writings have so alienated sincere Catholics that it has become immeasurably harder to engage in creative interfaith communication.[5]

William S. White, the well-known Washington correspondent, refers to this same tendency in Washington politics. He describes it as a mistaken notion of " objectivity," a " careful — indeed a meticulous — measuring out of absolutely evenhanded credit and blame to this man as against that, or to this movement as against another." He asserts that this sometimes puts " a curious veil over great and harsh issues," that it tends " to lump men and causes into some large and shapeless generality rather than to separate them for what they are — what each is, and each alone." Then he asks, "Is this not a national and not merely a Washington failure?" The answer is, of course, that this tendency is becoming a national weakness. Whatever the intention of those who use this procedure, its end effects are both to avoid and to cloak important issues.[6]

3. *Protestant Concessions to Catholicism.* The reader of Protestant books now coming off the presses soon has to accustom himself to the increasing number of concessions being made to Roman beliefs. Protestants have not waited for Roman Catholics to join them in choosing a common meeting place. On their own initiative they have chosen the ancient undivided church as such a place. To make their approaches more enticing, or as a sort of pledge in advance of their earnestness, they have indicated to what extent they are willing to modify their own beliefs, or to accept Roman beliefs, in order to induce Rome to agree to begin conversations toward union.

In succeeding chapters it will be explained how far some Protestants have moved in the direction of the Roman Catholic doctrines of the church, of the hierarchical sacerdotal priesthood, of polity, and of tradition. A number of writers have recently called attention to the veneration now being given to the Virgin Mary in certain Protestant circles. As a result of the liturgical movement there are large groups of Protestants who are promoting the use of sacramentals and ways of devotion that have previously been confined to Roman Catholicism. Monasticism is coming back rapidly in certain Protestant quarters, especially in Anglicanism.

Charles Boyer, a Roman Catholic author, who bases his hopes for a return of the separated churches to Rome partly on the changes that are taking place in Protestant thinking, specifically mentions the following changes: (*a*) the return to the cloistered life; (*b*) the recognition of the authority of tradition alongside the authority of the Scriptures; (*c*) the turning toward Rome on the part of the Anglo-Catholics; and (*d*) the recognition of the spiritual authority of the pope and of his place of honor and responsibility in the church universal.[7]

Roman Catholic theologians express delight but also amazement at the rapidity with which Protestants are moving closer and closer to historic Roman theology. The author just quoted enthusiastically declares:

> We can consider the present division between Protestantism and Catholicism as no more than the burdensome legacy of history. Are we not justified in hoping that many will refuse to bear the yoke of the past any longer, a yoke fashioned by the decisions of a few willful men of earlier centuries and for reasons that have now lost their cogency? [8]

4. *Protestant Optimism.* Another characteristic of the ecumenism of many Protestants is their optimism. In some instances this optimism is cautious because it is based upon developments taking place within certain areas of the Catholic Church that are being permitted but have not yet been approved by the Vatican. Therefore, the understandings between Protestants and Catholics that are envisaged as a result of these developments are at present mere *possibilities.* This type of optimism is found in Ernest B. Koenker's book *The Liturgical Renaissance in the Roman Catholic Church.*[9]

Koenker's book is an invaluable and illuminating study of the liturgical movement in the Roman Catholic Church. The purpose of his study is to show that the leaders of the movement are motivated by and actually putting into practice some evangelical beliefs that *could,* if allowed to continue, reform the church from within. He concludes his book with this optimistic summary:

> A climate of opinion appears to be forming in Rome conducive to the reform of the calendar and breviary, and, ultimately, the missal. The movement may go on to personalize, to individualize, and to Christianize the sacraments and sacramentals in such a way that the old magic sacramentalism of the Roman Catholic Church will be completely overcome. A new, evangelical spirit may be infused into the relationship between priest and people and their bishop; even the concept of the

papacy may be spiritualized and Christianized. If the renaissance can continue unhindered, there may be a new " Liturgical Springtime " of the Roman Catholic Church — an awakening, the importance of which many would not now dream. (P. 201.)

Being also well aware that the liturgical movements in the Protestant churches are, on the other hand, moving in the direction of Roman liturgical practices, he is enthusiastic about the possibilities of the liturgy paving the way for a Protestant *rapprochement* with Rome. (Pp. 181 ff.)

But for two reasons Koenker does not permit himself to do wishful thinking about the possibilities in the situation becoming actualities any time soon. These reasons are: (1) The pope has not yet given the leaders of the Roman liturgical movement official permission to go ahead with the changes they are now experimenting with on their own initiative; and (2) while he feels that the " irenic men in the liturgical apostolate who emphasize common ground deserve our love and gratitude," he also recognizes that " at times they arouse unfounded hopes " and "emphasize the fact that they are not representative of the hierarchy and the Holy See " (p. 194). So he forces himself to remember that the fate of this, as of all other reform movements in the Catholic Church, depends upon what the Vatican finally says about it. While discussing this aspect of Catholicism early in his book, he quotes Friedrich Heiler as saying:

> Contemporary Catholicism conceals within its bosom strong, promising currents of strength. But whoever knows Rome fears and trembles for them; whoever remembers the sad fate of so many promising movements in the Catholic Church cannot give way to any high hopes. The great, wide, Catholic idea has no protectress in Rome. (P. 21.)

The optimism of other Protestants is less restrained. Their optimism in large part grows out of the assumption and expectation that, since Protestants are willing to make concessions, compromises, and changes in order to achieve a united church, Roman Catholics can be counted upon to do likewise. These Protestants are aware of the difficulties and complexities of the problem, but they seem to feel certain that all obstacles can be removed and that the ecumenical church will assuredly come into being if kindly and patient negotiations continue long enough and if there is sufficient give-and-take on the part of both groups. So they are discussing changes they are willing to make and changes Rome must also make to ensure a united church, while they try zealously to envision the kind of church we are going to have when a modified Roman Catholicism and a modified Protestantism finally coalesce.

The position of two Protestant authors can be cited to illustrate this kind of optimism:

a. John Knox, whose position is found in a book referred to later in another connection, *The Early Church and the Coming Great Church*.[10] After expressing his willingness to accept certain beliefs in a form that might be acceptable to Rome, in order to bring about union with it, he specifies five things that the Roman Catholic on his part must do to achieve the same end: (1) The Catholic must be ready to acknowledge the validity and adequacy of the free churchman's ground for accepting the episcopacy (p. 144). (2) He must admit the "evangelical" distinction between the essential Spirit of the New Testament church and the forms that the later church developed (p. 146). (3) He must give "recognition in the united church to certain values in primitive Christianity which have been preserved and nurtured in denominations of the conciliar or congregational order" (p. 147). (4) He must "be more eager than he has often been to welcome fresh manifestations of the Spirit both in preaching and in worship" (p. 147). (5) He must not define the priestly significance of the ministry "so as to deny, theoretically or in practice, the freedom of access of the Christian man to the grace of God in Christ" (p. 148). He labels these five items "things of the Spirit" and says that they must be given precedence over ancient forms (p. 148).

He does not make clear how the Roman Catholic Church with its ancient forms might embody and give precedence to these five "things of the Spirit" that are so precious to evangelical Christians. Nor does he offer reasons why he thinks Rome might be willing to modify its forms in order to do this. Apparently he simply hopes that, like himself, Roman Catholics will be generous enough to make concessions in order to bring about a united church.

b. Geddes MacGregor, whose position is found in his book *The Vatican Revolution*.[11] In some ways MacGregor has made one of the most daring proposals yet devised by a Protestant ecumenist. His book is a study of the Vatican Council of 1870, at which the pope was declared infallible. He undertakes to prove three things, though not in this sequence: (1) Throughout medieval times the legal authority of the Roman Catholic Church was vested in the ecumenical councils. (2) Although the Roman Church is hierarchically organized, it is actually a "corporation," which, properly understood, is a form of democracy. (3) The Vatican Council of 1870 was not a true general (ecumenical) council of the church. Its declaration of the pope's infallibility was therefore illegal or unconstitutional from the viewpoint of medieval Roman Catholic law and practice.

What is his purpose in trying to establish these theses? That is stated early in his book:

If it could be shown . . . that the triumph of the papalist party in 1870 was an illegal triumph and that the opposition had law and history on its side, the prospect of a richer, purer, reunited Christendom would be much brighter. (P. 10.)

Precisely what does he mean by that? Simply this: if the bishops and laymen of the modern Roman Catholic Church would and could recover its essential medieval (conciliar) democracy, Protestants might find a sufficiently democratic Roman Church with which they could unite. At least he is convinced that "the only hope for eventual co-operation and friendship" with Rome lies in Rome itself recovering its democracy. (P. 152.)

In his discussion MacGregor anticipates certain questions from his Protestant readers, although he does not actually formulate them. For example, what about the Protestant doctrine of the authority of the New Testament church rather than the authority of church tradition and councils? He answers this question by referring to what is now commonly being said about the ancient church's antedating and getting along without the New Testament. " The earliest epistle in the New Testament," he observed, " was not written till nearly twenty years after the crucifixion," and if " all the apostles were dead before the New Testament was compiled in its present form," then " it can hardly be said that the New Testament has always been the indispensable rule of faith for every Christian " (pp. 81–82). In other words, if councils were as important as — or more important than — the New Testament once, they can be so again.

Again, how can you expect Protestants to accept the pope? He states frankly that he does not object to the pope as such. If the church were led by a " constitutional papacy in which the pope spoke as the mouthpiece of the church by the authority he derived from it " (p. 153), that conceivably might be democratic enough for Protestant Christians.

But what about the infallibility of the pope? He handles this subject adroitly. He thinks there is more than one kind of infallibility. " Not only the Roman Church, but every Christian society," including the New Testament church, " believes in some sense in its own infallibility " (p. 79). At least, every church believes in having God as its ultimate arbiter, and in that sense it possesses " spiritual infallibility." That the pope as the head of the church " shares somehow in the infallibility of the church is self-evident to all who admit that Christ's church is in any way divinely guided from error " (p. 90). Furthermore, " a spirit of humility and repentance is not incompatible with the possession of infallible guidance from the Holy Spirit " (p. 127).

The conclusion to which all of this leads is: Given the right kind of pope as its head, and with the " democratic " operation of a " democratic " ecumenical church back of him, we could conceivably envisage a form of episcopacy, headed by a pope, that would be acceptable to Protestants. Therefore, let the Roman Church restore its medieval democratic ideal, the constitutional rights of the church against the papacy, and " then, it is not inconceivable, the whole texture of the Roman Church might be altered, and her relations to the rest of Christendom immensely modified both to the advantage of Roman Catholics themselves and to other Christians in America and elsewhere who are outside the Roman fold " (p. 154). In effect, this is a pledge to Rome in advance that, if it would do these things, Protestants would accept the Roman Catholic Church as the one united universal church for which they are striving.

It is not certain that church historians will agree with Mac-Gregor's interpretation of the facts about the medieval catholic church. But no one can deny that he has contrived a dramatic and highly interesting proposal.

However, he leaves the reader with several unanswered questions. By what means would the present Vatican be changed from an absolute dictatorship to the form of democracy he envisages? Would it be by a peaceful or by a bloody revolution? Is it conceivable that the papacy would entertain any kind of democracy? Who knows whether the bishops themselves, or whether a substantial majority of the faithful, want such a change? By what constitutional methods and on what principles would Roman Catholics go about recovering the constitutional rights that are denied them by their dictator? What evidence is there that any large number of Protestants would agree that the kind of Roman Church he describes is sufficiently democratic to become the pattern for the Christian church? Would the setting up of a conciliar form of government assure the freedom to which Protestants have become accustomed? All these questions are left unanswered. Apparently he assumes that because he, as a Protestant, has so generously offered a way in which Roman Catholics can eliminate a major obstacle in the way of Protestant union with Rome, many Roman Catholics will reciprocate.

With the whole Protestant approach to Rome in this field of

ecumenism now before us, let us ask, "Are Protestants who are counting on the Roman hierarchy to change its theology, its policies, and its practices engaged in wishful thinking?" Perhaps a partial answer to that question can be found as we turn now to a consideration of the Roman Catholic side of the ecumenical picture.

ROMAN CATHOLIC ECUMENISM

For a long time Rome expressed no interest in, indeed expressed opposition to, the ecumenical movement. But Protestant longing for unity has become so intense, and so many Protestants have been giving concrete evidences of being in dead earnest and have made so many more concessions and changes than Rome could have dared to hope for or even dream of only a few decades ago, that at long last Rome has reportedly become greatly interested. At any rate, an increasing number of Catholic books on the subject have been coming off the presses. The contents of four of these books will be given briefly, not that there are many significant differences between them, but that the reader may have cumulative evidence of how leading Roman Catholics in different places are reacting to the movement.

1. *One and Holy*, by Karl Adam.[12] Adam is one of the foremost Catholic theologians in our time. His book consists of lectures delivered in 1947 to a large gathering of the *Una Sancta* movement in Germany. These lectures were addressed primarily to German Lutherans for the express purpose of trying to persuade them that they ought to return to Rome and could do so without giving up anything essential in their own faith.

He joins Protestants in expressing agony over disunity and yearning for unity. He censures the church of Christ for cruelly wounding the body of Christ with "the festering divisions among Christians unhealed," and for the "sin of scandalizing the non-Christian world with a shameful example of faction and conflict" (p. 2). He accepts for himself and other Roman Catholics a share of the blame for these divisions among Christians (p. 98). In a friendly and conciliatory spirit he lays down three basic principles

of reunion from the Roman Catholic viewpoint: (*a*) Each group
must take its own confession seriously. (*b*) Each group must give
itself unconditionally to Christ and his will. (*c*) Both groups,
filled with the love of Christ, must soften the antagonisms and
root out the loveless prejudices that exist between the two
churches (p. 111).

All this gives the impression that Rome, humbled because of
its sins and sense of guilt, is willing to rectify its wrongs, confess
its sins, and do its part to eliminate the barriers between itself
and Protestantism, and to meet Protestants halfway in an effort
to find a basis for union. But not so! Immediately he proceeds to
say:

> Because the Catholic Church knows that she is the one true
> means of salvation, that she is sufficient to herself, that she
> witnesses to herself as Christ's teacher, that she alone among
> all churches has received the totality of the Christian revela-
> tion and alone hands it on, *no* approach to her can be made on
> the basis of bargaining in matters of faith (*in rebus fidei*) and
> effecting compromises, by which she renounced certain truths
> and is conceded others in exchange. Because the truth of Christ
> is one, the church in her teaching must be intolerant to the
> utmost degree, to the very last article of faith. For truth is
> always intolerant. (P. 111.)

Again and again Adam makes it clear that when he speaks of
unity he means reunion with Rome. From this position he never
wavers for even a moment. " To admit even the possibility that
the final union of Christendom could take place other than in
her and through her," he asserts, " would be a denial and betrayal of her most precious knowledge that she is Christ's own
church. For her there is only one true union, reunion with herself." (P. 93.) He quotes Pope Pius XI as saying, "Whoever is not
united with it [the Roman Church] is united neither with the
church nor with Christ who is her head " (p. 96).

In the concluding section of his book, he resumes the humble,
conciliatory attitude with which he began. " We can say with

certainty," he declares, " that if ever a lasting union between the Catholic Church and the Protestant communions were to take place, there would be a giving and receiving of gifts on both sides." (Pp. 126–127.) Then, recognizing the difficulties ahead, he turns to prayer as the only hope for union. God, he says, will open roads to us. He may make us all " descend into the catacombs," that through terror and night we may come to understand and love each other. " If there cannot immediately be unity of faith, let there be at least unity of love," he pleads. (Pp. 129–130.)

This is the characteristic note on which practically all Roman Catholic books on unity end: if we pray long enough, suffer long enough, and through these experiences come to be bound together in heart as brothers and sisters, the final unity of faith will come. And always, always, that unity of faith to them means reunion with the Mother Church. There is not the slightest hint that through prayer and suffering and learning to love others they will be led to yield one iota of their own beliefs, or to make any concessions. What they pray for is not that they may see what they ought to do, but that all separated Christians will see clearly that it is their duty to come back to Rome.

2. *The Christian Dilemma,* by W. H. Van de Pol.[18] Van de Pol is a convert to Catholicism from the Reformed Church of Holland. He addresses himself to his brethren in that church, hoping to persuade them that the unity they seek will be found in the Roman Catholic Church.

He begins in the same way as Adam does. He confesses the guilt all Christians feel because of the dissensions and disunity among Christians. He assumes for the Roman Church its share of the blame for these dissensions. He proposes that Christians substitute friendly inquiry and mutual understanding and respect for controversy as a means to unity. He compares specific Roman Catholic and Protestant beliefs objectively. He has many helpful things to say about the ecumenical movement, especially about the psychological obstacles to union.

But at every stage he sets forth the same general conclusions as does Adam. He asserts that the Roman Catholic Church is the only true church, that it possesses absolute authority, and that every individual human being must submit himself to it without condition. (P. 53.) Catholics cannot engage in conferences, he says, to discuss points on which their church has already made final, infallible pronouncements. They can only provide information concerning those teachings. The idea of reaching "a common understanding" about such matters at a round-table conference is "unthinkable to a Catholic" (p. 59). The Catholic Church cannot have full communion with Protestant Christians until they profess the Catholic faith and return to full sacramental communion with Rome. (P. 264.) The Catholic Church "is not prepared to yield an inch in the matter of her authoritative preaching of the faith" (p. 268). "Never will there be any possibility of compromise or synthesis between the Catholic Church and the rest of Christendom." (P. 276.)

But, he goes on to state, this does not mean that faithful Catholics can do nothing toward unity. They can do penance, pray in secret, fast, sacrifice, and suffer with Protestants while Protestants are doing likewise in preparation for unity. All this spiritual agonizing is for what kind of unity? "Universal return" and "home-coming" of all the schismatics and separatists to the bosom of the Mother Church. (Pp. 284–285.)

3. *One Shepherd: The Problem of Christian Reunion,* by Charles Boyer.[14] Boyer is editor of *Unitas,* the international quarterly review representing the Unitas Association of leading theologians and other representatives of religious orders, organized in Rome with the authority of the pope. Their purpose is to explain and promote the Roman Catholic view of reunion. Generally speaking, he repeats what both Adam and Van de Pol say, the difference being that Boyer's statements can be considered more official than those of the other two writers.

He frankly declares that all conferences and meetings having to do with unity are designed, so far as Catholics are concerned, to prepare for the "return of dissidents to the common faith and their submission to Peter's successor" (p. 58). No Catholic writer has stated the official Roman Catholic attitude toward joint meetings in which unity is discussed more bluntly than has Boyer:

> We cannot expect the church to be guided by the principles of
> the Reformation. For her part, all she asks of Christians sepa-
> rated from her is that they study, recognize, and follow the
> will of Christ, as it is manifested in the sources of revelation.
> She prays and asks others to pray that this work of truth and
> grace may be accomplished. The church enjoins her priests and
> theologians to present on all occasions with competence, char-
> ity, and the greatest possible clarity, the proofs that she was
> founded and is preserved on the rock of Christ's own divine
> will. She also exhorts that light be thrown on incomprehen-
> sion, that confusion be prevented, and prejudice cleared away,
> as these all prevent many souls of good will from seeing her
> true countenance and recognizing her as their mother. Unless
> interfaith conferences, discussions, and meetings serve this end,
> what reason can there be for organizing or even attending
> them? Do our separated brothers expect anything from us ex-
> cept a clearer light on our Catholic faith? (Pp. 64-65.)

In the concluding chapters of the book he addresses himself to
the major non-Catholic churches. He reminds them of what Professor Florovsky said at Amsterdam in 1948: " No genuine ecumenical co-operation, no true Christian community, and no real
reunion of Christians can be achieved unless Rome can be included in it." He declares that both Catholics and non-Catholics
know that Rome cannot change and that " consequently the only
means of including it in the reunion of Christians is to accept the
faith of the church of Rome in its entirety " (pp. 115-116). And,
as with the other books mentioned, the concluding sentences of
the book are a prayer to God for the submission of all Christians
to the one, holy, universal, apostolic Roman Church.

4. *The Catholic Approach to Protestantism,* by George H. Tavard.[15] Tavard is a Roman priest now living in New York City.
Previous to his coming to this country a few years ago, he was

active in the organized Irenic Movement in France. His book is obviously intended to introduce this movement more fully to the American public and to promote its objectives from the Roman Catholic point of view. He speaks for a group of Catholics who believe that colloquies between them and Protestants, carried on with prudence and patience over a long period of time, will ultimately bring Protestants back into the Roman Church.

After quoting and discussing a statement of Hendrik Kraemer, director of the Ecumenical Institute of Bossey, Switzerland, which he feels contains the " basic conception of Protestant ecumenism," he declares flatly:

> Between Catholicism and ecumenical Protestantism we must therefore register that there is, from this standpoint, an unbridgeable gap, an out-and-out difference. They live in spiritual universes that are not compatible. . . . One may perhaps say that a union of opposites is being attempted, hardly easier than a squaring of a circle. (Pp. 78–79.)

Without hesitancy he affirms that when the ecumenical goal has finally been reached the Roman Catholic Church " will have the final role of opening herself to others as the harbor of their wandering and the term of their desire " (pp. 140–141).

As we have already seen, many others have said similar things upon many occasions. The distinctive value of his book is that, to a degree done by few other Roman writers, he openly reveals the methods Roman Catholics are using to guide Protestantism back to Rome. He lists and treats five such methods.

a. The first method is the generating of the appropriate mood in which to make the approach. In harmony with the general positions of the Irenic Movement, which he represents, he asserts that the chief hindrances to unity are not so much religious *truths* as religious *sensibilities*. He thinks Roman Catholics and Protestants are alien to each other because they do not understand or appreciate each other's deepest religious feelings. Their polemics are inspired by mutual irritations, antipathies, prejudices, and distrusts rather than by friendship, charity, and love. He urges his fellow Catholics to remember that unity can be effected by understanding rather than by condemning, and he offers them specific suggestions about how to generate the proper mood in which to approach Protestants. (Pp. 97, 132.)

b. The second method is the making use of the fact that all the churches — Eastern Orthodox, Anglican, Calvinistic, and Lutheran — rightly or wrongly " affirm that they have recovered doctrinal continuity in spite of, and even through, historical breaks " (p. 133) with the undivided church of the early fathers. He insists that there must be developed a group of Catholic scholars and theologians (" patrologists ") who are familiar with the theology of the patristic period and experts at comparing it with Catholic theology of later centuries and with the thought of all Protestant and Anglican theologians.

c. The third method is the convincing of Protestants that Roman Catholic doctrines and Protestant doctrines can be reconciled. This can best be done " among small circles where Catholic and other theologians have opportunity to exchange ideas and survey respective situations and problems " (p. 136). In these small colloquies, meeting regularly, Roman Catholic experts, carefully trained for this highly specialized work, can patiently compare Catholic and Protestant doctrines one by one and show how they may be harmonized.

d. The fourth method is the development of a new type of apostolate: a group of Catholic ecumenists who will " devote their life to spreading the ideas and concerns of the reunion of separated Christians and to encouraging prayer for unity " (p. 136). These apostles should be peculiarly equipped by temperament and training to maintain " a wide range of contacts with Protestantism on the levels of culture and spirituality . . . to acquire the feel of all the impressions, insights, likes, and dislikes that form the subconscious underground of Protestant thinking," and to explain Catholic doctrine to others. In short, they should accept as their vocation the task of making " the church and separated communions mutually understandable " (pp. 150–151). Undoubtedly, Tavard himself is such an apostle.

An important phase of this apostolate is the Catholic "move-ment of prayer," especially the annual " Octave of Prayer " from January 18–25, which parallels the Protestant annual "Universal Week of Prayer for Christian Unity." He expresses the faith, found in the other Catholic books we have considered, that a con-tinuous outpouring of prayer "will create on the face of the earth a spiritual power of cosmic dimensions that will some day be strong enough to break through human pride and reintegrate all Christians in the bosom of the one and only church " (pp. 139–140).

e. The fifth method is contained in a suggestion passed on from Father Mattias Loras that people in the various communities ought to join in " a fellowship of intellectual work," part of which would consist of

> *watching over classbooks, radio and TV programs, movies, and the press in order to purge any text or script that would slant the judgment of the public or sin against Christian charity* [italics mine] and, correspondingly, to assist every positive contribution to religious peace (p. 141).

Plainly stated, this envisages a co-operative campaign among all Christian bodies to censor all media of communication to make sure that nothing that anyone regards as uncharitable or critical of himself or of his religion appears therein.

That is to say, he believes that some such unhurried, persistent, and patient procedures as he has suggested will make Catholic doctrines palatable to Protestants, and Catholic practices familiar to them, thus " preparing a climate of creative peace that will prelude the final reunion of Christians." He enthusiastically joins voice and heart with the advocates of the " happy vision of peace that constitutes the ultimate goal of Catholic as of Protestant ecumenism " (p. 141) — all Christians regathered into the fold of the one, holy, catholic, and apostolic Roman Church, which is the deposit of the faith " once committed to the saints."

An Evaluation of Irenicism

Protestants have yet to look the facts about irenicism squarely in the eye. To do this, they need to ask themselves candidly and answer correctly some such questions as the following:

1. *Are Protestant anxieties about a divided Christendom wholesome and wise?*

The deep-seated sense of guilt among Protestants over the lack of unity among Christians could become morbid. It is producing an unhealthful mental and emotional state that may easily prevent rational behavior. They should somehow purge their souls of this disturbing mood.

The guilt should be analyzed to locate its causes, to discover whether it is real or imaginary, wise or foolish, justifiable or unjustifiable. Once the causes are identified, steps should be taken to eliminate them. Are we upset by the intolerance, hatred, bitterness, and unbrotherliness that have existed so often and so long among some Christians? Let all who have been guilty of these sins confess them, repent of them, and bring forth works that prove their repentance. Are we perturbed by the very existence of division? Division is not intrinsically sinful. It is not necessarily wrong to refuse to conform to beliefs and practices held by the great majority of Christians, to separate from others in order to worship God according to the dictates of one's conscience, or to organize a dissenting group for the purpose of emphasizing and preserving an essential but neglected Christian truth.

Are we agitated because the churches cannot reach an agreement on one particular kind of unity? Unity is not inherently good. There are several kinds of unity, some of which are desirable and some undesirable, some possible and some impossible of attainment, some essentially Christian in principle and some not. Our minds should be clearly made up concerning the kind of unity that is consistent with the peculiar nature of New Testament Christianity. Once that is done we should work for it with all our resources.

Are we disconcerted because Rome makes no response to our

brotherly overtures toward union? Jesus warned his followers to anticipate failure and opposition. He counseled them to keep their hearts free from anger and full of love for all, even their enemies. But he advised them not to be miserable over being unable to make others love them, and to live in peace with them. On one occasion he told them to make every effort to bring about reconciliation with a brother, but in case they failed, to let him "be to you as a Gentile and a tax collector" (Matt. 18:17). That I take to be the practical, common-sense Christian virtue of leaving people alone. If Rome will not negotiate concerning union, Protestants should leave the door open for it to enter any time it chooses, but leave it alone.

Is our disquietude due to the past failures of the church to achieve unity? This generation of Christians should not assume the responsibility for the last fifteen or more centuries of the church's failures. Only God is capable of bearing that heavy load. Anyway, God may be trying, through the negative results of the church's past experiences, to tell it that it has been on the wrong track. Possibly the church of our day needs someone to warn it at this point, as Gamaliel warned his Jewish contemporaries who tried to suppress Christianity, that we might "even be found opposing God!" (Acts 5:39). If that should be our trouble, we need only to harmonize ourselves with God, go along with him instead of fighting against him, to rid ourselves of our guilt complex.

Whatever the reason or reasons for their anxiety, it is foolish for Protestants to continue in a state of near-morbid guilt and frustration over the divisions among Christians. Until that mood is dissipated, the Protestant Church cannot hope to be properly equipped emotionally to make its maximum contribution to whatever ecumenical church is in the offing.

2. *What kind of ecumenical church should Protestants be working for?*

Some Protestants apparently take for granted the fact that God desires and that the gospel requires an organic, structural union of Christian bodies. But sentiment is increasing that the spiritual unity of the New Testament times, which will be described in

Chapter II of this study, when rightly understood and properly implemented in the modern world, is all that is required by the gospel and is sufficient to enable the Christian church to fulfill its divine purpose on the earth.

Christians of the apostolic times were formed into a universal fellowship of those who were " one in Christ ": one in their personal commitment to him as Lord and to his way of life; one in their acceptance of the tasks laid upon them by him; one in their willingness to suffer in order to serve and redeem mankind; one in their manifestations of the fruits of the Spirit in their lives and relationships. Manifestly, to be successful even this kind of unity would require considerable practical co-operation, administratively and otherwise, between large and small groups of Christians. Such co-operation is now taking place among the churches and will undoubtedly increase in the coming years. But the success of this co-operation does not depend upon or require an organic corporate body with rigid uniformity of administrative structure, authority, doctrine, and worship.

The conviction is also mounting among Protestants that an organic union of Christian churches is not possible. In a recent significant book, *The Quest and Character of a United Church,* Winfred E. Garrison gives the history of Christian unity from the New Testament period to the present time. That history proves conclusively that the efforts to achieve unity through uniformity have been tried and have failed " more disastrously and more inevitably than anything else the church has tried to do " (p. 13). After describing the fruitless efforts over the centuries to " produce a solid doctrinal consensus," Garrison asserts:

Only a dreamer or a naïvely optimistic dogmatist can hope that any complete and detailed system of religious belief and behavior will ever be unanimously approved by a world of free and thinking men. (P. 170.) . . . Any who think that theological agreement can now be reached by a few more conferences and commissions and " study groups " may profitably remember that this method has been tried continuously for centuries and that the net result has been the proliferation of diverse opinions now strongly held by devoted and presumably intelligent Christians. (P. 197.) [16]

In his recent book on church unity, *The Christian Tradition and the Unity We Seek,*[17] Albert C. Outler makes this unqualified statement:

There is simply no prospect whatever that we shall reduce the different church traditions to a universal uniformity. (P. 134.)

Such a church, according to any existing pattern, or some other conceivable pattern, is no more possible, and never will be, than a world political organization that seeks to eliminate all variety of customs and capacities, level all distinctions of race and language among peoples, and absorb the responsibilities for governing all local communities.

Furthermore, the desirability of an organic union of the churches is now frequently questioned. The very size of such a church, as the archbishop of Canterbury recently pointed out, would be a danger to freedom. To differ with the majority in a church of that proportions, so the archbishop pointed out, would be hazardous. But it would also be a danger to the church's vitality and spiritual life. The antisacerdotal sects preceding the Reformation, the Salvation Army in our time, and other minority groups, large and small, all of which were once regarded, and some of which are still regarded, as fanatical and heretical, have saved the church from losing or forgetting quietism, pietism, evangelism, missions and the love of God, the doctrines of the Holy Spirit and of the Second Birth, and many of the social implications of the gospel. Even if we could suppress such groups, it would be neither prudent nor Christian to do so. They are essential for the periodic rebirth, regeneration, and revival of the church for its spiritual soundness.

The constituent churches of the National and World Councils of Churches should direct their energies toward improving and increasing the degree of spiritual unity they have already achieved through the ecumenical conferences. There is no valid Christian reason why these conferences should seek a uniformity of theological opinions, of polities, and of forms of worship. But they should and can result in

> more unity, more love, more fellowship, more bearing of one another's burdens, more participation in one another's joys and sorrows, more concerted action in common causes. These things are not merely manifestations of unity: they are constituent elements of the church's unity. (P. 219.) [18]

As a matter of fact, it is now common knowledge that some of the Protestant leaders of the ecumenical movement are saying quite openly that the ecumenical movement has reached a stalemate. They are convinced that organic union of the Protestant churches is not in the picture for the foreseeable future. They assert that for the time being the constituent bodies of the movement should be content to re-examine and give witness to their historic beliefs, and endeavor to understand and appreciate one another's distinctive contributions, while they seek ways of cooperating. That is to say, the time has come to be realistic, to strive for a *unity* that is possible rather than consume energies on a *union* that is impossible. If union of Protestants is unrealistic, then union of Protestants and Roman Catholics is doubly so.

Conceivably a fellowship of this kind could develop to such a degree of intensity that an interchangeable ministry and membership, intercommunion, co-operative agencies along educational, missionary, and benevolent lines would be possible, yet leave complete freedom of organizational structure, doctrine, and worship. This is substantially the kind of unity Garrison proposes in his recent book as the goal of Christianity.

The delegates to the Oberlin Conference of 1957 drafted a Message to the Churches of North America in which they made seven statements describing the nature of the unity we should seek. Two statements deal with unity of faith. While these were quite general, they seemingly embody the old concept of unity of uniformity. One statement speaks of worship in the somewhat general phrase, "a unity in adoration." Three statements definitely refer to a unity of a different kind:

> A unity of bearing one another's burdens and sharing one another's joys. . . . A unity in mission to the world. . . . A unity possessing rich variety in worship, life, and organization.

Still another reads:

> A unity in which every ministry is a ministry of and for all the members, bound together in a worshiping and sacramental community.

Although the last statement is not entirely clear, it seems to endorse the policy of an interchangeable ministry. As a whole, therefore, the portion of the Message dealing specifically with the nature of unity seems to open the way for a frank acceptance of diversity as a fundamental principle of unity.

A public declaration by Protestants that their goal is a unity of diversity, of spirit, of purpose, and of service would clarify the issues between the various Protestant bodies as well as between Protestantism and Roman Catholicism. Some such declaration would release the energies of Protestants for a concerted effort for the development of the only kind of unity that is possible or desirable. At the same time, it would apprise the Roman Catholics of the only basis upon which ecumenical conversations with them could take place. Would not this prevent all talk of union with Rome? It would undoubtedly stop all talk of organic union with Rome. But it would not necessarily prevent efforts to find ways of co-operating with Rome on projects of other kinds.

3. *What is the judicious and Christian attitude toward the kindliness that now so generally characterizes religious discussions?*

There can be no doubt that kindliness deserves an important place in the list of Christian graces. But it is not an unqualified virtue, independent of all others. In short, it is not absolute. Every Christian virtue must be balanced up with other virtues; otherwise it runs the risk of becoming a wrong or an untruth. This is true even of love, the greatest of the graces. Love that does not include justice, judgment, and discipline is weak and ungodlike. Psychiatrists, psychologists, and educators are now recognizing that kindness in the training of children and youth becomes an unkindness to them if not accompanied by firm discipline. Similarly, tenderness in religious discussion does harm if it prevents a frank discussion of facts or an adequate defense of truth.

The immoderate kindliness that Protestants are manifesting toward Roman Catholics has been doing that very thing. With the best of intentions Protestants are becoming parties to an unofficial but hazardous form of censorship. Their desire not to hurt the feelings of their Catholic brethren is unwittingly a refusal to face the real issues involved in Protestant–Roman Catholic relations. This can be illustrated by what happened at and following the meeting of the Central Committee of the World Council of Churches at New Haven in August, 1957.

One of the items considered by that Committee was the suppression of religious liberty in Colombia, a country that is predominantly Roman Catholic. The facts about this suppression have been well publicized in recent years, and yet it has not ceased. So an effort was made to get the Central Committee, which was made up of 165 representatives of Protestant, Anglican, and Orthodox churches in 50 countries, to make a strong pronouncement about conditions in Colombia. But after considerable debate it was finally decided not to speak "too roughly" about the situation. In fact, the Committee decided not to speak specifically about Colombia at all, but to speak in general terms about the need of making a study of "the problem of religious liberty arising in Roman Catholic and other countries." By this means they hoped to avoid offending Roman Catholics and jeopardizing ecumenical approaches to them.

Yet, when this cautiously worded — temperate, moderate, conciliatory — statement was made public, it was immediately attacked by the National Catholic Welfare Conference in an article published by *The New York Times,* which claimed that the discussions and pronouncement of the Central Committee of the World Council had done " great damage to Catholic-Protestant relationships throughout the world." This statement by the Catholic group was so unfair that Henry P. Van Dusen, president of Union Theological Seminary, New York City, chairman of the Division of Foreign Missions of the National Council of Churches, who had recently visited Colombia and had on-the-spot information about what was happening there, wrote a letter to the editor of the *Times* stating the facts about the situation in Colombia that were back of the pronouncement of the Committee. The *Times* refused to publish the letter on the ground that such " religious matters are not discussed in our ' Letter ' column." The editor of that newspaper has been making a heroic fight in recent years for freedom of the press. But in this instance he betrayed freedom of speech by giving only one side, and that a distorted side, of an important issue. All of this was done in the name of kindliness.

Incidentally, more damage was done Catholic-Protestant relations in the United States by this roundabout censorship than could possibly have been done by a straightforward airing of the facts. No service is ever rendered any cause by a suppression of facts or a refusal to hear both sides of a question.

The trouble about trying to eliminate all so-called unfair statements from a public discussion of religious issues is the difficulty of determining who is to classify the statements. Is everything to be eliminated that anyone regards as unfair to him and his point of view? If so, anyone disposed to do so could prevent a free and fair discussion by labeling as uncharitable an appraisal of any of his beliefs.

That is exactly what many Roman Catholics are continually trying to do. This is illustrated by an incident that took place in Kansas City in the summer of 1956. Glenn L. Archer, a prominent Protestant lawyer, who is executive director of Protestants and Other Americans United for Separation of Church and State (POAU), delivered an address before eight thousand Southern Baptist messengers at their national convention in that city. His address was a calm, carefully documented analysis of current threats to the American principle of separation of church and state by the policies of the Roman Catholic Church. His address was unfairly attacked in the daily press by the Catholic archbishop of Kansas City, Edwin V. O'Hara, who did not hear the address.

At the request of Protestant leaders in the city, Mr. Archer returned later to reply to the archbishop. Shortly before the opening of the meeting at the Second Presbyterian Church, where Archer spoke to a crowded house, two policemen arrived and announced they were there to keep watch on an " agitator from out of town." Indignant protests were made to public officials about the presence of these policemen at the meeting. The next day (August 27) the *Kansas City Times* reported that the policemen were sent to the meeting at the suggestion of a Mr. Gremley, a Roman Catholic, who is the executive director of the Kansas City Commission on Human Relations. According to the newspaper, Gremley had reported to police headquarters that " a troublemaker was coming in from out of town, and it might be well to have some men there."

This episode raises questions of serious import. Here an attempt was made to censor a public meeting in a Protestant church in which something was sure to be said with which Roman Catholics would not agree and which they could easily label unkind and undesirable from their point of view. Unfortunately, this incident does not stand alone. It is one of a series of incidents that prove that the Roman Catholic hierarchy is engaged in a censorship effort of major proportions. Earlier in this chapter attention was called to the fact that, as one main project of the Irenic Movement, which he represents, Father Tavard suggested a cooperative campaign to censor all media of communications to make sure nothing that anyone regards as a " sin against Christian charity " appears therein. Roman Catholics now have such a censorship campaign in full swing across the country.

The campaign is carried on in two main ways. First, every criticism of the Roman Catholic Church of whatever nature and for whatever purpose by anyone is, by them, labeled as " prejudice," "uncharitable," "religious bigotry," "offensive," or "unbrotherly." Secondly, pressures are brought to bear upon newspapers and magazines, publishers, booksellers, radio and television stations, to see that all such statements do not occur. These pressures often take the form of mass telephone calls, letters of protest, and sometimes threats of boycott. These telephone calls are now described by some TV stations as "bigot calls," since all protest in the same language against what is labeled "bigotry." When it was announced that Paul Blanshard was scheduled to appear on a program over station WABD (New York) early in 1957, 187 "bigot calls" came in before the program and 250 after the program.

By these methods Roman Catholics have sometimes prevented the public from reading or hearing a discussion of their church's beliefs and practices. One of the outstanding examples of this Roman Catholic censorship is the story of the manner in which the hierarchy of that church succeeded in preventing the newspapers, bookstores, libraries, and publishers of the country from advertising, reviewing, purchasing, or even accepting as a gift, copies of the first edition of Paul Blanshard's *American Freedom and Catholic Power*.[19] In spite of this censorship, more than a quarter of a million copies of the book were sold.

Roman Catholics are thus taking advantage of a so-called charitable spirit among religious groups to silence their critics and to prevent an honest discussion of the issues between them and other bodies. Is this use of Christian good will legitimate? Should the irenic spirit be used for any such ulterior purpose? Did Christ intend that his gospel of love become a tool for destroying free discussion of the truth?

Pope Pius XII issued an encyclical on September 8, 1957, asking for social and moral censorship of movies, radio, and television. He called upon both industry and the state to co-operate with the church to help "these new arts make their proper and natural contribution to the right fashioning of minds." According to the newspaper report of the encyclical, he also called for special " ecclesiastical offices to be set up in every country to co-ordinate Catholic activities in the fields of radio and television." When this encyclical is further implemented in America, as it surely will be soon, the form of censorship just described can be expected to increase rapidly.

Unfortunately, censorship is not confined to utterances about Roman Catholics. Efforts to censor utterances on other religious subjects are all too common. When *The Atlantic Monthly* published an article by Reinhold Niebuhr about Billy Graham, the magazine was deluged with subscription cancellations and Niebuhr received the most violent and disturbing mail of his whole writing career.[20] Frederick C. Grant, the noted New Testament scholar, recently revealed how he had tried without success to redraft certain religious articles that he had written at the request of the editors of a well-known encyclopedia. They failed to satisfy representatives of Jewish and Christian bodies who were appointed to make sure that they contained nothing objectionable to them.[21]

The gravity of the situation is still further underscored by the fact that censorship of public utterances in fields other than religion has such a firm hold on the American people. In an article in *This Week*, October 27, 1957, George Gobel tells about the protests television stations receive from viewers about the jokes used on his programs. Jokes involving various classes of people, of animals, and of birds, and a variety of terms such as " schizophrenic " and " silly," are protested so vigorously as being unfair or unkind to someone or to somebody's pet that television offices now kill all such jokes in rehearsals to avoid injuring somebody's feelings.

In an article in the " Easy Chair " section of *Harper's Magazine*, October, 1957, Leo Rosten describes a similar censorship. In a national contest, sixteen stories were chosen by a panel of illustrious judges as suitable for use in television programs. They were also examined critically by representatives of the television industry and classified as excellent for this purpose. But when they were offered unconditionally to nine producers, all but two of the stories were declined for reasons such as these: "We can't use material which puts the police in a bad light"; "Of course, television can't touch stories about segregation, you understand"; "Unfortunately, each of the cases involves some malpractice of justice which would meet with disapproval from our sponsor" (p. 19).

Early in 1958, *Life* magazine published a series of articles entitled "Crisis in Education." The series was a worthy attempt to give an honest and fair report of the condition of our American school system. The headquarters of the National Association of Secondary School Principals were so incensed at some of the adverse criticisms of schools that they sent letters to twenty thousand members, urging them to threaten to cancel school subscriptions to *Life* and *Time* for being opposed to education.[22]

Letters to editors of magazines in which readers take issue with and attack the authors of articles are commonplace and are to be expected. But the increasing number of letters by readers who object to the writing and the publication of points of view with which they disagree is disturbing.[23]

For several years social scientists at Purdue University have been making a study of what American young people are thinking. The results of their studies were recently published in a book entitled *The American Teenager*.[24] Their investigations revealed, among other things, that an alarmingly high percentage of American youth endorse censorship of books, newspapers, magazines, and other media of communication.

These facts indicate that a wall of censorship has already been built in our country. That wall must be broken through to prevent freedom of speech from being seriously abridged. Protestants are prepared in historic traditions, in principles, in theological convictions, and in practice, to become the spearhead of a campaign for this purpose. They have always believed in "free trade in ideas," to use an expression of Justice Oliver Wendell Holmes. Throughout their history in America they have stood for "open covenants openly arrived at," for complete airing of facts and honest expression of opinion. They have had a long experience in maintaining freedom of speech among themselves, though not without some failures. They have yielded to others the liberties they have asked for themselves. They have worked for all freedoms as consistently as they have for religious freedom on the principle that ultimately all freedoms stand or fall together. They are, therefore, in a highly strategic position to take the lead in a campaign for the preservation of freedom.

This campaign would need to make clear that freedom is both an end and a means. Freedom cannot be attained as an objective unless free discussion is employed as the way to that objective. All media of communication must be kept open to a discussion of issues in all areas of our national life, including religion. There are honest conflicts of convictions and judgments in the field of religion as in the field of politics. It is just as dangerous to our freedom to label religious discussion as bigotry or prejudice as it would be to paste the same label on political discussion. The arbitrary exclusion of religious ideas from the free markets of thought is a form of prejudice. These things Protestants will have to say and keep on saying — to insist upon the right to say — until prejudice against the free flow of religious thought is eliminated, until the behind-the-scenes censorship of religious ideas by newspapers and other media of public discussion has been broken down, until the taboo against religious debate has been dissipated.

Protestants would render a valuable service for which there is pressing need if they would announce to the American people a national policy on irenicism. First, they should express their opposition to a form of irenicism that is actually a cloak for censorship. Such concealed censorship is a sure way to destroy freedom of speech and to prevent open discussion and dissemination of facts. One wonders what will become of freedom of speech if the present misguided wave of good will, designed to be tender with the feelings of everybody, continues unabated. Secondly, they should declare their intention to engage in a sound and discriminating irenicism in which there is a free, frank, and fearless discussion of truth and airing of facts through all media of communication. This is the only attitude that is fair to all concerned, including future generations, and the only attitude that will ensure a safe, secure, and democratic society. There can be little doubt that such a pronouncement would be welcomed by all who believe in freedom to speak, to read, and to hear: by editors of newspapers and magazines, librarians, radio and television stations, book publishers and sellers, and citizens in general, including many Roman Catholics.

4. *On what basis can Protestants engage in fruitful religious conversations with Roman Catholics?*

On the basis that they are met together to discover ways and means of peaceful coexistence. The main purpose of such meetings should not be merely to generate good will. Yet throughout the discussions both groups should be guided by Peter's exhortation, "Always be prepared to make a defense to any one who calls you to account for the hope that is in you, yet do it with gentleness and reverence" (I Peter 3:15). This statement implies that one should also be willing in the same spirit to hear the other person give reasons for his hope. The search for, and the explanation and examination of, truth should always take place "in love" (Eph. 4:15).

Participants in these conversations should meet around the table as equals. The continual declaration by Roman Catholics previous to such meetings that they will not alter their beliefs as a result of the exchange of views, but that they hope ultimately to bring Protestants back into the Roman fold, is not very inviting. Few Protestants relish the idea of carrying on conversations that can move only in one direction and lead only to one predetermined and prearranged goal: accepting the other person's views. All ulterior motives and goals should be eliminated. There should be mutual respect for the convictions and integrity of all who participate.

The expression of opinions should be unrestrained. No effort should be made to avoid or evade issues, to withhold or suppress facts, to censor utterances, to prevent any person from having his opportunity to speak. All should be encouraged to speak their sentiments without aggressiveness and hostility, on the one hand,

and bland, soft talk, on the other. " Men are never so likely to settle a question rightly," said Macaulay, " as when they discuss it
freely."

Or, to put it in a nutshell, it should be understood that they
are met to make an honest, serious, unhampered, clear-cut effort,
without double talk or double-dealing or mental reservations, to
discover where they agree and disagree, what views can be reconciled and what are irreconcilable, where they can work together
for their common good and where they cannot, and what is required of all if they are going to live side by side in peace and
concord.

When the religious controversies of his day were at the height
of their intensity, Richard Baxter, the seventeenth-century Puritan, proposed the following course of action, which might well
become the policy for religious discussions in our day:

> To come as near together as we can possibly in our principles,
> and when we cannot, yet to unite as far as may be in our prac-
> tice, though on different principles; and where that cannot
> be, yet to agree on the most loving, peaceable course in this
> way of carrying on our different practices.

Nothing is gained by saying " ' Peace, peace,' when there is no
peace " (Jer. 6:14). Frank and honest talk about differences that
separate Protestants and Roman Catholics is always best. To side-
step or evade or keep silent about the real differences, or to draft
ambiguous formulas designed to secure a superficial agreement
or an insincere truce, are unworthy, render no good service to the
cause of Christ, and carry the seeds of their own failure.

If peaceful coexistence is attained on a secure and lasting basis,
then both groups must practice tolerance. Religious freedom and
tolerance are interdependent and inseparable. One cannot exist
without the other. If I am to be free, others must tolerate my convictions. If others are to be free, I must tolerate their convictions.
The word " tolerate " can best be aptly defined in negative terms.
To tolerate is to permit by not preventing. Specifically, then, religious freedom means being allowed to profess and practice a faith

without any attempt being made by anyone to hinder or prevent it.

Charlotte Cushman, the noted actress, used to greet her friends at her villa with the words, " This is Liberty Hall: everybody does as I please." Under such conditions, liberty is a farce. Freedom can never be a one-way street or a unilateral agreement. It applies alike to the majority and to the minority. Or, as William Penn used to say, " We must yield the liberties we demand." The unrestrained expression of all sorts of religious opinions can safely be tolerated in America only if all of us adhere to the unwritten agreement to defend to the death the other person's right to profess a faith that we wholly disapprove of.

5. *Are Protestants realistic in expecting union with Rome?*

Much loose talk is going on in Protestant circles to the effect that great changes are taking place in the Roman Church, that the ecumenical movement is making a tremendous impact upon it, that it cannot indefinitely resist its appeal, that in the not-too-distant future it is bound, for its own good, to join our united effort. This talk is engendering false hopes.

There are some laymen and possibly some priests in the Roman Church who are willing to meet Protestants halfway in order to bring about a united Christendom. But they are in no position whatever to influence the official policies of the Roman hierarchy. That official group, headed by the pope, and that group alone, formulates the policies of the Roman Church. And Roman officialdom is not changing. Protestantism is doing all the changing.

Rome is not compromising. As yet, it has conceded nothing. All concessions and compromises thus far made have been made by Protestants. Rome is not coming our way. The ecumenical movement is going down a one-way street in Rome's direction. Any union with it will take place on its terms, not on ours. The sooner the rank and file of our Protestant churches face these bald, hard facts about the status of negotiations with Rome, the better it will be for all Christendom. The time has come for Protestants to speak frankly to one another about these matters.

Protestants who are paying compliments to Rome, engaging in

conciliatory conversations with its representatives, criticizing themselves, compromising their beliefs, changing their practices, and modifying their traditional theological doctrines, in the hope of persuading Rome to reciprocate, thus making an ecumenical church possible, are engaged in wishful thinking. None of these things has yet, or can or will, affect the historic positions of the papacy. One has only to read any good history of the papacy [25] to convince oneself that such a miracle as a reformed, evangelical, democratic papacy is not possible in the foreseeable future.

The Vatican has accommodated itself to the forms of government and the types of rulers and movements that have not threatened its position or interfered with what it claims to be its rights and prerogatives. When forced to do so, it has made the best concordat possible with hostile governments, while it has bided its time, consolidated its forces, and planned its strategy. Any apparent modifications of its positions have been designed to aid in the realization of its goal of a world-wide society subject to its oversight.

The pope is supreme in his church. His power is absolute. As a last resort, he has only to condemn the liberal movements that threaten to lessen his power or limit his authority, and the loyal members of his hierarchy and his faithful subjects, who have sworn allegiance to him, will yield their obedience. Thus far he has succeeded in retaining a strong enough hold on enough people to perpetuate his regime.

We must never forget that Luther intended to reform Rome from the inside, not to start a new church. But he discovered that the only way to secure for the evangelical faith a chance to express itself freely was to separate from Rome. The Roman Catholic Church is stronger now, the Vatican far more efficiently organized and equipped with far more resources, the pope far more entrenched and more popular with the faithful, than in the days of Luther. What valid grounds do modern Protestants have for supposing that they can succeed in doing from the outside what Luther and all associated with him could not do from the inside? Another revolution of major proportions or a world upheaval of some kind, the nature of which cannot now be foretold or foreseen, will be necessary before a union with Rome that is compatible with the evangelical faith is possible. When and how that will occur must be left in the hands of God.

But in the meantime the duty and strategy of Protestants are clear. They should continue friendly conversations with Rome on the bases suggested, remembering always to be as "innocent as doves" but also as "wise as serpents" (Matt. 10:16). They should not permit themselves to imagine that papal policies pursued throughout the centuries, and now well entrenched behind a powerful, closely knit, well-equipped, and well-organized dictatorship, will be modified or surrendered without prolonged and complex internal struggles. They should improve the quality and extent of their unitive and co-operative efforts now being made through the National and World Councils of Churches with the proper ends in view. They should continue to profess, proclaim, and practice their evangelical faith with *enlightened zeal* (cf. Rom. 10:2).

Perhaps we, whom our transcendental different have historicized Judaism. This is surely and be brought deeper Jesus a just than to my and as it would been, and us open a thin in your Jesus, religious and Judaism, the most relation of this but it also essential to an understanding of his

Chapter II
New Testament Christianity

Most of the major issues between Protestantism and Roman Catholicism in our day have their roots in the New Testament. This means two things: First, that these issues grow out of the fact that the two groups interpret the New Testament differently; and secondly, that in many instances these issues can be traced back specifically to the conflict between Judaism and Christianity as that is described in the New Testament.

In order to understand the differences between Protestantism and Roman Catholicism, we must, therefore, make a study of the movement inaugurated by Jesus as it is described in the New Testament documents.

THE CONFLICT BETWEEN JUDAISM AND CHRISTIANITY

The Christian movement originated within Judaism. The appreciation of this fact is essential to an understanding of the New Testament. Jesus was a Jew. He was brought up in the world of ideas found in our Old Testament. He spoke first and primarily to his own people. He recruited his early followers from among his fellow countrymen. The Christian Scriptures were produced for the most part by writers whose minds were saturated with the history, the traditions, the hopes and dreams, that are embodied in the Jewish Scriptures. The Old and New Testaments both move in the same general realm of ideas. No one in any age or place can grasp the true meaning of the gospel without coming to it through the Old Testament. As one scholar puts it, the clue to the understanding of both the mission and the message of Jesus is found in the Old Testament. John Knox goes so far as to say that "the event of Christ is inconceivable in any connection other than the Jewish culture and in the course of Jewish history. Located anywhere else it would have been a profoundly different — indeed another — event." [1]

But even so, there are fundamental differences between Christianity and Judaism. This is recognized by Jewish and Christian scholars alike. From the outset of his public ministry there was open conflict between Jesus' movement and Judaism. The appreciation of this fact is also essential to an understanding of the New Testament.

Differences of opinion quickly arose among the Jews concerning Jesus and his religious movement. Some of the strict Jews regarded his teachings as dangerous and subversive. They soon sensed that if these teachings were accepted, many of their cherished religious beliefs must be discarded or radically revised. So they rushed to the defense of their traditional beliefs by attacking him. They regarded him as a dangerous innovator, opposed him and his movement at every turn, and ultimately succeeded in securing his death. Later, when the followers of Jesus undertook to preach his gospel throughout the Roman Empire, they were violently opposed and persecuted by Jews who shared this point of view.

Fortunately, some Jews became disciples of Jesus, though not all of them with the same degree of enthusiasm. At first, the ardent followers of Jesus did not intend, nor suppose that Jesus himself intended, to organize a separate and competing religious movement. They accepted him as their often-predicted and long-expected Messiah under whose leadership the divine destiny of the Jews would be brought to fulfillment. But at the outset few of this group had an adequate grasp of what this fulfillment would involve. In fact, not until after Jesus' death and resurrection did his followers begin fully to realize the significance of his ministry. As this began to happen, his supporters became divided into two groups that may be labeled conservatives and liberals.

The conservatives sought to make changes either slowly and slightly or not at all. They wanted to save many of their traditional institutions and customs by incorporating them into the new movement. The liberals, on the other hand, were willing to discard or revise old customs and beliefs if necessary in order to carry the teachings of Jesus to their logical conclusions.

Differences of opinion between the two groups grew tense and came to a head when Christian missionaries, who were scattered abroad by persecution, began to preach with amazing success to Gentiles as well as to Jews and to Jewish proselytes. The question then arose, Should Gentiles be required to become Jews in order to become Christians? That is, should they be required to be circumcised and to adopt other Jewish customs as a condition of membership in the Christian fellowship?

These questions were the chief items on the agenda of the council of Jerusalem, which is briefly described in the fifteenth chapter of The Acts. On the surface the decision of the council appears to be a compromise. But actually it was a partial victory for the liberals. The council voted, in effect, that Gentiles desiring to become Christians should be required to adopt only the minimum Jewish practices ordinarily expected of Jewish proselytes. Circumcision was not on the list. (Acts 15:29.) The import of this decision was that Christianity was not a mere sect or phase of Judaism, that it was not to be restricted or tied down to the rites and customs of that religion, but must be given freedom to develop according to its own genius. The council at Jerusalem is, therefore, regarded by many scholars as a turning point in the history of early Christianity. There Christianity ceased to be a Jewish cult and became a universal religion.

From that time on, the tensions between the two groups of Jewish Christians increased and at times developed into open conflicts. The conservatives became known as Judaizers and are referred to here and there in the New Testament primarily as troublemakers. They tried unsuccessfully to perpetuate in Christianity the observances of Jewish customs that were regarded by other Jewish Christians as outgrown. Nevertheless, most of the New

Testament bears either direct or indirect evidence that the Judaizers were active and influential throughout New Testament times.

An outstanding piece of evidence of their activity is Paul's letter to the Galatians. The Judaizers at work in the Galatian churches were successfully persuading Christians to observe Jewish rites in order to become full-fledged Christians. They had attacked not only Paul himself but the gospel he preached. Paul wrote his letter to vindicate both his apostleship and his gospel of justification by faith alone instead of by means of the Jewish ceremonial law. The book of Hebrews was also evoked by the work of the Judaizers. The purpose of the author of this treatise was to explain precisely and in what ways Christianity is superior to Judaism.

Paul soon became the leader of the liberal Jewish Christians. This group was responsible for transforming Christianity into a Gentile religion. They became the dominant force in forming the Christian church and determining its nature. Much of the New Testament was written and used by these early Christians in their teaching and preaching to counteract the effort of the Judaizers to burden the new religion with old Jewish rites and customs. At the same time that they were opposing the Judaizers, they were formulating their own Christian beliefs and developing their own distinctive institutions and customs.

In general, the New Testament documents were written with two basic purposes in mind: to persuade the Jews that Christianity was the fulfillment of their ancestral faith, and to persuade both Jews and Gentiles that Christianity had emerged from its Jewish chrysalis and had become a universal religion, the final religion for all mankind. The writers achieved their purposes by showing how, in the process of fulfilling historic Judaism, Christianity replaced or superseded the older beliefs and institutions with those so different and so much farther advanced as to make Christianity a new religion. When these writings were chosen as the official Christian Scriptures, they were called the *New* Testament to distinguish them from the Jewish Scriptures, which they called the *Old* Testament. The Christian Scriptures were called *new,* not because they were absolutely original, or unrelated to what had been thought hitherto, but because they carried religious truth so far beyond what anyone previously had conceived.

Nor was the new truth a mere natural development or evolution from the old. Rather, it was a jump forward that left a gap between the old and the new. Take, as an example, the New Testament doctrine of the Messiah. New Testament Messianism has a long history, going back through the noncanonical writings of the postexilic period of Judaism and the Old Testament. One cannot understand Christian Messianism apart from that history. But in the alchemy of Christ's mind Jewish Messianism became something of a different order. No one who lived before New Testament times could have predicted what turn that concept would take or what pattern it would follow when taken up into Christ's gospel. At this point Christianity took a great leap forward similar to the leap God took when he created man distinct from the animals. When Christianity is compared point by point with Judaism, therefore, it appears not to be a gradual variation from the old religion but a sudden mutation emerging therefrom, a *spiritual mutation*.

FORM CRITICISM

Within the last thirty or thirty-five years a group of Biblical scholars has developed a new approach to the study of the Gospels known as Form Criticism. This type of criticism has provoked considerable discussion both favorable and unfavorable. Whatever the final outcome of that discussion may be, it appears that this school of critics has given the Christian church a tool for better understanding the problem we have been discussing: how and why the New Testament took its present form. Our concern here is with that tool, not with the details of the method.[2]

This group of scholars believes that the material in the Gospels was first circulated among Christians, probably by word of mouth, in small units. These units were used by them to study their newfound faith, to teach it, and to defend it in religious controversies.

These independent units were later put together in written form in our present Gospels. Different scholars have made different classifications of the material and formulated different theories about how it finally reached its present forms and about the uses to which it was put. By a hurried check of the Gospel of Matthew, the reader can identify some of these units for himself. For example, there is the Sermon on the Mount, Matt., chs. 5 to 7 (cf. Luke, chs. 6 and 12); the instructions of Jesus to his twelve apostles as he sent them on their mission, Matt., ch. 10; the parables of Jesus, Matt., chs. 13 and 25 (cf. Luke, ch. 15); Jesus' teaching concerning little children, Matt., ch. 18; and his teaching about the last things, Matt., ch. 24 (cf. Mark, ch. 13, and Luke, ch. 21).

This material in the Gospels became the basis upon which the apostolic church organized its institutions, regulated its life and practice, and formulated its theology. Thus the Gospels are a primary source for the study of the book of The Acts and the Epistles. That is, in the Gospels we find the clue to an understanding of the remainder of the New Testament.

Let us now proceed to examine the New Testament — first the Gospels and then the records of the early church — for the purpose of ascertaining what kind of church the early Christians were trying to build.

Some Teachings of the Apostolic Church

A. *New Testament Ministry and Polity.* These two topics are considered together because they are so closely interwoven in the New Testament and in the life of the modern church.

Jesus said very little specifically about either church officers or church government. But many of the things he said, as well as the whole tenor of his gospel, have implications for the nature of the ministry and the form of government of the church. His teaching about who is greatest in the Kingdom of Heaven (Matt. 18:1 ff. and parallels in Mark 9:33 ff. and Luke 9:46 ff.; Matt. 20:20 ff. and parallels in Mark 10:42 ff., Luke 22:24 ff., and John 13:12 ff.) and his public rebuke of the Jewish leaders

(Matt., ch. 23) indicate a distinct conception of the ministry and of the government of the church. They imply, on the one hand, that Jesus opposed authoritarianism, distinctions in ranks, lording it over others, and other characteristics of an autocratic government, and, on the other hand, that he sanctioned a brotherly fellowship in which, as we Americans express it, democratic attitudes and processes prevail.

His followers remembered these sayings of Jesus, put them into practice while they were organizing the church and choosing its leaders, and preserved them for the guidance of future generations.

1. *The apostles.* The early Christians gave deference to the apostles appointed by Jesus, but neither they nor the apostles thought of the apostleship as carrying with it the right to slavish obedience from others or the right to exercise authority over the life and thought of the church. Sometimes it is surmised that the apostles acted as a college of bishops or a sort of " supreme court " to which all questions were referred for settlement. But there is scant evidence to show that they even remained for long or at one place as a compact group.

The New Testament reveals no such thing as a chairman of the apostles or a single ruling apostle. The successor to Judas was chosen, not by the Eleven, but by the whole group of disciples (Acts 1:15 f.). The general council at Jerusalem (ch. 15) was presided over by James, who was not an apostle. The delegates were welcomed by the whole assembly (vs. 4, 12). The pronouncement was signed by both apostles and elders (v. 23). Peter was freely criticized by the people (ch. 11:2).

The apostles did not claim or exercise the right exclusively to ordain church officers. The whole church at Antioch chose and commissioned Paul and Barnabas as missionaries. (Acts 13:1-3.) Timothy was ordained by a group of elders. (I Tim. 4:14.) The New Testament does not lend support to a doctrine of apostolic succession in the sense of passing office and authority on to others. In fact, the term " apostle " is used both in the narrower sense of the Twelve chosen by Jesus and in the broader sense of ambassador or emissary. (Cf. Acts 14:14; Rom. 16:7; I Cor. 4:6, 9; Gal. 1:19.) For this reason some declare that the term means simply " missionary," not an order of ministry at all.

2. *Church workers.* As the situation evolved and the necessity arose, a variety of workers appeared in the church. Paul gives a list of these in I Cor. 12:28. This is sometimes regarded as a hierarchy of *offices.* But most scholars would agree with John Knox that the least it can be is a hierarchy of *functions.* " For Paul," Knox declares, " there were teachers and prophets, but hardly the *offices* of teacher and prophet." [3] Some feel that here Paul was speaking not about officers as such but about spiritual services. The reader should observe that bishops, elders, and deacons do not appear in Paul's list.

The officers most frequently spoken of are elders and bishops. The consensus among New Testament scholars is that these words are used interchangeably and undoubtedly refer to the same office. The word " elder " is of Jewish origin; the word " bishop," of unknown origin. Both bear the same general connotations. There seems to be little basis in the records for the position that bishops were a distinct order in the Christian ministry from the beginning, or that they were the successors to the apostles and invested by them with the authority they themselves had received directly from Christ. Each church in the New Testament seemingly had several elders (bishops) but none had a single bishop (elder).

There has long been an uncertainty about the precise meaning of the office of deacon, which is mentioned twice in the New Testament (Phil. 1:1 and I Tim. 3:8). The " seven " (Acts 6:1-6) were not called deacons and are generally believed by scholars not to be so classified. There are few Jewish parallels to the office. The use of the word " women " in the midst of what is said in I Tim. 3:8-13 about the qualifications for deacons may mean that some deacons were women. Phoebe is called a " deaconess " in the Revised Standard Version (Rom. 16:1). Some kind of special officer to take care of the widows in the church may be implied in I Tim. 5:3-16.

3. *Method of commissioning church workers.* There is no certainty about how some of these workers were appointed to office, though the method of appointing others, especially elders, is clearly described. At least one group was self-appointed, "the household of Stephanas" (I Cor. 16:15-16). These are said to have "devoted themselves," meaning "appointed themselves," or assumed an important service voluntarily.

The precise meaning of the act of ordination is also unclear. There was no regular, standardized, officially recognized procedure. The nearest thing to this is found in Acts 6:1 ff., which tells how the seven were appointed to "serve tables." The Twelve "summoned the body of the disciples" and requested that body to choose seven men for the task, whom they, in turn, would appoint. The group chose the men and set them before the apostles, who prayed and laid their hands upon them. This might conceivably be regarded as the usual procedure in commissioning workers. But the same sequence of actions is not found in all cases. (Cf. Acts 13:2-3; 14:23; II Cor. 8:19; I Tim. 5:22.)

The laying on of hands was used for a variety of purposes both in the Old Testament and in the New Testament: by fathers as they blessed their sons, by Jesus as he healed the sick and blessed little children, by the disciples when they healed the sick, and by one group of workers when it set apart other workers for the church. (Cf. Acts 6:6; 13:2-3; 14:23; I Tim. 5:22.) It can be argued with some justification that the act of laying on of hands meant little more than a prayer for God's benediction or for the presence of the power of the Spirit. That is, the laying on of hands was a symbol of prayer: the prayer articulated the symbol. (Cf. Acts 8:17; 19:6.)

Upon first reading, the record seems to say that certain gifts were imparted to Timothy by his ordination. (Cf. I Tim. 1:18; 4:14; II Tim. 1:6.) But these passages may just as easily be interpreted to mean that Timothy first showed by prophetic utterance that he possessed divine gifts, that this was taken to indicate God's call, whereupon the ordination took place as a confirmation of both the call and the gift. That is, the ordination did not confer, but rather recognized, the gift. At any rate, there is no certain evidence in the Christian Scriptures that anyone was chosen for any work until he first demonstrated that he possessed the spiritual gifts for that work.

4. *Christian priests?* The Gospels do not state that Jesus himself intended the twelve apostles to be a distinct order of men who would become a Christian priesthood, paralleling the Jewish priesthood, to perform sacerdotal functions and to mediate divine grace. The records of the New Testament church do not indicate that the apostles thought of themselves as such an order, or that the Christian church set up such an order during the New Testament times, or that there were any sacerdotal functions for such an order of priests to perform. The hierarchical and hereditary priesthood of the Jewish Temple was discarded by the early Christians and played no part in the organization and administration of the church.

5. *Christian laymen.* Paul urged the members of the church to be " subject . . . to every fellow worker and laborer " and to give recognition to such leaders (I Cor. 16:15-16). The workers referred to were the household of Stephanas, who were not ordained at all, unless, as some think, they ordained themselves. The person who, on his own volition, showed ability to serve was to be submitted to, even though he was an unordained layman. This submission was not to an office but to a proved leader. This seems to indicate that no distinction was made between laymen and ministers as such.

Another fact pointing in the same direction is that the performance of tasks in the early church was not limited to specified individuals or officials. Others performed the same type of services as those performed by the apostles. In successive sentences Paul urges the Thessalonians to respect officers who admonish them and to admonish one another (I Thess. 5:12, 14). Admonition, then, was not the exclusive function of a particular official. Everyone who wished to do so could preach. No special leader of worship was mentioned by Paul in I Cor., ch. 14. All worshipers were free to make their individual contributions. No one was officially appointed to baptize. (Cf. Acts 8:12, 38.) There is no suggestion that the Lord's Supper was administered only by officially appointed persons. Paul appealed to the entire church to purge the observance of the Supper of its pagan elements and to see that it was observed with proper dignity and restraint. (I Cor., ch. 11.) The records contain no hint that only when any of these acts was performed by properly appointed or ordained persons could it be considered valid.

6. *The nature of the New Testament ministry and polity.* On the basis of the above facts it is not possible to declare that the New Testament sets forth the precise form of government and ministry for the Christian church. But from these facts may be drawn certain principles to guide the church in devising its polity and choosing its ministry. Both of these must conform to those principles if a church is to be considered fully Christian in the New Testament sense.

These principles may be formulated somewhat as follows: The authority in the church belongs to its members as a whole, not to any individual or group. The authority of an official is not inherent in his office, but is delegated by the body that appoints him. To that body he is responsible for the exercise of his duties. There can be no distinction in order between laymen and clergymen and no such thing as a hierarchy either of officials or of functions. There can be only a division and delegation of duties and responsibilities. Ordination does not confer grace or transmit authority. It recognizes the training and possession of spiritual gifts that qualify individuals for certain services and sets them aside for specific tasks. It is an act of brotherly acceptance into and a sharing of responsibilities of office by those already holding that office. Christian ministers are not priests in the ordinary meaning of that term. They perform only ministerial functions, not sacerdotal functions.

Such are the truths divinely revealed in the New Testament about ministry and polity for the guidance of the church of succeeding ages. How they shall be incorporated in the life of a church of a particular age or place is a matter of experience, experimentation, and judgment. But these truths constitute the authoritative standard for the church of all ages.

7. *Current trends in Protestant thinking about ministry and polity.* One cannot keep in touch with what is happening in our times without being impressed that radical changes are taking place rapidly in the traditional thinking of Protestants about the church's ministry and government. The modern liturgical movement has restored to the vocabulary of large segments of Protestantism the word " priest," a term that was displaced by the New Testament word " minister " by practically all the Reformers. But it is more than a restored word: it is a restored office. On all hands one sees in Protestant churches priestly functions being performed by ministers in priestly attire decorated with priestly symbols. There is a decided return also of distinctions in ranks and symbols of differences in ranks among ministers in Protestantism.

Currently there is considerable sentiment, both in America and abroad, for the adoption of the historic episcopacy as the form of government for the coming ecumenical church, even among those churches which throughout their history have been opposed to bishops in any form. One of the main conclusions of John Knox, in his recent book on the ecumenical church, referred to earlier, is, " I simply cannot conceive of the union of Christendom except on the ground of a polity which, while not failing to embody the invaluable contributions of groups with a presbyterial or congregational tradition, yet involves the full acceptance of the historic episcopate." [4] He makes it quite clear that he is thinking of the episcopacy in the special sense of " a distinct order of ministry, superior to the presbyterate and diaconate, and as standing in a particular historic succession." [5]

The Presbyterian Church of Scotland is now engaged in a heated debate over a proposal to introduce bishops into its form of government. This proposal was made by representatives of the Churches of England and Scotland as a result of meetings designed to bring the two bodies closer together. The same group proposed that the Church of England institute a new office of laymen akin to the elders of the Presbyterian Church. The Protestant scholar Geddes MacGregor has proposed to the Roman Catholic Church that it go back to the medieval government in which, according to his interpretation of medievalism, the church was controlled by ecumenical councils, and in which the pope spoke by the authority he received from the whole church. If that were done, he thinks, the present episcopal polity of the Roman Catholic Church, pope and all, including some form of infallibility, would be democratic enough to suit modern Protestants.[6]

Of course, there is nothing intrinsically sacred about words or terms such as bishop, elder, deacon, synod, conference, presbytery, house, assembly, episcopacy, congregation. The important thing is the content of these words and the kind of relationships and attitudes that exist in the Christian community using them. But there can be no doubt that the trends just mentioned show that Protestants are moving away from their historic positions and toward a high-church-Anglican and Roman Catholic position concerning the ministry and polity of the church. In order to approve these changes a Protestant must either adopt and justify an interpretation of the New Testament other than the one traditionally held by Reformed theologians, or else find his authoritative standard for ministry and polity elsewhere than in the New Testament.

B. *New Testament Worship*. There were two main religious institutions among the Jews in New Testament times, the Temple and the synagogue. There was only one Temple, located at Jerusalem. But hundreds of synagogues were scattered throughout the Roman Empire, one in each community where there was a sufficient number of Jews to support it. The Temple was the national shrine, and it was visited occasionally by the loyal Jews at the time of annual festivals or for some other special purpose. The prevailing type of worship in the Temple was sacrifice-worship, presided over by the priests. But daily prayers, the chanting of psalms, and possibly other liturgical uses of the Jewish Scriptures also took place there.

The Jews congregated weekly in their local synagogues for a

nonsacrifice worship. In connection with the synagogue they and their children received a portion of their religious instruction in schools conducted by the rabbis. For all practical religious purposes, the synagogue, therefore, was the more important of the two institutions, for it was the peoples' local church. The synagogue service of worship was organized around the reading and exposition of their sacred Scriptures. The various uses of the Scriptures were framed with singings, responses, and prayers. The whole procedure was carefully prescribed and meticulously followed.

Jesus came into conflict with the leaders of both institutions during his brief public ministry. But he criticized the practices of the scribes and Pharisees more often than those of the priests. He scathingly denounced the scribal system of casuistry in the interpretation of the law and their burdensome rules. (Matt., ch. 23.) He openly criticized and, in some instances, disobeyed their Sabbath regulations. (Matt. 12:1 ff.) He opposed their substitution of traditions of the elders for the word of God. (Matt. 15:1-20.) Openly and indirectly in many of his parables he clashed with and challenged the practices and teachings of the scribes and Pharisees. (Cf. Matt., ch. 22, and large sections of the Gospel of John.) He warned his followers that they would face bitter opposition in the synagogues and be persecuted and killed by its leaders. (Cf. Matt. 10:16 ff.; Mark 13:9 ff.; Luke 12:1 ff.) As a substitute for the scribal legalistic system, and as its fulfillment, he set forth the law of love written on the heart. (Matt., chs. 5 to 7; Luke, ch. 6.)

The scribes and Pharisees opposed Jesus not only because they believed he was threatening their institutions, but also because he said sharp things about prayers (Matt. 6:5-14), alms-giving and fastings (Matt. 6:2-4, 16-18), and other rabbinical practices.

The priests opposed him because they decided that his teachings were undermining their systems of sacrifices and of ceremonial holiness. The reasons for their apprehensions may be found in such passages as the following: Jesus' driving the traders from the Temple (Matt. 21:12 ff.; Mark 11:15 ff.; Luke 19:45 ff.;

John 2:13 ff.), his utterances while teaching in the Temple (Matt., chs. 21 to 23; Mark, chs. 11; 12; Luke, chs. 19 to 21), what he said about ceremonial washings and how they were interpreted (Mark 7:3 ff.), his parables of new patches and new wine skins (Mark 2:21-22), his references at the Last Supper to the "new covenant" (Luke 22:20, margin; cf. Matt. 26:28; Mark 14:24), and what he said about spiritual worship—where and how to worship God (John 4:7 ff.).

His followers utilized all these passages in their study and teaching of Christian worship. As a result of this, they apparently concluded that the acceptance and application of Jesus' teaching demanded a new kind of worship. For they proceeded quite early to depart radically at many points from their traditional Jewish worship and to create a more advanced spiritual worship.

1 *Terminology of New Testament worship.* Upon a first rapid reading of the New Testament one is likely to get the impression that Christian worship was a mere continuation of Jewish worship. This is due to the wide use by New Testament writers of terms customarily associated with Jewish worship. One finds references in the New Testament to priest, high priest, sacrifice, altar, tithes and offerings, bread, wine, blood, atonement, and lamb—to name only a few such terms.

But it would be a mistake to conclude from this that Christians molded their worship after the pattern of the worship to which they were accustomed. Neither Jesus nor his disciples had any other choice than to make use of Jewish terminology, and to do their thinking in the same general realm of ideas as their hearers, if they expected to succeed in communicating their new ideas. We may be quite certain that neither Jesus nor his followers had ever heard of the modern, psychological term "apperception." Nevertheless, they made use of the teaching procedure that that term describes, namely, new ideas must be presented to people in terms of the knowledge they have previously acquired. In so doing, these Christian writers were not molding the new worship after the pattern, the thought, and the conceptions of the old. They were using the terminology of the old worship primarily as analogies, as figures of speech, to elucidate a worship to be distinguished sharply from what those same terms represented in the old system. Let us examine a few of those terms.

a. *Sacrifice.* Christians used the word " sacrifice," but always to indicate a different type of sacrifice from, and superior to, Temple sacrifices. As previously stated, after the death and resurrection of Jesus, when the full significance of his words and work came to be understood by the disciples, they discarded the Temple system of sacrifices. They believed that the sacrifice of Christ made unnecessary the old sacrifices that the priests offered on behalf of the people. All justification for the existence of material sacrifices was swept away in Christ's one sacrifice of himself.

This is one of the important teachings of the book of Hebrews. The author of that letter discusses the Old Testament sacrifices at some length. He shows wherein they were ineffectual and states that they were typical only of the real sacrifice that was offered in the death of Christ. Hence, they were transitory in nature. He discusses also the nature of Christ's sacrifice. He shows that it is superior to the animal sacrifices because it is a spiritual instead of a material offering, and because Christ offered his perfect sinless self instead of the blood of animals. He " offered for all time a single sacrifice for sins " (ch. 10:12), thus fulfilling the intentions of all other sacrifices and making the repetition of his own sacrifice unnecessary (cf. chs. 7 to 10).

The New Testament speaks of sacrifices other than material sacrifices that Christians themselves should offer to God; e.g., " living sacrifice " (Rom. 12:1), " spiritual sacrifices " (I Peter 2:5), " sacrifice of praise " and of good works (Heb. 13:15-16), sacrifice of generous gifts (Phil. 4:18), and sacrifice of unselfish labors (Phil. 2:27 ff.). All these sacrifices are *spiritual,* that is, they involve the spirit, the mind, the heart, the life of those who offer them. Such sacrifices are of a higher quality than are material sacrifices. A new and nobler kind of sacrifices supersedes the old sacrifices.

b. *High priest.* In developing his theory of the atonement in the first nine chapters of his book, the author of Hebrews applies the term "high priest" to Christ. Having done that, he proceeds to describe an entirely different high priesthood from that of the Temple system. The essence of what he says is: the Jewish high priest appeared once a year before the Holy of Holies to offer, not his own blood, but the blood of animals, as a sacrifice for the sins of his people. Jesus offered himself, not repeatedly but once, and for all the sins of the world. After his resurrection, he "entered, not into a sanctuary made with hands, a copy of the true one, but into heaven itself, now to appear in the presence of God on our behalf" (Heb. 9:24), or, as was expressed earlier, "he always lives to make intercession for" us (chs. 7:25; cf. chs. 4:14 ff.; 6:20; 7:14 ff.; 8:1 ff.). Thus he makes a comparison of two priesthoods to show their dissimilarities or to show how they are to be distinguished radically from each other.

c. *Altar.* In his comparisons of the old and the new sacrifices the author of Hebrews makes the statement, "We have an altar" (ch. 13:10). First and last, this statement has been the center of much attention and the subject of considerable discussion. After examining the exegeses of this verse in its larger setting by Alexander C. Purdy in *The Interpreter's Bible*, James Moffatt in *The International Critical Commentary*, A. S. Peake in *The New Century Bible*, and Marcus Dods in *The Expositor's Greek Testament*, I am convinced that the statement means, not "We Christians have an altar," but rather, "We Christians do not have an altar in the Old Testament meaning of that word."

These scholars agree that the author of Hebrews is not referring to an altar in a place of worship but to the altar in the heavenly sanctuary. Purdy's exegesis goes little beyond this. But the other three agree: (1) that the point the author is making is that in real Christian worship there is no sacrificial meal such as is found in paganism; (2) that no material sacrifices are required to bring us into fellowship with Christ; and (3) that the author was not referring at all to the Lord's Supper. Moffatt goes so far as to say that the author does not allude to the Eucharist anywhere in his book.

If these scholars are correct, then clearly the expression "We have an altar " cannot be used to support the position, now current among Protestants, that the Lord's Supper is the Christian counterpart of the Jewish sacrificial system and that the table is an altar on which the elements are offered as our sacrifice to God. The table represents something significant and distinctive in Christianity. But the New Testament gives no substantial support to its being considered an altar on which the communicants literally or symbolically make sacrificial offerings for their sins.

d. *Circumcision.* The acceptance of circumcision by some members of the Galatian churches was one of the problems that provoked Paul's letter to the Galatians. In that brief but important treatise Paul rejected circumcision and the system of Jewish rites and ceremonies that it symbolized. He expressed amazement that the Galatians, who, by accepting the gospel, had been set free from rites and ceremonies of their former heathenism, were so quickly becoming enslaved to another form of heathenism in Judaism (Gal. 4:9). He urged them to stand fast in their Christian freedom, and not to submit again to a " yoke of slavery " (ch. 5:1). To those who were receiving circumcision he specifically said: " You who would be justified by the law; you have fallen away from grace. . . . In Christ Jesus neither circumcision nor uncircumcision is of any avail, but faith working through love " (vs. 4, 6). He exhorted them to live and walk by the Spirit as free men in Christ. In short, Paul, himself reared as a devout Jew, renounced the Jewish system of ceremonial holiness as primitive practices of an immature religion that were no longer of any consequence either to Jews or to Gentiles who walk by faith and live by the Spirit.

Although Paul thus rejected circumcision, he used it as a figure of speech with which to explain an essential Christian teaching. Circumcision was the *outward* mark of a Jew. Paul used this to stress, by contrast, the *inner* mark of a Christian: a spiritual quality of life. (Cf. Rom. 2:28-29; Phil. 3:3; Col. 2:11.)

Many Protestant writers now commonly assert that baptism in the Christian system is a substitute for circumcision in the old system. According to Winfred E. Garrison, this idea first emerged long after apostolic times. It is not found in the New Testament.[7] Christian baptism was a symbol of the inner cleansing of the heart by the working of the Spirit, as well as a ritual by which, after professing his Christian faith, a person was received into the Christian fellowship. The distinctive *mark* of a Christian, however, was a regenerated heart evinced by a new life. Of course, this is not to say that it is improper to draw a parallel between the way in which a Jew uses circumcision to prove that he is a Jew and the way a Christian treats his admission into the church as proof that he is a Christian.

2. *The elements of New Testament worship.* Let us now turn from the negative to the positive side of the subject, to a discussion of what elements the Christians included in their worship.

For the first few weeks or months after the death and resurrection of Jesus, the Christians who remained or lived in Jerusalem went to the Temple for prayers. (Cf. Luke 24:53; Acts 2:46-47; 3:1; 5:42.) Later other Jewish Christians, including Paul, are said to have gone to the Temple to offer sacrifices. Wherever Christian missionaries went, they attended worship in synagogues and participated in the discussions that took place there. But when their numbers increased they also began to hold worship services of their own on the first day of the week. When a full-scale mission for the conversion of Gentiles was undertaken, when persecution of Christians by the Jewish authorities started, and after Jerusalem and the Temple were destroyed and the Jewish Christians of Palestine fled to Pella and practically vanished from the scene, Christians separated themselves completely from Judaism and all its institutions and began to develop their own services of worship on Sunday only.

The records are silent concerning who led in public worship, or what order of service they developed, except that Paul describes the actions of Jesus at the Last Supper (I Cor., ch. 11). Presumably this became their procedure in the observance of the Supper, but at approximately what time this became prevalent is not known. The only things that can be compared even remotely to rubrics are the five principles stated by Paul in I Cor., ch. 14:

(1) "I will pray with the spirit and I will pray with the mind also; I will sing with the spirit and I will sing with the mind also" (v. 15); (2) "Let all things be done for edification" (v. 26); (3) "If a revelation is made to another sitting by, let the first be silent," a suggestion of mutual deference (v. 30); (4) "For God is not a God of confusion but of peace" (v. 33); and (5) "All things should be done decently and in order" (v. 40).

However, a number of the acts of worship or elements used in worship are mentioned throughout the book of The Acts and the epistles. So many references are made to the preaching, teaching, study, and reception of "the word" (cf. Acts 13:49; 17:11) that it seems certain that when they met for worship the reading, preaching, and teaching of the Jewish Scriptures as well as devotion to "the apostles' teaching" (ch. 2:42) took place regularly. Singing of one type or another is mentioned by Paul several times. (Cf. I Cor. 14:26; Eph. 5:19; Col. 3.16.) "The prayers" (probably common prayers) are mentioned (Acts 2:42) as are also several kinds of prayers: "supplications, prayers, intercessions, and thanksgiving" (I Tim. 2:1). A form of spontaneous or free prayer is manifestly referred to in I Cor. 14:16. Giving (I Cor. 16:1-2; I Tim. 6:18), the peoples' "Amen" (I Cor. 14:16), a confession of faith (possibly meant in I Tim. 6:2), the kiss of peace (Rom. 16:16; I Cor. 16:20; I Thess. 5:26; I Peter 5:14), contributions by individual worshipers (I Cor. 14:26), speaking in tongues (I Cor., ch. 14) — all are referred to here and there. The breaking of bread (the agape, or love feast), a communal meal similar to our modern potluck or "favorite-dish" meals, and the Lord's Supper are mentioned as having taken place together, but never separately, in their services of worship. (I Cor., ch. 11.)

We have no way of knowing whether all these various items were used regularly in every service of worship, and if so, in what sequence. But some things are clear enough to suggest the general type of worship in which they engaged.

3. *The nature of New Testament worship*. As described by Paul in I Cor., ch. 14, Christian worship was more like Scripture-prayer worship of the synagogue, in which laymen, and possibly

lay women, participated without the leadership of the same person each time, than like the Temple worship. Although some of the same elements found in the synagogue and Temple services were used in Christian worship, there was a spiritual fervor or enthusiasm in their singing, praying, giving, preaching, and agape-Supper that must be considered a *new* ingredient or quality in worship. This is what Paul called singing and praying with both " the spirit " and the mind. This fervor had to be curbed. Their emotions had to be restrained. They had to be urged to worship in a more orderly manner and in a quieter mood. But Christian worship can be distinguished from other worship partly by the presence of this new ingredient.

When all the known facts are considered together, we can say both negatively and positively how New Testament worship is to be characterized. It was *not* sacerdotal, or sacrificial, or priestly, or completely fixed or ritualistic, or formal worship. It *was* lay-participation, Scripture-centered, prayer-and-preaching, free, spirit-filled worship.

To say that New Testament worship is of this particular type does not preclude the possibility, even the necessity, of developing an orderly, more or less liturgical, worship, under the direction of a leader trained and set aside for that purpose, and of continually improving and refining all the elements used in worship. But it does preclude the development of a type of worship that the New Testament discarded, or that excludes the distinguishing characteristics of New Testament worship itself.

The worship of the New Testament church is the standard by which the worship of all future periods of the church — the church of the first three or four centuries, the medieval church, and every modern church — is to be judged, not as to all details, but as to type.

4. *Modern trends in Protestant interpretations of New Testament worship.* The modern liturgical revival, beginning about 1850 and moving with increasing tempo in this century, especially since the appearance of the ecumenical movement, has brought a number of changes in Protestant interpretations of the

New Testament worship. Increasingly the tendency has been to soften or minimize the differences between Jewish worship and Christian worship; to assert that the traditional Protestant interpretation of New Testament worship went too far; to declare that the New Testament church did not depart radically from the formal and liturgical worship of the Temple and synagogue; to interpret the Lord's Supper as a New Testament form of sacrifice, a substitute for the Temple sacrifices, and to consider baptism as a substitute for circumcision; to emphasize the *objective* worship of God to such a degree and in such a manner as to eliminate the *subjective* or spontaneous or emotional features of New Testament worship; to restore the more dramatic and colorful symbolism and ceremonialism and some of the rites of ancient religions, both Jewish and pagan.

These trends clearly indicate that historic Protestant worship is being reshaped in certain crucial respects into a type of worship that is becoming more like Roman Catholic and ancient Jewish worship and less like New Testament worship. Admittedly differences in worship practices constitute one of the chief barriers between Protestantism and Roman Catholicism. Until these practices are brought more nearly into harmony a *rapprochement* between the two bodies is not possible. The expressed purpose back of the trends just described, therefore, is to pave the way for a better understanding and ultimately a union of the two. Are these trends to be considered progress or retrogression? Does the modern Protestant church find itself in the same position as the Galatians who were described by Paul as turning back " again to the weak and beggarly elemental spirits," a submitting again " to a yoke of slavery " from which Christ set them free (Gal. 4:9; 5:1) ? Or is the church moving forward under the leadership of God's Spirit into a worship that is more nearly in harmony with God's revelation in Christ? Protestants have yet to find the true answers to these questions.

C. *The New Testament Church.* Jesus is reported to have used the word " church " only three times. Once he used " my church "

(Matt. 16:18) and twice he used " the church " (ch. 18:17). About all the Gospels reveal are that the disciples of Jesus were loosely organized around him, that his movement was supported by the gifts of at least a few women (Luke 8:2-3), and that Judas was the treasurer of the group (John 12:6; 13:29). But without a doubt the records leave the distinct impression that Jesus expected his followers to organize themselves for their divine mission. They were expected to be " the light of the world," " the salt of the earth." They were to belong to and help build the Kingdom of God. They were commissioned to go into all the world and preach and teach the gospel. (Matt. 28:18-20.) But he gave them no specific instructions about what kind of organization to set up. Nor did he offer any suggestions about drafting a doctrine of the church.

This, however, does not mean that when the early Christians faced the task of organizing themselves they had to start *de novo,* without anything to guide them. As already stated, when they came to decide on the ministry, the polity, and the worship of the church, they remembered and took into consideration many things Jesus said. Similarly they were guided by many things he said when they formulated their conception of the nature and function of the church.

Chief among the things that influenced them at this point was what John the Baptist and Jesus both criticized in Judaism, namely, the beliefs, too widely held, that the Jewish church had exclusive claims upon God, that salvation was to be found only in membership in the Jewish community, and that the revelation of God was confined largely to the Jewish people.

They remembered and recorded the warning of John the Baptist to his fellow Israelites, " Do not presume to say to yourselves, ' We have Abraham as our father '; for I tell you, God is able from these stones to raise up children to Abraham " (Matt. 3:9). Likewise they recalled: (1) the times Jesus said that faith is not limited to Israel, that some non-Israelites, even some tax collectors and harlots, will come into the Kingdom of God while the " sons of the kingdom " will be cast out (Matt. 8:10-12;

Luke 13:30; Matt. 21:31); (2) the parable of the Last Judgment, in which Jesus said many who proudly boast of being his followers will find that they do not belong to him, while many who are not aware of it will find they are among his people; and (3) the occasion when Jesus declared, " I have other sheep, that are not of this fold " (John 10:16). They were careful to include in the Gospels Jesus' criticisms and chastisements of the scribes and Pharisees for blocking the entrance to the Kingdom of God (Matt., ch. 23). They would have been strangely indifferent, if not disloyal, to their Master's teaching if they had proceeded to devise a church patterned after the very beliefs and practices of the Jewish church that he condemned. We could hardly expect them, with these utterances of John and Jesus vividly before them, to organize a church that claimed to have a monopoly upon God.

Now let us seek to discover what was the New Testament teaching concerning the church. The modern doctrine of the church usually revolves around three phrases used or implied to describe the church in the New Testament: (1) " The new Israel," (2) " The people of God," and (3) " The body of Christ."

1. *The new Israel.* The exact expression " new Israel " is not found in the New Testament. The nearest thing to it is the expression " the Israel of God," used by Paul to describe all those, Jews and Gentiles alike, who recognize that in the sight of God nothing counts except " a new creation " (Gal. 6:15-16). But the idea can be implied from a number of places where Judaism is compared with Christianity. The idea that the Christian church is the new Israel can be helpful toward understanding what the New Testament teaches about the church, provided both the word " new " and the word " Israel " are properly explained within the context of apostolic Christianity.

Certainly the records reveal that the early Christians did not think of the church as an exact reproduction of the old Israel. Many things in the old Israel were openly discarded, or modified, or incorporated in a radically different form in the new religion.

On the other hand, there are a number of parallels between the two religions. Modern writers quite properly call attention to these parallels. They help us, as they helped ancient folk, to understand who Christ was and what God revealed in him and his gospel. But if these parallels are taken too literally, they can become misleading, especially to the uninformed, casual readers, and average church members, who are not equipped to evaluate the comparisons between Judaism and Christianity.

One of the comparisons most often made between the two is the one between the Old and New Covenants. The two Covenants are said to follow the same general patterns of grace, compassion, election, and deliverance. Although a similar pattern in the two revelations can be discerned, the revelations cannot be equated. The grace of God revealed in the person and work of Christ is on a higher level than his grace manifested in the deliverance of Israel from Egypt. The two events may be similar in principle, but they are unlike in content and in quality. After comparing the two revelations in some detail, Rowley finds that they are given under "different conditions" and in "different terms," and that the new revelation brings a "new message" and a "new power." He goes on to assert that no one could deduce the pattern of the New Covenant "from the Old. And there cannot be the slightest suggestion that by the careful study of the Old Testament anyone could have written the New before its context of history took place." [8]

The term "elect" is applied in one way or another to Christians several times. Paul declares in Ephesians that God "chose us in him [Christ] before the foundation of the world. . . . He destined us in love to be his sons through Jesus Christ" (Eph. 1:3-5). That is a tremendous thought. It gives a cosmic setting for every man's little life. But that view of election is far and away broader in scope than the Old Testament doctrine of election.

Paul refers often to the promises of God made to Abraham and his offspring. He claims that these promises are fulfilled in Christ for the Jews and that Gentile Christians also partake of them.

(Gal. 3:29; 4:28; II Cor. 1:20; Eph. 3:6.) On the basis of these
and similar passages Gregory Dix declares:

> We utterly misunderstand St. Paul if we imagine him as en-
> gaged in founding a new "Gentile Christianity." To himself
> he seemed only to be extending the single "Israel of God,"
> with every conversion, whether of Jew or Gentile. He cannot
> even conceive of the salvation of the Gentiles except by their
> becoming children "of Abram our father, to whom was the
> promise that he should be the heir of the world" (Rom. 4:13).
> He has not the faintest question in his mind that *all* the prom-
> ises of God to, and all the covenants of God with, all the
> Jewish Fathers are renewed and fulfilled in the Messiah.[9]

One cannot read Rom., chs. 2 to 4 and 9, Gal., chs. 3 to 5, and
Eph., chs. 1 to 3, and agree fully with that statement. In the
thought of Paul, Gentiles were not saved by becoming children of
Abraham, except by sharing his faith in God, any more than
Jews were saved merely because they were the offspring of Abraham. Both Jews and Gentiles were saved on the same new terms
of the gospel: justification by faith and reconciliation through the
cross. According to Paul, Christ made Jews and Gentiles one
"by abolishing in his flesh the law of commandments and ordi-
nances, that he might create in himself *one new man* in place of
the *two* . . . and might reconcile us *both* to God . . . through
the cross . . . , for through him we *both* have access in one Spirit
to the Father" (Eph. 2:15-18, italics supplied).

Hence, in Christ both share together the promises God made
to Abraham and in the additional promises God vouchsafes to
his children in the New Covenant. But Paul does not imply here
or elsewhere that the Christian church is to be thought of merely
as another or as a renewed or a reconstituted Israel.

Both Israel and the Christian church have a common fund of
ideas, as has already been noted. But the church is not another
Israel. It is a fuller revelation of what God had in mind for all
peoples since the dawn of creation. The revelation that was only
partially understood by Israel and incorporated in its laws and

traditions is now more completely understood and incorporated in a *new* form in the Christian church. It is seriously to be questioned whether the church can fitly be thought of as *an* Israel. The distinguishing description of a Christian church is that it is the fellowship of people who are spiritually united to Christ.

The genius of Christianity is Christ. As Garrison rightly asserts: " The rootage of Christianity in Hebrew history is deep, and undoubtedly a continuing purpose of God runs through both. But the church was a new thing. . . . No religion before Christianity ever had a church." [10]

2. *The people of God.* By virtue of the mere fact that they were in Abraham, in the line of his descendants, bearing the mark of circumcision, many Jews believed they belonged to the chosen and favored people of God. By virtue of the same fact, they believed they inherited and shared in the divine promises of God given exclusively to Abraham, and that they were therefore a holy people, a sacred community of the elect, set apart from all other peoples.

In a number of places in the New Testament Christians are likewise spoken of as the people, or the household, of God. (Eph. 2:19; Gal. 6:10; I Peter 2:9-10; 4:17.) How are these expressions to be understood? Did these Christian writers mean to claim that Christians had superseded the Jews as the only and exclusive people of God? In all probability they did not intend to make such a claim. Christians claimed to be those who were " in Christ," that is, who had accepted him by faith, found in him a new moral and spiritual power, and had convenanted to live a new life in him. But being " in Christ " was different from being " in Abraham."

This becomes clear when I Peter 2:9-10 is considered in its full context. That passage reads, " You are a chosen race, a royal priesthood, a holy nation, God's own people." The writer is exhorting his readers who are Christians, and therefore chosen and sanctified for obedience to Christ, and now scattered abroad in an unchristian world (ch. 1:1-2), to remember what type of people they are supposed to be in the society in which they live. They are to be a " spiritual house," a priesthood that offers " spiritual sacrifices acceptable to God through Jesus Christ " (ch. 2:5). The writer was evidently thinking not of a particular and limited race of people like the Jews, but of a new mankind in Christ, a spiritual race, a people born not of flesh and blood but of the Spirit. " A new people were coming forward who could no longer be called Jewish, Greek, Scythians, or Barbarian, but were indeed a ' third race ' at the side of Gentiles and Jews." [11]

The author of I Peter at the moment apparently had in mind not the ecclesiastical body called the church, but that new mankind in Christ from among all peoples of earth. He was urging his readers to demonstrate that they belong to that new race. All who are " in Christ " are chosen or elected to be members of that universal household of God. No restrictions, racial or otherwise, apply to that household. But note that the *broad* Christian concept grew out of the figurative use of the old *narrow* Jewish term " the people of God."

3. *The body of Christ.* The expression " body of Christ " in certain places in the New Testament refers to the literal body of Christ, in which he was incarnated and which died on the cross. (Rom. 7:4; 8:3; Eph. 2:10 ff.; Col. 1:22; Heb. 10:10; I Peter 2:24.) But in the letters of Paul, Christians, or Christians composing the church, are called the " body of Christ." This occurs in four of his letters: Rom., ch. 12; I Cor., ch. 12; Eph., chs. 4 and 5; and Col., chs. 1 to 3. Is that statement to be taken literally or metaphorically?

A controversy is going on over the answer to that question, which is reminiscent of the Eucharistic controversies among the Reformers over whether the saying of Jesus at the Last Supper " This is my body " is to be taken literally or symbolically. The controversy may prove to be equally as tragic for the Protestant church as were its predecessors.

When considered in the context of the passages just mentioned, the expression is unquestionably a figure of speech. In all these passages Paul *compares* the members of the church to the members of the human body, though not to the same degree or in the same manner in each. But the general idea is this: as there is one body, with many members, each of which has a different function to perform, and as all members work together harmoniously, so Christians, though many, should function together smoothly in the church.

In all four instances, however, his main concern is not about the organization called the church, nor about its offices and officers, but about the spiritual gifts possessed by its members. He begins and ends each discussion with spiritual gifts. In each context where he uses the phrase he spends a great deal of time exhorting his readers to manifest the Spirit of God in their living, to put off the old nature and all its ways, and to put on the new nature in Christ with all the virtues and graces that should characterize new men in Christ. His main, almost his sole, interest is that the members of the church be " in Christ."

This interest is most noticeable in Eph., ch. 4. In fact, the expression " in Christ " is used more than thirteen times in the book of Ephesians. In each connection in which Paul uses the word " body " in Colossians, his interest is manifestly that his readers might live " in Christ," that they might be " rooted and built up in him " (ch. 2:7), " raised with Christ," " hid with Christ in God " (ch. 3:1-3).

After studying the phrase in its larger settings in each epistle, it is difficult to believe that Paul was making an ecclesiastical statement at all. His concern was spiritual and not ecclesiastical.[12]

But many do believe that Paul was using the expression to describe the church as an ecclesiastical organization. They take it more or less literally. Then they use it as the focal point around which to develop a conception of the church as an organic or corporate personality in which individuals are more or less submerged and apart from which they can have no Christian life. John Knox declared recently that the expression " The church is the body of Christ " is to be taken literally, not metaphorically. As used here, the word " body " means " the spatial-temporal locus of personal existence." Hence, " Christ is actually embodied in the church. . . . It is his body. Not only is he known there: he

can be known only there. This means that we can know nothing
that is distinctly Christian except in or through the church. Indeed we can go further than this and say that nothing such
exists." In another connection he says, " The access to God is
available to individuals *within* the church," and nowhere else.[13]

Some years ago Cecil Northcott reported that it is now commonly accepted in British theology " that salvation is salvation
into the life of the Spirit of the community," and " that the relationship of the believer to Christ is always a relationship within
the church. ' Christian experience is ecclesiastical experience.' "[14]
That statement has been amply confirmed by later utterances of
British writers. Alan Richardson declared that there is " no such
thing as a private, personal relationship between God and the
individual apart from his membership in the covenant-folk.
Throughout the Bible it is consistently taught that outside the
church there is no salvation."[15] William Neil asserts, " Salvation
is not a private transaction with God based on acceptance of
Scriptural truth, but life lived in obedience to God within the
church and illumined and sustained alike by living worship and
written word."[16] This is also the point of view of many American Protestant writers. For example, Claude Welch says in his
recent book, *The Reality of the Church:*

> One is never alone in Christ. Membership in him is at the
> same time membership in one another. There is no purely
> private Christianity, for to be in Christ is to be in the church,
> and to be in the church is to be in Christ, and any attempt to
> separate relation to Christ in faith from membership in the
> church is a perversion of the New Testament understand-
> ing.[17]

The most extreme statements by an American Protestant along
this line have been made by William Robinson in *The Biblical
Doctrine of the Church*.[18] His position is that Christ and the
church " are, in some sense, identified " (pp. 115, 116); that " the
church is Christ manifest in the flesh, as Jesus of Nazareth was
God manifest in the flesh " (p. 117); that the church is the " con-

tinuation " (p. 117), or "perpetuation " (p. 119), of the incarnation; and that "neither the Bible nor classical Protestantism knows anything of Christianity without the church " (p. 207).

If the church is literally the body of Christ, if no one can belong to Christ unless he belongs to the church, or experience Christ except within the church, then, to all effects and purposes, the church *is* Christ. That position comes dangerously near to deifying the church. Certainly it limits the work of Christ on this earth to the church.

Moreover, those Protestants who subscribe to this doctrine of the church swing over toward the Roman Catholic view. The classical Protestant position is that the individual believer's relation to the church follows and depends upon his personal relation to Christ. The traditional Roman Catholic position is that the individual believer's relation to Christ follows and is dependent upon his relation to the church. Aside from the literal interpretation of the analogy of the church as the body of Christ, there is little in the New Testament itself to support the Roman Catholic position.

Nowhere in the New Testament is the church called Christ or identified with Christ or with the Holy Spirit. The New Testament tells us that we are saved by Christ, not by the church; that grace is from Christ, not from the church; that Christ, and not the church, is our reconciliation. The organic conception of the church, the thought of a group of people possessing a " corporate personality " like a human body, is suggestive. But there is nothing in the New Testament to justify a view of the church that requires the individual personality to be submerged in the group.

Salvation is described in the New Testament not as being an organic relation to the church but as a personal relation to Christ, an acceptance of and commitment to Christ, by individuals. In the book of The Acts there are many references to the salvation of individuals in which the church itself is not mentioned at all, or not mentioned as a factor in their salvation; for example, there is the salvation of those on Pentecost (Acts 2:37 ff.); of the Ethiopian eunuch (ch. 8:35 ff.); of Saul (ch. 9:17-18); of the household of Cornelius (ch. 10:44 ff.); of those at Antioch (ch. 11:21); of those at Antioch of Pisidia (ch. 13:48); of the Philippian jailer (ch. 16:29 ff.); of those at Athens (ch. 17:34); and of those of Corinth (ch. 18:8). After individuals had believed, had been baptized, and, as the case might be, the Holy Spirit had come upon them — that is, after they had been saved — they were added to the fellowship. But there are no instances of individuals joining the church and then being saved. Individuals qualified for membership in the church by first believing in Christ and experiencing the power of the Holy Spirit.

In short, there is no substantial basis in the New Testament for the claims that Christian experience was only ecclesiastical experience, or experience in the church; that individuals could not have a private or personal relationship with God or Christ except within the church. Emphasis in the apostolic church was upon those who were *in Christ,* not upon those who were *in the church.* Wherever Christ became a living presence in any group of people, there the church was found. Or, to state it the other way round, the church was found only where Christ was living *in people.*

Aside from everything else that has been said, it is inadvisable to build the doctrine of the church around only one figure of speech in the New Testament. In the same books in which Paul uses the analogy of the body, he uses other analogies equally as fruitful and meaningful; we find, for example, " building up the body of Christ " (Eph. 4:12-16; Col. 2:7); " the bride of Christ," implied but not stated (Eph. 5:21 ff.); and " the temple of God " (I Cor. 3:16-17). To these could be added " the vine and the branches," used by Jesus (John, ch. 15); " living stones," used by the author of I Peter (ch. 2:5); and " flock," used by Jesus (Luke 12:32), by Paul (Acts 20:28-29), and by the author of I Peter (ch. 5:2-3). One could quite as justifiably base his whole doctrine of the church on one of the other figures as to base it on the single figure of the body.

This is especially true of the figure of a building or a house, since the New Testament is teeming with passages containing that metaphor. (Matt. 7:24 ff.; 21:42; I Cor. 3:11; II Cor. 5:1; Eph. 2:19-22; Col. 2:7; Heb. 11:10; I Peter 2:5; Rev., ch. 21.) The comparison of the union of Christ and his followers to the union of a husband and wife is the basis for the use of the term " spouse of Christ " found in both Roman and Reformed creedal statements about the church. No single figure of speech, no matter how enlightening, is capable of carrying the whole weight of the Christian doctrine of the church.

This corporate view of the church, as it is now being reformulated in Protestant circles, is approaching the Roman Catholic view of the church as the perfect and visible community of the saved, and as the only vehicle of God's grace in the world. That concept in its Jewish form of an exclusive community of God's people was rejected by the New Testament church. The same concept in its extreme Roman Catholic form was rejected by the leaders of the Protestant Reformation. This view of the church, as is the case with the new Protestant views of the ministry, of polity, and of worship, dealt with earlier, apparently is adopted by many Protestants on the ground that it may aid in bringing about a united Christendom. Again, Protestants must stop and ask whether in doing this they are going backward or forward.

THE AUTHORITY OF THE NEW TESTAMENT

One of the main historic issues between Protestantism and Roman Catholicism is their difference of opinion about the relative authority of the New Testament and of the church's tradition. One of the cardinal doctrines of the Reformed churches has been that the Bible is the sole and sufficient authority. This includes the subsidiary doctrine that the New Testament is the standard for the church of all ages and for all phases of the church's life. The Roman Catholic Church teaches that the tradition of the church is also an authoritative standard.

When both Scripture and tradition are rightly understood there is, or should be, no antithesis between them. Tradition has been described as " the living stream of the church's life "; that is, it includes the experiences of the church throughout its history: its theological discussions and creeds, its experiments in creating forms of worship and of administration, its evangelistic, educational, and missionary enterprises, its varied efforts toward building the Kingdom of God. Or to state it another way, tradition embraces all the lessons learned, all the values accrued, from the history of the church. All groups of Christians have believed in the indispensable and inestimable value of tradition when it is thus explained. All have believed that the Holy Spirit works through history, that God speaks to the church through its experiences.

But a difference of opinion arises about whether tradition can add anything essential to our faith, anything not found in the original revelation in the New Testament. The Roman Catholic Church teaches that some truths are revealed through the tradition of the church that are not contained explicitly in the Scriptures, that the church under the guidance and discipline of the Holy Spirit developed or discovered these truths as its experience expanded, and that the church has the authority from Christ to declare such truths to be as binding as the truths in Scripture, and, in some instances, to declare them necessary to salvation. The well-known Roman theologian, Karl Adam, states it this way:

The other truths of faith which have been formulated in the course of centuries by the church though not expressed in the Bible . . . are all contained at least in germ (implicitly) in a revealed truth already clearly held and proclaimed by the church. . . . The Catholic Church lives and breathes in the consciousness that by her apostolic succession founded upon Peter she stands in that stream of tradition which leads straight from Christ through the apostles, down to the present. With this before her eyes she knows herself as divine tradition *incarnate,* as the visible embodiment of those powers of our Lord's resurrection which are forever penetrating the world whether they were set down by the finger of God in Holy Writ or not. The church has no need of witnesses. She witnesses to herself by the " divine tradition " in which she stands and by which she lives, indeed, which she *is*.[19]

The historic Protestant position is that all the traditions of the church — its creeds, its administrative standards, its worship forms, its practices, and its programs — are to be judged by whether or not they are in harmony with the fundamental truths and principles revealed in the Scriptures. The traditions of the church need to be amended and revised over the years, but always in the light of a better understanding of the original revelation in the Scriptures. Traditions are to be judged, ultimately, not by what any one church or council of churches declares but by whether these are found to be in conformity with the Word of God. The church finds its faith in the Scriptures, not in its own traditions.

When Paul wrote his epistles the Gospels were probably still being circulated by word of mouth. He undertook to lay it upon the consciences of all Christians, leaders and followers alike, that it was their sacred duty to see that the gospel was handed down without mutilation or corruption, as the rabbis had guarded and transmitted the tradition of the elders. So in a number of places he urged that the gospel be received and transmitted accurately. (Cf. I Thess. 2:16; I Cor. 11:2; cf. also I Tim. 6:20; II Tim. 1:14.) Protestants have always believed that the early Christians performed this obligation faithfully.

Why the early church decided to transmit the Gospels in the precise manner they did, we shall never know. Why they chose for their purposes certain portions of the teachings of Jesus only, will probably always remain a mystery. Manifestly they were not thinking of answering all the questions future critics would raise about these documents. They were concerned to hand down *the gospel* itself. Protestants have always believed that they succeeded in doing just that. Much was not included. But the New Testament gives us a true picture of what the gospel was and is.

The evidence seems to prove clearly that they made their choices on the basis of the principle of *apostolicity*.[20] They sought out those people or writings, as the case might be, that were nearest the events being reported. Some of their sources were eyewitnesses; some were facts gathered by careful historians. Documents were chosen not because they represented the theological viewpoint of the church at the moment, but because they represented the original facts of the apostolic era. When they finished, they had compiled the Christian Scriptures, the New Testament, which Forsythe rightly called " the apostolic deposit." But they did not create it: they canonized it! The New Testament was produced *within* the church, but not *by* the church.

The New Testament is the record of events, episodes in history, not a mere growth of tradition. Its documents, taken together, tell a story of what happened. Not as we would have told it had we been there, nor as we wish they had told it, but a consistent, reliable story, competent for the purposes intended, namely, to hand down *the gospel* itself to future generations. The *kērygma* and *didachē* of the New Testament give us the only record, the unchangeable record, the sufficient record of evangelical Christianity. That is where we go to discover God's full revelation in Christ. That is the criterion by which the churches and their traditions are judged and measured. At least, that is the historic Protestant doctrine of the authority of the New Testament.

The Protestant and Roman Catholic views of tradition have been all but irreconcilable until the recent rise of the ecumenical movement. As a result of that movement, and in order, if possible, to bring the Roman Catholic Church into it, many Protestants have been modifying their conception of tradition to bring it more nearly into harmony with the Roman view. This particular change in Protestant thinking, as many have observed, is one of the remarkable, if not astounding, features of the ecumenical movement. Roman Catholics have welcomed the change with enthusiasm and regard it as confirmation of their position. Charles Boyer warns Protestants that once they have taken steps in the direction of the Roman doctrine of tradition, they must go all the way, for there is no turning back. He declares:

If one admits that a truth may be contained in substance in Scripture or in tradition — even though not explicitly — one recognizes the principle that justifies the whole doctrinal development that has occurred in the Roman Catholic Church. There can no longer be any distinction between the fundamental truths and the others. Neither the councils nor the popes have ever defined any matter of faith that is not in substance, at least implicitly, in the sacred books or in the teaching of the fathers. (P. 87.) [21]

Are Protestants willing to go all the way with Roman Catholics at this point? If not, where do they stop and on the basis of what principle?

The Unity of the New Testament Church

The New Testament churches did not have an authoritative Scripture or an authoritative group of officials or a uniform administrative structure to hold them together. Neither did they have a formal theological statement or creed to which they were all expected to subscribe. But they did have a common faith, a common experience, a common purpose, and a common spirit, which bound them together into one brotherhood.

A few passages in the New Testament seem to refer to some kind of confession. (II Cor. 9:13; Heb. 4:14; 10:23; I Tim. 6:13.) But these can scarcely indicate the existence of a well-articulated creed that was used at the time of their baptism or when they were received into the church or that was recited in connection with public worship. Nevertheless, they had a common faith, simple, to be sure, but vital and common to all. That faith can be stated in the words, " I accept Jesus as Lord " (cf. Acts 2:38; 16:31).

This simple act of faith, however, was actually made up of several things: an acceptance of facts about the life, death, and resurrection of Christ; a personal commitment to him and to his teaching as a new way of life; and a vital experience of being new men in Christ or of being empowered and sustained by his living, spiritual presence. The experience of his presence was what they meant by receiving the Holy Spirit. The two things were identical. All these things put together constituted what they called the " Way," the Christian way of living. (Acts 9:2; 19:9, 23; 22:4; 24:14, 22.) That Way, rather than a written creed or a particular administrative setup, identified them with and bound them to all other Christians. All Christians were united by this common evangelical experience.

There cannot be the least doubt that the Christians of all the churches, which were widely scattered throughout the Roman Empire, were bound together into a spiritual fellowship of those who shared the Christian experience and were walking in the Christian Way. That fellowship was the distinctive characteristic of Christianity, a new phenomenon in religion, amazing alike to the Christians themselves and to outsiders.

John Knox says the church was not united in a " visible unity in the apostolic age." But he strongly insists that it was united in what he calls a " shared life," or a " shared faith," which was a " recognizable cultural phenomenon " wherever Christianity was found, and that " every Christian group was deeply aware of its own identity within the movement that included all the rest." [22] Here Knox identifies and emphasizes the importance of that *spiritual unity* which was the primary concern of both Jesus and Paul.

In his prayer for his followers (John, ch. 17) Jesus does not mention the church or its officers or its organization. He prays that his disciples might possess that kind of harmony that existed between him and the Father, " that they may be one, even as we are one." The community of thought, of purpose, of character, of spirit, for which Jesus prayed is also that for which Paul pleaded in that familiar passage in Ephesians: " The unity of the Spirit in the bond of peace," " one body," " one Spirit," " one hope," " one Lord," " one faith," " one baptism," " one God and Father " (Eph. 4:1-6).

Does not the *spiritual ecumenical fellowship* of the New Testament church, which amazed Christians who experienced it and non-Christians who observed it, provide us with the clue to the kind of unity that the church of our day should seek? Is not the New Testament our standard in this respect as in all other respects?

Chapter III

The Ancient Undivided Church

Anyone who has a modest acquaintance with the religious books published in recent years must have been impressed by the frequency with which writers dealing with church unity have been referring to the undivided church of the third and fourth centuries. There seems to be a general unofficial agreement that the standards for the ecumenical church of the future — its polity, its theology, its worship, and its unity — are to be found in the church of that period. So the spotlights are being thrown upon the writings of the postapostolic, ante-Nicene, and post-Nicene fathers. A steady stream of books about these leaders, some by Protestants and some by Roman Catholics, is flowing from the presses.[1] It is of prime importance, therefore, for the rank and file of our Protestant churches to inform themselves about this church of the early centuries and try to discover why it has been assigned such a crucial role.

The dates assigned to this church are roughly A.D. 100–400. The information about it is spotty, being generally meager for the first half of the period and more plentiful for the last half. Following the New Testament times there was a period of years — of fifty years at the very least, of possibly one hundred years at the most — about which very little is known. Some scholars like to say that the church passed through a tunnel from about A.D. 75 to 150. Furthermore, the church worshiped secretly for at least one hundred years from about A.D. 250 to 350. This period may be thought of as another kind of tunnel through which the church passed, for so long as secret worship prevailed, Christian documents gave scant information about many of their practices. The New Testament itself gives us a fairly detailed account of what the church was like when it entered the first tunnel. From the writings now extant we can gather what happened during the century after it emerged from that tunnel. We also have a fairly clear picture of what it was like when it came out at the other end of the second tunnel. But we do not know for certain what developments took place while it was going through the tunnels. Even so, there is little disagreement about the available facts, only differences of opinion about the meaning of those facts.

THE MINISTRY OF THE POSTAPOSTOLIC CHURCH

Many significant changes in the organization of the church took place in this period. Philip Schaff summarizes these changes as follows:

> The distinction of clergy and laity, and the sacerdotal view of the ministry becomes prominent and fixed; subordinate church officers are multiplied; the episcopate arises; the beginning of the Roman primacy appears; and the exclusive unity of the Catholic church develops itself in opposition to heretics and schismatics. The apostolical organization of the first century now gives place to the old Catholic episcopal system; and this, in its turn, passes into the metropolitan, and after the fourth century into the patriarchal. Here the Greek church stopped, and is governed to this day by a hierarchical oligarchy of patriarchs equal in rank and jurisdiction; while the Latin church went a step further, and produced in the Middle Ages the papal monarchy. The germs of this papacy likewise betray themselves even in our present period, particularly in Cyprian, together with a protest against it.[2]

The accuracy of this summary, so far as the ministry is concerned, is substantiated by a recent book, *The Ministry in Historical Perspectives*,[3] in which the evolution of the ministry in this period is given in considerable detail by a group of outstanding scholars. Their conclusions are essentially the same as Schaff's.

Some of the changes that occurred were made surprisingly early. In his first letter to the Corinthian church (ca. A.D. 96), Clement, the chief presbyter-bishop of Rome, in behalf of the Roman church, exercised authority that later grew into papal primacy. Through him the Roman church, proud of being the church of Peter and Paul (I Cor., ch. 5), and apparently also of being in the imperial capital, assumed the prerogative of directing the church at Corinth to keep its elected bishops and deacons for life, instead of distributing this responsibility by substituting other officials of their own choosing (ch. 44:2-6). When Clement declared that the time, place, personnel, and life office of those officiating at worship were prescribed by God (ch. 40:1-3), that their authority had been handed down through the apostles to their successors (ch. 42:1-4), and that it was a grave sin to transgress these divine regulations (ch. 44:4), the doctrine of apostolic succession appeared and Roman Catholic canon law was born. He restored to the church the hierarchical-sacerdotal priesthood of the Old Testament when he regarded the chief bishop who celebrated the Lord's Supper as the type of the Aaronic high priest, the other ministers as priests, and the deacons as Levites (ch. 40:5). He made a clear distinction between clergy and laity by asserting, "The layman is bound by the layman's code" (ch. 40:5).

The letters of Ignatius of Antioch, who died a martyr about A.D. 116, strongly urged Christians to hold together by submitting to the bishops, presbyters, and deacons. This is the first clear description of the threefold ministry. Obedience to them, he says, is obedience to Christ, who appointed them, and disobedience to them is disobedience to Christ. The bishop presides in the place of God, the presbyter in the place of the council of apostles, and the deacons perform the "ministry of Jesus Christ." He urges all three groups of ministers alike to do nothing without the bishop. When the people come together where the bishop is, even as wherever Jesus Christ is, there is the Catholic church. The laity are supposed to be subject to the deacons, the deacons to the presbyters, the presbyters to the bishop, and the bishop to Christ.[4] The Martyrdom of Polycarp, the account of the death of the presbyter-bishop of Smyrna, which occurred about A.D. 155, gave great impetus to martyrology, the extravagant veneration of saints and relics that bordered on idolatry.

Mariology began to develop before the end of the second century. About the end of that century the small noncanonical Book of James appeared. In this book the perpetual virginity of Mary, the belief that the brothers of Jesus were sons of Joseph by a previous marriage, and a hint that Mary was miraculously conceived, were set forth in a series of fictional narratives.

During the same period of years when Calixtus as bishop of Rome (A.D. 217–222) claimed that the " power of the keys " was granted to Peter and, presumably, to his successors at Rome, many legends about Peter appeared in the noncanonical Acts of Peter. Although Tertullian (ca. A.D. 220) was a strong adherent of the Catholic movement then developing and directed North Africans among whom he labored as a presbyter to look to the Roman church for guidance, he protested against the growing laxity of the Roman church, and bitterly assailed Calixtus for declaring that the church could forgive sins committed after baptism, whereas hitherto it had been held that only God could forgive such sins. Cyprian, bishop of Carthage in North Africa (died about A.D. 258), advocated the supremacy of the papacy. He " called the Roman church the chair of Peter, and the fountain of priestly unity, the root, also, and mother of the Catholic church. But on the other side, he asserted with equal energy the equality and relative independence of the bishops, as successors to the apostles, who had all an equal direct appointment from Christ." [5] The point of all this is that by the year A.D. 250 the primacy of the bishop at Rome and many of the legends, stories, etc., associated with it, were already developing.

After the persecution of the church ceased and Christianity was favored by Constantine, bishops all but became leading officers of the state. Certainly they exercised a tremendous, if not a controlling, influence in political and civil affairs. Constantine not only worked closely with the bishops but looked upon himself as one of them. Eusebius reports that he said to an assembly of bishops, " You have been installed bishops for the inner affairs of the church, but I have been installed bishop by God for its outer affairs." Political intrigues and methods soon thereafter quickly got mixed up with bishops and their ecclesiastical labors.

After the middle of the fourth century, celibacy was becoming the outward mark of the clergyman, and asceticism was coming more and more into prominence. Monasticism began to spread rapidly over the whole church. Monastics soon developed into a third order of ministers as a rival to the regular priesthood. Some of these became the " holy men " known as hermits, who lived in caves, desert places, and on tops of pillars, and engaged in many forms of excessive self-punishment. Here appeared a new form of morality that was supposed to be a higher degree than the ordinary virtues of common, everyday life. This widened still farther the gulf between clergy and laity.

In this same general period the tonsure, or short-cropped hair, appeared, and the wearing of a distinctive garb, and other accoutrements of dress, such as certain kinds of sandals, rings, pallia, and maniples, denoting distinctions in ranks, became customary. These distinguishing insignia and articles of attire corresponded to similar symbols of ranks among the citizens in the secular society. Within the highest rank (the *illustres*) there were five grades, the next to the highest (*nobilissimi,* or those of royal blood) being the *glorissimi.* At the Synod of Arles in the fourth century the Roman pope was addressed as *glorissime.* In this process of division into ranks a group of clergymen became known as " the *lower* clergy." Included in this group were readers, exorcists, acolytes, doorkeepers, subdeacons, and deaconesses.[6]

As just indicated, some of these symbols of rank seem to have been adopted by the clergy in imitation of Roman society, but others seem to have been bestowed upon them by the Roman emperor. Before the fourth century came to a close, the *cathedra* (chair), symbolizing the teaching function of the bishop, became his throne to correspond to the emperor's throne.[7]

In short, throughout this period there was a proliferation of types and gradations of ministers that developed into a hierarchy of officers unknown in the New Testament. As we shall see in the next section, the conception of the functions of the minister likewise was modified radically from its original New Testament form.

Two questions arise at this point: (1) Were these developments a natural or normal process of maturation, or, in the process was the essential nature of the New Testament church changed? (2) If some of these developments are regarded as still valid for the church of our day, and others as accretions that are inharmonious with Christianity, on what principle, or by what criterion, are the two groups thus differentiated from each other? We shall refer to these questions again.

WORSHIP IN THE POSTAPOSTOLIC CHURCH

A. *In the Second Century.* How did the Christians of this period worship? A satisfactory answer to that question is made difficult by the fact, already mentioned in the previous section, that between the apostolic era and the middle or latter part of the second century, the church went through a tunnel. Between the New Testament period and A.D. 200 there are extant only five or six documents that throw any light on this question, and there is considerable difference of opinion about how these should be interpreted. All but one of these documents contain little more than fragmentary hints of what was taking place.

1. At the close of his first letter to the Corinthians (ca. A.D. 96), Clement gives a prayer in which a number of phrases occur that are similar to those found in the liturgies of the fourth century. There is no indication that it was a fixed prayer, but it has often been regarded, without much justification, as an early form of the fixed Eucharistic prayer of later centuries. He also used the expression, " Holy, holy, holy is the Lord of Hosts; every creature is full of thy glory," which is taken to mean that the Sanctus, in a brief form, was coming into use at this early date.

2. The letter of Pliny the Younger, Roman governor of

Bithynia in Asia Minor, in which he was reporting his observations about Christians to his Emperor Trajan (ca. A.D. 112), contains one of the earliest mentions of Christians worshiping at sunrise. It also states that they sang a song to Christ as God, responsively, or antiphonally, and " afterwards " (time not specified, possibly in the evening) assembled to eat " ordinary and innocent food." The latter undoubtedly refers to the same service as the " breaking of bread," or " agape," in the New Testament.

3. The Didache, or Teaching of the Twelve Apostles (ca. A.D. 130), reveals that the Lord's Supper was still observed in the early form of the agape, or with it, and gives a few brief prayers of thanksgiving, apparently common prayers, after which, it states, " The prophets were permitted to give thanks as they wish " (free prayers).

4. The " apology " of Justin Martyr to the Emperor Antoninus Pius (ca. A.D. 140) describes two separate services: a celebration of the Lord's Supper, which followed public baptism, and what appears to be a regular Sunday service at which the Supper was also celebrated. He mentions " the prayers " after which they greeted one another with " the brotherly kiss," the reading from " the Memoirs of the Apostles and the writings of the Prophets," a discourse and exhortation by " the president," and the Lord's Supper. The " president of the brethren " officiated. In one account he states that the president offered prayers after which the people said " Amen." In the other account he states that the president offered thanks " according to the power given him " (free prayer), but also that " we all rise in common prayer." He also mentions the blessing or consecration of the elements by a word of prayer, the distribution of the elements by the deacons, and, following the Communion, freewill offerings for the poor and needy, which were deposited with the president. This gives us a fairly clear picture of a slowly expanding, but still simple, order of service.

One statement of Justin's deserves special emphasis. He said that Christians thought of the elements as " the flesh and blood of the incarnate Jesus." This is one of the earliest indications of what later developed into one important phase of the Eucharistic controversy that has divided and harassed Christians ever since, namely, the question of whether the elements are to be thought of in a literal or in a figurative sense.

5. During the last quarter of the second century Irenaeus compared the Lord's Supper to the pagan sacrifice, called it the "Eucharistic gift," and spoke of it as being offered at an altar. But, like the writer of Hebrews, he seems to have been thinking of the altar in heaven. However, according to Niebuhr and Williams, the apocryphal Acts of John, written before the end of the second century, first called the table an altar in the common meaning of that term. Once that practice began, the officiating "president," as he was called by Justin, came to be spoken of as a priest. Polycrates, the bishop of Ephesus (ca. A.D. 190), was the first, apparently, to refer to the Christian minister as a priest. He did it by speaking of the apostle John as a priest "who wore the sacerdotal tiara." [8]

6. The Apostolic Tradition, supposedly compiled by Hippolytus of Rome about A.D. 200, contains the full text of the Eucharistic prayer, or prayer of consecration, which has also been the subject of much discussion. The question is whether that prayer almost from New Testament times was a fixed prayer of a particular structure, and whether, therefore, it must always continue to be so in order to be effective and perform its consecratory function validly. Hippolytus specifically states that it was not a fixed prayer. His exact words are, " It is not necessary for him [the president] to recite the same words, but, according to his own ability, so each one is to give thanks."

The above are practically all the known facts on which to form an opinion of the way Christians worshiped between A.D. 100 and 200. All in all the evidence points to a simple but orderly worship containing the main elements of New Testament worship, except that fundamental changes in the meaning of the Lord's Supper had made their appearance.

B. *In the Third and Fourth Centuries.* When we come to the third and fourth centuries the problem of discovering how Christians worshiped is made difficult by the century of secret worship mentioned above. A number of explanations have been offered for this practice: that Christians were imitating the secrecy of the mystery religions that were rife in that period throughout the Roman Empire; that it was a device for protecting Christianity against pagan profanation; that it resulted from the growing tendency to look upon the Lord's Supper as a mysterious, awesome, holy thing; that it was a practical step for their own personal safety during a period of violent persecutions. In all probability, each of these explanations has some basis in fact. At any rate, the secret worship lasted for at least a hundred years, from about A.D. 250–350. This explains why it is so difficult to determine approximate dates and places where new practices originated or old ones ended.

In A.D. 313, Constantine issued his famous edict of Milan, which gave Christians complete freedom to practice their religion. Christian worship could once more take place in the open. When that happened it soon became evident that many changes had taken place during the period of their " captivity." The sense of freedom and the fact that Constantine showered special favors upon Christianity brought even more changes before the end of the fourth century. Reference has already been made to the manner in which their organization and ministry imitated, or were influenced by, Roman customs. Other important developments also took place and will now be described briefly.

1. *Worship began to take the form of public spectacles.* Church buildings became more numerous and more expensive. Constantine himself built magnificent churches in Jerusalem, Bethlehem, and Constantinople. Furnishings and appointments became more lavish and ostentatious. Gregory Dix mentions a document submitted as evidence about A.D. 303 in courts that contained a list of articles used in worship. This list included such things.as expensive chalices, bowls, lamps, tunics, veils, slippers, and so on, showing how pretentious worship was becoming. Church festivals

multiplied rapidly and were celebrated with pomp, ceremonials, processionals, and extravagant symbolism.

2. *The liturgy became longer and more complicated.* This is vividly illustrated by the earliest complete Christian liturgy preserved to modern times, the so-called Clementine liturgy. This liturgy is found in Books II and VIII of the Apostolic Constitutions, which is dated about A.D. 380 by most scholars. Although opinions are divided about whether it was ever a " living " liturgy, scholars generally agree that it probably represents Christian worship as it took place in the city of Antioch and elsewhere in Syria about A.D. 350–380. Actually it is a compilation of church laws, usages, and liturgical formulations that had been gradually developing since the days of the apostles, and, purportedly, on the authority of their practices. At the time, it was not accepted as authoritative by all parts of the church. But it was so accepted by the Eastern Church, with the result that one can attend a service of worship in an Orthodox church today and feel that he is observing with few changes the same general kind of service that prevailed in Syria possibly as early as the fourth century, certainly as early as the sixth.

In fact, the modern Orthodox Church has unbroken continuity with the church of the fourth century not only in worship but also in theology and polity. Hence it can roughly be thought of in many respects as the kind of church the ecumenical church is supposed to follow as a pattern if it is to be like the church of the early centuries.[9] In this study, however, we are concerned with the Western, or Roman Catholic, Church only.

William D. Maxwell has given a clear and concise reconstruction of the liturgy and an explanation of the procedures followed as the worship continued.[10] He estimates that the increased number and length of the Scripture readings, the increased number, kinds, and length of prayers, the addition of such new features as salutations, litanies, responses, and versicles, and the use of dramatic and symbolic ceremonials resulted in a service three hours in length.

One has only to compare this service with the simple, short

service indicated by Justin Martyr (A.D. 150) to see how far Christian worship had changed in the course of two centuries.

3. *Changes were made in the Lord's Supper.* By this time the Supper was regarded as more sacred, more holy, of a different quality, than the other parts of the service. It was now beginning to be approached with awe, the elements treated almost with superstitious fear, and thought of as possessing miraculous power. The elements were conceived of as a sacrifice. The table was considered an altar. The ministers were vested priests. The doctrine of transubstantiation of the elements into the actual blood and body of Christ was nearing completion by the end of the fourth century. The Supper overshadowed the other parts of the service. Everything that went before the Supper was thought of as preparing for the Communion. The culminating act of worship was the moment when the priest offered the sacrifice and elevated the elements and, just a bit later, when the miracle of transubstantiation occurred.

Thus by the end of the fourth century, the church of the post-apostolic fathers had developed worship into a great public spectacle, embodying most of the features of medieval worship, which it immediately preceded, and incorporating much of the theology that characterizes Roman Catholic worship at the present time. Again certain questions emerge: (*a*) Was this a natural development of the more or less rudimentary worship of the New Testament, or was it the formation of a type of worship incongruous in many respects with New Testament worship? (*b*) On what bases is one's answer to that question to be determined?

C. *Reading History Backward.* Before this section on the worship of the patristic church is concluded, attention should be called to a practice, common in modern histories of worship, of using this worship as the clue to understanding the worship of the New Testament. This is accomplished by the simple procedure of reading history backward from the fourth century. According to Oscar Cullmann, this procedure is laid down by H. Lietzmann as a principle of historical method in liturgics. Lietzmann says the starting point should "be made in the later sources and from there the way back be sought to the time of the first beginnings where the sources are few and far between and development is still going on." Cullmann adds: "Although this method is on the whole to be approved, warning must be given of the danger of a too one-sided application. It carries with it very easily the temptation to want to find willy nilly later developments in earliest times, at least in embryo." [11]

This is how the method operates. The service of worship in 380 clearly consisted of two separate and different kinds of worship. With this pattern in mind as the key, and by the use of a moderate amount of imagination, one can leap backward over the long periods in which there is scant evidence as to what was taking place, and reconstruct the fragmentary evidence of previous periods into a similar scheme. For example, in 150, more than two hundred years previously, Justin stated that no one was permitted to partake of the Supper except believers. With the key provided by the Clementine liturgy, one can imagine that to refer to a division into two parts. Similarly, one can easily suppose that Pliny was describing two distinct parts of one service, not two different services, when, in 112, he reported that Christians had a brief service and then stated that *afterward* they assembled to eat " ordinary and innocent food."

By a similar application of this principle many writers find in the New Testament the same liturgical order of service presided over by the same types of ministers in the same architectural setting as that found in the church of the late fourth century. For example, Cullmann makes a passing reference to "the book of Revelation, which, *as we know* [italics added] correlates the present [meaning the then current] service of worship as its fulfillment in the events of the last days." [12] What he is saying may be stated more pointedly thus: "We [scholars] now know that John's description in Revelation of the worship of God by the heavenly beings is patterned after the maner in which Christians were accustomed to worship on earth in those days."

Of course, he does not mean that scholars actually *know* this for certain. Rather, he means that, beginning with the Clementine liturgy as the clue, scholars now move back, through Justin Martyr, Pliny, Ignatius, and Clement, to Revelation, and by a large amount of ingenious interpretation of the cryptic figures, and of the bizarre language of Revelation, *discover* that John was describing a heavenly liturgy in the framework of the liturgy with which he and his readers were familiar in their weekly worship.

The limitations and dangers of this method of interpreting history are obvious. It is often important to know where religious beliefs originated, especially if those forms are to be considered normative. But everything that develops from an original germ-idea cannot be accepted as valid merely because it can be traced back to the original. The validity of an emergent is determined by whether its nature is compatible with the nature of the original sources. Assuredly the nature of the original Christianity cannot be established by studying what later emerged from it. The essential nature of the Christian religion can be discovered only by a study of what it was at its beginning. By the use of the principle suggested by Lietzmann, namely, that later developments can be used as the clue to the first beginnings of Christianity, one could justify as true everything that has grown out of early Christianity. This only serves to re-emphasize the validity of what was stated earlier: that the criterion by which we judge all that has taken place since apostolic times is whether it is in harmony with the essential nature of New Testament Christianity.

The Unity of the Postapostolic Church

As stated at the beginning of this chapter, there seems to be a general unofficial agreement that the pattern for the kind of unity required for the ecumenical church of our day is found in the postapostolic church. Those who take this position, of course, find it necessary to assert that the New Testament churches were too loosely associated together outwardly or visibly to be taken as a model for the modern church. John Knox declares categorically: " The diversity and division in early Christianity cannot be taken as normative. The united church of tomorrow cannot be modeled after the divided church of the first century." [13] So he turns to the postapostolic church in which he finds the *visible* unity that he believes to be essential to an ecumenical church.

Since that church supposedly included all the churches then in existence, it is called the old *catholic* church. Because previous to this time the separate churches were presumably too loosely associated together to be regarded as either united or divided, this church is called the *undivided* ancient church. The assumption seems to be: if we could get the modern Christian bodies to agree to return to the condition of the Christian church when it was for the first time really united, and before it had been divided over basic issues, we would have a solid foundation on which to build one modern catholic church. Let us therefore try to ascertain the kind, the amount, and the value of the unity that was attained in those centuries.

Before the end of the first century, Christians were threatened from without by persecution as a dangerous and subversive minority, and from within by theological disputes and divisions. They sought to defend themselves against erroneous charges, to hold their own in debates with the apologists of other religions, and to protect themselves from the infiltration of non-Christian beliefs and practices. The contest was with both Judaism and heathenism. The fight was long, continuous, and bitter, and the success was uneven. In the struggle the episcopal form of government grew apace; the Christian Scriptures were officially gathered together into the New Testament; Christian doctrines were formulated by Christian apologists; and an elaborate system of worship was rapidly developed.

But a complete and satisfactory unity was not attained. The first councils of the church were not catholic. They were diocesan and provincial synods. But even these councils are not mentioned in the records until the third century. So it would appear that the church operated somewhat satisfactorily for more than a century without any kind of general council. The first councils seem to have been democratic in nature and were attended and participated in freely by both clergy and laity in the area. They dealt with controversies and matters of morals, discipline, and worship. Decisions, known as canons, were adopted. Discipline was purely moral in nature and had nothing to do with civil punishment. When it seemed necessary, offenders were simply expelled from the church. The bishops exercised the discipline and excommunicated heretics in behalf of the synod.

There is little to indicate that the canons of one synod were necessarily or usually followed by other synods. On the contrary, available evidence seems to show that there was no such thing in the church of this period as unanimous co-operation or uniformity of action or unanimity of belief among the churches in the several areas of the Empire. Each synod had to deal with its own schisms and heresies. In time some of the controversies spread to all parts of the church and came to be dealt with by most of the synods. Even then, unanimity of action, practice, and belief was seldom achieved by the whole church. In general each bishop felt himself supreme within his own diocese. Jealousy and competition between the bishops developed quite early and continued throughout this period and on into later centuries until the final split between the eastern and western sections came.

Excommunication of those considered heretics did not fully succeed in its purpose. This was largely because some of the so-called heresies were not unmixed errors. On the one hand, these heretics were fighting to preserve in the church certain New Testament truths and principles, and on the other were opposing inclusion in the church of certain things alien to New Testament Christianity.

For example, take Montanism, one of the most important of the early heresies. Bishops and synods of Asia Minor excommunicated Montanists from their fellowship, but Montanism found supporters, even open supporters, elsewhere in the church. The most noted of these supporters was Tertullian, who advocated its beliefs without either seceding from the church or being excommunicated from it. In spite of laws enacted against them until well into the sixth century, they continued to draw many adherents, especially in the Eastern Church. And even after they ceased to be of any importance as an organized group, some of their beliefs kept springing up in different forms and places and have continued to do so to the present time. At the conclusion of his study of Montanism, Schaff says:

> The religious earnestness which animated it, its prophecies and visions, its millenarianism, and the fanatical extremes into which it ran, have since reappeared, under various names and forms, and in new combinations, in Novatianism, Donatism, the spiritualism of the Franciscans, Anabaptists, the Camisard enthusiasm, Puritanism, Quakerism, Quietism, Pietism, Second Adventism, Irvingism, and so on, by way of protest and wholesome reaction against various evils in the church.[14]

Winfred E. Garrison has recently called attention to the fact that Arianism, which was supposed to have been driven out of the church in the early fourth century, continued to be a factor within the church for a long time thereafter:

> A synod in Seleucia in 360, a full generation after Nicaea, rejected both *homo-* and *homoi-ousion* as contrary to Scripture. Ulfilas, the missionary to the Goths, converted that aggressive nation of "barbarians" to Arian Christianity. Alaric's Goths, who captured Rome in 410 and thereby stirred Augustine to write *The City of God,* were Arian Christians. Theodoric, who founded the Ostrogothic kingdom of Italy, and ruled it for nearly forty years until 526, was an Arian, and his enlightened administration did credit to the cause. The Visigoths carried Arianism into Spain.[15]

These facts provoke the question whether it will ever be possible, or, if possible, whether it will be necessary or desirable, to establish a church in which there is uniformity of theological thought about our basic Christian doctrines.

When ecumenical councils arose, of which the Council of Nicaea (A.D. 325) was the first, church unity assumed a different form. The bishops began to take full control and councils became clerical dictatorships, with bishops the only voting members. These bishops were not elected by those whom they were supposed to represent, but assumed the right to rule by virtue of their apostolic authority. After the persecution of Christianity ceased under Constantine, the bishops more and more began trying to suppress heresy by calling upon the state to enforce their edicts and canons. By the end of the fourth century the church, with the full support of the state, was actually seeking to exterminate paganism. The successors to Constantine issued decrees upon decrees forbidding pagan sacrifices, closing pagan temples, confiscating heretical meetinghouses, imposing fines on heretical clergy, and so on.

Some church historians rejoice in this apparent victory of Christianity over paganism by the use of force. Others justify it as a historical necessity under the circumstances then prevailing. But this form of unity is alien to New Testament Christianity. This particular concept of unity is the natural outgrowth of a doctrine of the church that had been in process of formation since the late decades of the second century. Irenaeus (ca. 190) taught that "where the church is, there is the Spirit of God, and where the Spirit of God is, there is all grace." He left no doubt that he meant by this: that we find the Holy Spirit only in the church; that to be separated from it is to be separated from the Spirit; and that all heretics are sons of Satan.

Tertullian a few years later compared the church to Noah's ark, out of which no person can find salvation. About the middle of the third century, Origen wrote his famous words: "Out of the church no man can be saved." In the year A.D. 251, Cyprian brought this doctrine of the church to completion in his classical tract *De Unitate Ecclesiae*. His views in this tract are explained by Schaff as follows:

> The catholic church was founded from the first by Christ on St. Peter alone. . . . She has since remained one, in unbroken episcopal succession. . . . Out of this empirical orthodox church, episcopally organized and centralized in Rome, Cyp-

rian can imagine no Christianity at all. . . . Whoever sepa-
rates himself from the catholic church is a foreigner, a pro-
fane person, an enemy, condemns himself, and must be
shunned. No one can have God for his father, who has not
the church for his mother. As well might one out of the ark
of Noah have escaped the Flood, as one out of the church be
saved; because she alone is the bearer of the Holy Spirit and
of all grace.[16]

This was written a hundred years before the joint campaign of
the bishops and the Roman state to exterminate all non-Christians. Within that century this medieval, Roman Catholic view
of the church was taking root in the minds of leading churchmen
who were preparing, consciously or unconsciously, to make good
use of it. By the end of the fourth century — the end of the
period of the old, catholic, undivided church under consideration — this doctrine had become official and was the basis upon
which all dissenting thought was suppressed. Yet this doctrine of
the church had no standing in New Testament times. Neither
Christ nor the apostolic church attempted to command or coerce
the wills and minds of men. Neither used nor sanctioned the use
of force to secure confessions of faith or to punish nonbelievers.
No effort was made in the apostolic church to secure uniformity
in the formulations of the Christian faith. Church membership
at no time depended upon the acceptance of a creed drafted by a
church council.

What then shall we say of the unity of the church of the fourth
century? Such unity as existed was maintained at the expense of
free thought and free speech, by excommunications, by the power
of the state that suppressed all opposition and forced submission
and obedience, by persecutions, and, if necessary, by death. Unity
was not genuine or deep. Dissent was driven underground only
to appear in still more serious controversies and schisms later.
Post-Nicene Christianity preceded and paved the way for medieval Christianity, which was, so to speak, just around the corner.

The facts do not justify speaking of *the* unity of the church of the fathers. There were several degrees and kinds of unity during that period. Precisely which of these types of unity is in the minds of those who ask the whole of Christendom to accept the ancient catholic church as the standard for the one universal church? The unity of the second century, which was more or less voluntary but not actually universal? or the unity of the third century, which was achieved by moral discipline? or the unity of the fourth century, which was gained by compulsion and persecution? Answers to those questions are not given clearly. Protestants had better be clear about this before they commit themselves to accept the ancient church as normative.

Non-Christian Influences in the Postapostolic Church

Two non-Christian influences, other than those which have been mentioned already, or mentioned only briefly, will now be considered.

A. *Judaism.* It is commonly supposed that the Judaizers mentioned in the New Testament were conquered by the apostolic church and that their successors played no significant part in Christianity after the Jewish Christians fled to Pella when Jerusalem was destroyed by Titus in A.D. 70. The facts do not support this position, unless one is thinking only of the part Judaism played through well-organized groups.

Many scholars have analyzed the theology of Clement of Rome and found it more Hebraic than Christian in nature. The Epistle of Barnabas, usually dated in the early part of the second century, had essentially the same objective as the book of Hebrews: to show that Christianity abrogated Judaism. The writer warned Christians against adopting Jewish ideas and practices. In that same period Ignatius warned the Magnesians, " For if we still go on observing Judaism, we admit we never received grace " (ch. 8:1), and " It is monstrous to talk Jesus Christ and to live like a Jew " (ch. 10:3). The movement known as Marcionism separated from the main stream of Christianity, beginning in A.D. 140, in order to repudiate several Old Testament features that had been incorporated into the early church, and to try to restore Christianity to its primitive apostolic form. A number of Judaistic heresies known as the Nazarenes and Ebionites passed off the scene after many ups and downs, leaving their imprint upon the church.

Attention has already been called to the fact that beginning with Clement of Rome the idea of a Christian hierarchy, in imitation of the Old Testament hierarchical priesthood and distinct from the laity, was introduced into the church. Although the polity of the Christian church was partly of Roman origin, it can be said that the ministry of the church was a new form of the Jewish priesthood. Niebuhr and Williams state that within four centuries the hereditary priesthood of Israel had been replaced by another form of Christian indelible priesthood known as the apostolic succession, the ordination to which " represented a tactile succession going back to the apostles." [17]

The Christian year and many of the festivals connected with it were partly of Jewish origin. Some of the most violent controversies of the ancient church were known as the Paschal controversies, and had to do with the time of the celebration of the death and resurrection of Jesus, which came to be known as the Christian Passover. The issue was: should the Jewish Paschal day or the Christian first day of the week determine the time and meaning of that festival? The details of the controversies do not concern us here. They began about A.D. 150 and were officially settled by the Council of Nicaea. That council decreed that it was not becoming of Christians to follow the Jewish usage, that the date of Easter should be movable, and that it should always be held after the Jewish Passover. That decree did not alter the fact that Christians took over a Jewish festival. Pentecost also rested on a Jewish feast, the feast of harvest.

Earlier we showed that the Christian church, in time, and contrary to New Testament thought, came to interpret the Lord's Supper as a Christian form of the Old Testament sacrificial system. The elaborated symbolic, ceremonial, and ritualistic worship of the late fourth century is more like Old Testament worship than New Testament worship. The conception of the church, described above as underlying the combined efforts of the Roman emperors and the bishops of the Christian church to impose Christianity by force upon the entire Empire, is traceable to, or certainly parallels, the Old Testament idea of an exclusive, corporate community of God's people to which all members of the community are compelled to belong. In fact, one appeal made about A.D. 350 to the sons of Constantine to exterminate paganism by force was justified on the basis of Deut. 13:6-10, where God commanded that any person who enticed others to worship false gods should be shown no pity, but should be put to death.

Many of the features of the church of the fathers that are alien to New Testament Christianity must, therefore, be thought of as being due to the continuing influence of Judaizers in the church.

B. *Paganism*. Other practices alien to New Testament Christianity were due to the influence of the pagan society in which the church existed. For example, festivities celebrating the birth of Jesus on December 25 were deliberately set up in imitation of and to take the place of pagan festivities in connection with observances of the birth of the sun. The date of Epiphany was set as January 6 to imitate and supersede festivities connected with the worship of Osiris and Dionysius. Mariology, which began to develop in this period, was substituted for the worship of Osiris and Isis.

Without doubt the mystery religions, which flourished in the Mediterranean world for at least a thousand years beginning in 700 B.C., influenced Christian beliefs and practices. These religions had impressive rituals, ceremonies, symbolism, and sacramental rites in connection with their worship. They observed a baptism of purification and regeneration, a symbolic meal with their gods, rituals portraying death, resurrection, and the future life, etc. Few scholars would affirm categorically that Christianity incorporated the practices of the mystery religions bodily in their own system of worship. But most of them are convinced that Christians developed their own rites and rituals for the express purpose of competing with, and in imitation of, the fascinating rites and rituals of paganism, and that in the process Christianity itself became partially paganized.

This paganizing process came to its climax, or at least was nearing completion, by A.D. 400. Confirmation of this is found in a recent Roman Catholic book.[18] The author states that his study is based on the teaching of the first Christian centuries and consists " of an interpretation of the symbolism of Christian worship according to the fathers of the church " (p. 4). The fathers whose writings are used as sources are almost exclusively those of the first four centuries. He confines his study to the symbolism of three sacraments, Baptism, Confirmation, and the Holy Eucharist, and of the Christian week of the liturgical year. He frankly admits that the church borrowed some of these symbols from the customs of the Greek world about them. But he also insists that they were grafted on to a " primitive stock " of symbols that may be found in the Bible, principally in the Old Testament. He also states candidly that he finds these symbols in the Bible by a typological interpretation of the documents.

The purpose of our study would not be served by going into the details of his treatment. Suffice it to say that he confirms the views long held by Protestants that much of the theology and many of the symbolic practices associated with Roman Catholic worship, which Protestants regard as semipagan, are of non-Christian origin, although, of course, by his method of typological interpretation, he always finds them at least " in germ " somewhere in the Bible. Attention is called to these facts in order that the reader may understand clearly from one more angle of approach exactly the kind of church that is being held before modern Christians as a norm.

This church contained, not in germ merely, but in a well-developed form, practically all the characteristic features of the later medieval church, including its hierarchy, with the bishop of Rome at the top claiming to be the successor of Peter; its worship, with its elaborate rituals, symbolism, sacramentals, and supper-sacrifice; its many and varied traditions and doctrines, many of which were later repudiated by the Reformers. This is the church that is supposed to be the pattern for the coming ecumenical church!

Two Concluding Questions

A. *How are we to judge the changes that took place in the postapostolic church?* Are we to think of the church as having gradually departed from New Testament principles, or as having developed those principles to their mature conclusion? One's answer to this question depends upon his doctrine of the authority of the New Testament. If he believes, as I do, that the New Testament contains sufficient and reliable information on which to discover the nature of the church as God intended it, his answer will be that in many ways and at the specific points indicated as we have proceeded, the church departed from, or developed characteristics out of harmony with, New Testament principles. The church was by no means wholly apostate, else it could not have accomplished its divine mission in the world to the degree that it has throughout the centuries. But it failed to develop its doctrines, organization, administration, and worship fully according to New Testament principles, and this prevented it from achieving more fully its divine destiny in the world.

A distinction should always be made between the nature of the church and the manner in which that nature is expressed, between the principles of the New Testament church and the policies and procedures embodying those principles. One who believes that the New Testament contains the authoritative standard for the nature of the church does not claim that the manner in which that church originally organized for business, so to speak, provides a blueprint for the church's organization to the end of time. He acknowledges that the church needs to change its policies, methods, and procedures in order to meet changing conditions and to embody the results of its growing experiences and experiments. But he declares that through all changing and growing experiences the church should retain its original characteristics as revealed in the New Testament.

On the other hand, if one believes that the nature of and God-given purpose for the church can be discovered, not solely in its early origins but also in its later developments, his answer will be that in the first four hundred years of its existence the church grew from childhood to maturity. Those who hold this position claim that the church was not only established by God but continues to develop under the guidance of his Holy Spirit. That, of course, is all but universally believed, except that this leaves us with the problem of deciding how we can discover which developments were guided by the Spirit and which were not. Or else, it forces us to say that the Spirit guides all developments that take place in history. Some criterion or standard must exist by which to judge whether events are man-made or God-made. What is that standard if not the New Testament?

If the beliefs and practices of the fourth-century church are normative, why are not the practices of the church of any or all ensuing centuries also normative? On what principle or principles do we declare the church of the third and fourth centuries to be standard rather than the church of the Reformation, or of the twentieth century? And of the churches in the twentieth century, which is normative: the Orthodox, Roman Catholic, United Church of India, Anglican, Lutheran, or some other? Or, is there a standard by which all churches, past and present, are to be measured? The history of the church is not its own judge: it is judged by the New Testament.

B. *Why have Protestants chosen the ancient church of the fathers as normative for the ecumenical church?* The answer to that question seems to be: because they hope this will help bring the Roman Catholic Church into the ecumenical movement. At least this is the reason openly expressed in numerous books by Protestants. They know beforehand that Rome will not agree to negotiate on the basis of either the New Testament church or the Reformation church, and that Protestants will not negotiate on the basis of the medieval church. So they have chosen the church of the fathers as the place to begin ecumenical discussions, hoping that it may become the liaison between the two groups.

No one can understand or appraise properly the Protestant–Roman Catholic phase of the ecumenical movement unless he takes into consideration this basic motivation which prompts the thinking of Protestants and determines the course they are pursuing.

Chapter IV
Some Essential Protestant Doctrines

The alacrity with which many Protestants are agreeing to bypass the Reformation and return to the church of the patristic period for their standards is disturbing for several reasons. That ancient church, as shown in the last chapter, was, in a number of respects, almost as inharmonious with Protestantism as the medieval church that followed. Furthermore, a return to the ancient church would take the unwise step of trying to turn the clock backward. The processes of history cannot be reversed. The accumulated experiences of fifteen hundred years cannot wisely be discarded lightly. We cannot afford to close our ears to what God has to say to the church of our century through its history since the first four or five centuries.

Again, to return to that church as a pattern is equivalent to admitting that no significant contribution toward a better understanding of the nature of Christianity has been made by Protestants in the four and a half centuries of their separate existence. There is no factual or rational reason for making such an admission. God took more than a thousand years to pave the way for the Reformation of the sixteenth century. Even then the process of restoration, rejuvenation, and renewal was only begun. Two hundred years passed before Reformed Christians rediscovered and achieved to a significant degree the freedom that is inherent in the nature of the gospel. As a result of their slowly maturing experiences, Protestants have developed a Christian church that, with all its imperfections, is in many ways more nearly in accord with the principles of the New Testament than any church since apostolic times. And the work of the Reformation is still not complete.

In this connection certain crucial questions arise that Protestants must face: Has Protestant Christianity in its present form ceased to be relevant to the modern situation, or, to use another's expression, are we now living in " post-Protestant times "? Does Protestantism represent or embody any distinctive truths that justify a separate existence? Have its distinguishing testimony and its divine contribution been made? Has evangelical Christianity become such a vital and virile force within the Roman Church that non-Roman evangelical Christian bodies are no longer necessary? Is God trying through the ecumenical movement to tell Protestants that the time has come for them to disband and lose their identity in a new type of church that more nearly conforms to the genius of the Christian gospel? The present trends in Protestant thinking, if continued unchecked, would seem to require an affirmative answer to all these questions.

But before these affirmative answers are given, let us take a fresh look at some of the essential beliefs of Protestants that must be given a chance to live and thrive and do their creative work in any future Christian church. As we do this, let us keep asking ourselves another question or two: How can evangelical Christians best keep their characteristic beliefs free to make their full, unimpeded witness in the world? By giving them up in whole or in part in order to form an ecumenical church that includes the present Roman Church? Or by continuing their separate existence?

Students of the Reformation are generally agreed that the Reformers of the sixteenth century were seeking to restore Christianity to its New Testament type. David Schaff has said that the Reformation went back to the " fountainhead of Christianity itself," that it was a " deeper plunge into the meaning of the gospel " than had been made by any previous age of the church.[1]

The Reformers had no intention of initiating a new form of **Christianity. In separating from Rome they were getting back** into the stream of original Christianity. As Luther said upon one occasion, the Roman Catholics, not the Reformers, were the ones who had played the apostate. In so far as the Reformers succeeded in their purpose they could rightly claim to be in the direct apostolic succession, to represent apostolic Christianity.

Protestants, therefore, can trace their lineage back through all the intervening centuries to the New Testament period. Evangelical Christianity never died out completely, but existed in one group or another, to one degree or another, through all the centuries preceding the sixteenth. Indeed, some of its tenets may be found in all the churches of Christendom. But it was released by the Reformation and given a maximum opportunity to perform its divine function in the world. Until the present time Protestantism is the main guardian of the essential doctrines of that Christianity.

The ecumenical movement of our times is forcing Protestants to consider whether they can be faithful to their sacred trust if they seek a union with Rome that requires the surrender or radical alteration of their essential beliefs. What is involved is not simply their continued existence as a religious organization or the perpetuation of a mere name, but the preservation and transmission of certain evangelical truths of which, until the present time, they have been the principal representatives and custodians.

Protestants and Roman Catholics have many of the same items in their creeds. Both groups avow belief in God, in Christ, in the Holy Spirit, in the Bible, in the church, in redemption, in worship, in prayer, in the life hereafter, in the Christian way of life, in Christian evangelism, and in missions. But they believe quite differently about some of these matters. Some of their doctrines, though bearing the same general titles, are, when spelled out, dissimilar, diverse, and even disparate in nature. Both are Christian bodies, but they represent in many ways different kinds of Christianity.

I shall now proceed to state what I consider to be some of the cardinal doctrines of Protestantism. This statement is not an attempt to produce a comprehensive, historical, systematic summary of Protestant theology that is acceptable to various Protestant bodies. Rather, it is one person's explanation of crucial evangelical beliefs that hosts of Protestants are unwilling to waive or weaken as the price of union with Rome. In order to accomplish this purpose adequately, it will be necessary to indicate that Protestants deny or reject certain Roman Catholic beliefs. This procedure is inevitable. Under the limitations of human thought and communication, there is no way to explain freely and positively what one believes without at the same time stating in negative terms what he disavows.[2]

The Authority and Sufficiency of the Scriptures

This doctrine was considered at some length in Chapter II. As there stated, Protestants affirm that the Bible is the sole and sufficient authority for the church. This means that the Word of God is the standard for the church of all ages, its court of last resort; and that the church and its beliefs, organizations, practices, and enterprises are to be judged by whether they are in harmony with the fundamental principles and truths revealed in the Scriptures, as those principles and truths are fulfilled in the New Testament.

This does not mean that the church remains static. The church's formulation and understanding of the gospel, its applications and implementations of the gospel, the institutions, organizations, and programs it creates for the proclamation and propagation of the gospel — all these are continuously undergoing criticism, revision, and change. This accumulating and changing body of the church's thinking and experiences is known as traditions. Valuable as these traditions are, they can neither add anything to nor subtract anything from the *essential nature* of the original gospel as it is recorded in the Bible.

Because Protestants believe thus in the authority and sufficiency of the Scriptures, they find it necessary to disavow the Roman Catholic teaching that tradition is of equal authority with the revelation of God in the Scriptures. The Council of Trent, meeting about the middle of the sixteenth century, made this doctrine official when it declared "that unwritten traditions in the church are all to be accepted with respect and veneration equal to that which is due to the Scriptures." Once the validity of this doctrine is admitted, there is no way to prevent non-Christian and anti-Christian elements from penetrating the life and thought of the church. For the church's teaching cannot then be evaluated by any external authority. It becomes the sole judge of the dogmas that it promulgates.

When the attention of Pius IX was called to the fact that the tradition of the church for a thousand years preceding 1870 was against the doctrine of the infallibility of the pope, he declared, "I am tradition." The noted Roman Catholic historian, Lord Acton, who opposed the dogma of infallibility, said of the Roman doctrine of tradition: "The existence of tradition has nothing to do with evidence, and objections taken from history are not valid when contradicted by ecclesiastical decrees. Authority must conquer history." [3] Given a pope, or a series of popes, with the disposition to attempt it, Christianity could be changed by the use of tradition into another kind of religion.

This is precisely what has happened. Original Christianity has been changed at certain points. Operating in accordance with its doctrine of tradition, the Roman Church declared as dogmas, which all the faithful are expected to accept as true, the immaculate conception of the Virgin Mary (1854), the infallibility of the pope (1870), and the bodily assumption of the Virgin Mary into heaven (1950). None of these has any support in the New Testament. As we shall see in the next section of this chapter, in actual practice the Virgin Mary for great numbers of Roman Catholics has taken the place of Jesus Christ as the mediator between God and man. The Roman Catholic writer, Juniper B. Carol, recently frankly admitted that most of the Roman Church's teaching about Mary is not found in the Bible. He defines tradition as "the body of revealed truth not contained in the Bible, but transmitted from generation to generation under the guidance of the magisterium or teaching authority of the church." Then he adds, "It is well known that the teaching of tradition has played a major role in the progressive development of Mariology; hence its importance cannot be overestimated." [4]

Protestants feel obligated, therefore, to reject the non-Christian and anti-Christian accretions of the Roman Church and to repudiate the doctrine by means of which primarily they enter that church's theology.

THE ACCESSIBILITY, SOVEREIGNTY, AND FREEDOM OF GOD

The Protestant doctrine of God is based squarely upon the New Testament teaching that God revealed himself fully and completely in Jesus. So we can say that, when one fully understands all that Jesus was, said, and did, one understands the nature, the character, and the attributes of God, as well as how God feels toward human beings and how he deals with them. (Cf. John 1:14 and ch. 14:9; Heb. 1:3; II Cor. 4:4.) That is to say, the early Christians believed that God is like Christ. Or to state it more fully still, they believed that God *is* what Christ *was* — a living, loving, forgiving, redeeming, ever-present God.

Protestants believe that God loves people, values people, treats people as Jesus did. We believe that in the death of Jesus, God suffered for the redemption of mankind. In that act God removed all barriers between him and his children except the barriers they themselves erect. (Cf. Rom. 5:2; Eph. 2:18; 3:12; Heb. 10:19 f.)

At all times God is immediately accessible to men. They do not have to go to any special place, or engage in any special ritual, or speak in any special formula, or summon the assistance of any other being, earthly or heavenly, to get into the presence of God. In Christ and through Christ, God has made himself forever available to the human souls who seek him. " When you pray," said Jesus, " go into your room and shut the door and pray to your Father who is in secret; and your Father who sees in secret will reward you." (Matt. 6:6.) The Spirit of God and the spirit of man can meet! They can meet as easily, as simply, as naturally, as a child goes into the presence of his mother or father.

Furthermore, Protestants believe that God is sovereign. He is alive in history, but not bound by it. He is always Lord of heaven and of earth. He has not abdicated his throne in favor of any person or people, any society or institution. He rules over all nations and all social orders. He has not turned over to anyone his divine authorities, prerogatives, and powers. His Spirit works where and when and how he pleases. God established his church, but he is not confined or restricted to what the church does. The church is not God's Kingdom. He works through the church but also through other institutions. The church is his instrument. He is not the church's instrument. He chooses and uses men as his agents, but this does not prevent him from participating directly in the affairs of men and of nations. No person or institution can claim to have a monopoly on God or on ways to God. God is forever Lord! He is forever free!

Because Protestants believe these things they reject three fundamental doctrines of the Roman Catholic Church: the doctrines of the pope, of Mary, and of the priesthood.

1. *The doctrine of the pope.* The official formulation of this doctrine is found in Chapter III of the First Dogmatic Constitution of the Church of Christ in the Vatican Decrees.[5] This chapter, entitled "On the Power and Nature of the Primacy of the Roman Pontiff," declares:

> All the faithful of Christ must believe that the holy Apostolic See and the Roman pontiff possesses the primacy over the whole world, and that the Roman pontiff is . . . true vicar of Christ, and head of the whole church. . . . [To his power] all . . . both pastors and faithful, both individually and collectively, are bound . . . to submit not only in matters which belong to faith and morals, but also in those that appertain to the discipline and government of the church throughout the world. . . . None may reopen the judgment of the Apostolic See, than whose authority there is no greater, nor can any lawfully review its judgment. (Pp. 189, 191.)

The chapter concludes by pronouncing anathema upon all who deny these claims.

Pius IX was pope when these decrees were issued. His immediate successor, Leo XIII, in his encyclical *Satis cognitum,* declared that the Roman pontiffs have supreme power in the church by divine right (*jure divino*), that "Christ assigned to Peter and his successors that they would be His Vicars and would forever exercise the same power in the Church that He Himself exercised in His mortal life." Pius X, the next pope in line, issued a compendium, *The Catholic Faith,* in which he claimed that the "Roman pontiff is the vicar of Jesus Christ because he represents him upon earth and takes his place in the government of the church." Modern Catholics are taught, through pamphlets widely distributed, to believe:

> The Vatican is the home of Jesus the teacher. . . . From this sanctuary the Lord Jesus now speaks to the world by the mouth of his vicar. . . . When we fall at the pope's feet and offer him the homage of our mind, and to accept his teaching, it is again in a certain way Jesus Christ whom we adore in his doctrinal presence. . . . God wills and commands it because the pope wills and commands it.[6]

A recent Catholic book states with great pride, "Whereas the Reformation bows before the inaccessible majesty of God, Rome substitutes itself for God and claims his powers."[7]

At the coronation of Pope John XXIII, in 1958, a triple tiara was placed upon his head, and then a cardinal deacon said, "Receive the tiara adorned with three crowns and know that thou art the Father of princes and kings, Ruler of the world, Vicar of our Savior Jesus Christ, to whom is honor and glory, world without end. Amen." According to the *Catholic Dictionary,* the first crown symbolizes the pope's "universal episcopate"; the second, his "supremacy of jurisdiction"; and the third, his "temporal supremacy."

Protestants deny that Jesus gave, or could have given, the popes any such authority to govern the church. From the very beginning of his ministry Jesus refused to assert power to rule. He rejected this possibility in his temptation. That is the significance of the temptation story. His ministry was a disappointment to the Jewish leaders, because he refused to exercise the usual power and authority of an earthly king. He did not pretend to come as a world power, an imperial magistrate; nor did he claim to dominate the earth. To Pilate he said, " My kingship is not of this world " (John 18:36). Yet the Roman Church declares him to be the head of a priestly ruling dynasty, the kind of king he refused to be on earth, and the kind of ruler he warned his followers from trying to become. (Matt. 23:8-12.)

These tremendous claims of the Roman pontiff are based primarily upon the incident recorded in Matt. 16:15 ff. After Peter had confessed Jesus to be the Christ, Jesus is reported to have said to him:

> Blessed are you, Simon Bar-Jona! For flesh and blood has not revealed this to you, but my Father who is in heaven. And I tell you, you are Peter, and upon this rock I will build my church, and the powers of death shall not prevail against it. I will give you the keys of the kingdom of heaven, and whatever you bind on earth shall be bound in heaven, and whatever you loose on earth shall be loosed in heaven. (Vs. 17-19.)

About this passage Protestants have the following things to say:

a. Many Biblical scholars question the authenticity of this passage.

b. Immediately after these words were spoken, Matthew reports that Peter rebuked Jesus for saying that he was soon to suffer death in Jerusalem. Whereupon Jesus in turn rebuked Peter strongly, saying: " Get behind me, Satan! You are a hindrance to me; for you are not on the side of God, but of men." This was indeed a strange thing for Jesus to say if he had meant to assign infallible and sovereign authority over the church to Peter.

c. In Matt. 18:18, the same words about binding and loosing are spoken to all the disciples. If both passages are historical, the first one can hardly be properly interpreted to mean that Peter was to be given authority not possessed by the whole group.

d. The interpretation of Matt. 16:15 ff., favored by the great majority of the church fathers and of modern scholars, does not support the Roman interpretation. They believe that "this" (revealed truth) in v. 17, and "this rock" in v. 18, are the same; that is, the rock upon which the church of Christ is built is not Peter but the revealed truth he uttered.

e. Jesus said nothing about authority and power, or about these being transferable to Peter's successors. In fact, he did not here or elsewhere so much as intimate that there were to be successors to Peter or to the office of apostle. The founders of institutions, foundation stones of buildings, the first person to profess a faith — none of these can have successors any more than Adam could have had a successor as the first man, or Sputnik could have a successor as the first artificial satellite.

f. There is no historical evidence to support the claim that Peter was ever the bishop at Rome or that during his lifetime the Roman Church had a bishop to whom he could pass on his supposed authority.

g. The claims of Rome, based on this passage, are so far out of line with the rest of his gospel and the teaching of the New Testament as a whole that it must be rejected as being out of harmony with the whole spirit and tenor of the New Testament.

2. *The doctrine of Mary.* The teaching of the Roman Catholic Church concerning Mary has developed farther than the average Protestant realizes. That teaching, as found in Juniper Carol's *Fundamentals of Mariology,*[8] will now be summarized. According to Carol, the teaching concerns the mission and the prerogatives of Mary. Her singular mission is fourfold: (*a*) She is the "physical" mother of God. (*b*) She is the "spiritual" mother of angels and men (p. 43). (*c*) She exercises universal mediation. She is the "Mediatrix," the "Co-Redemptrix" with Christ . . . the "Dispenser of all graces" (p. 66). "All favors," without exception, "granted by God to all men are granted in view and because of Mary's intercession. . . . We say *all* men, without exception, regardless of any circumstances of time or space. Those living after the Redemption. . . . Those living before that time" (p. 66). (*d*) She exercises universal queenship. "She has a right

to that title both as Mother of the King [Christ], and as his intimate consort. . . . Like earthly queens in their own sphere, Mary rules her spiritual subjects mostly through the efficacy of her influence over the heart of the King [insinuations, suggestions, powerful intercession on behalf of the subject]." (Pp. 74–75.)

Mary's singular prerogatives are divided into three classes: (a) Prerogatives conferred on her at the beginning of her life. These are the immaculate conception and her fullness of grace. "At the first instant of her conception [she] was preserved from all stain of sin." (P. 87.) (b) Prerogatives conferred on her during the course of her life. These are her immunity from actual sin, her perpetual virginity, and her knowledge. Her immunity from sin means that she "was preserved free from all actual sin during the entire course of her life" (p. 135). Of her perpetual virginity the Roman Church teaches that she was a virgin before the birth of Christ, during his birth — "As the light goes through a glass without breaking it, so Christ passed through our Lady's body into the outside world without any detriment to her virginal seal" — and after his birth. (Pp. 143, 147, 150–151.) (c) Prerogatives conferred at the end of her life. These are immunity from corruption, and anticipated resurrection, her bodily assumption (declared a dogma by Pope Pius XII, on Nov. 1, 1950), and her glorification in heaven. The author explains these prerogatives thus: "After our Lady died, her sacred body remained miraculously incorrupt in the tomb until in time, when, reunited with her soul, it was taken to the glory of heaven where she enjoys the beatific vision and reigns with her divine Son as Queen of the universe" (p. 182).

Having explained these "sublime prerogatives which Almighty God has so liberally bestowed" on Mary, the author declares: "It is obvious that she is entitled to receive a distinct cult from all her children. This cult, which consists essentially in a grateful recognition of her unique dignity and exalted privileges, is technically called *hyperdulia*." *Hyperdulia* is below *latria,* the worship given to God, and above *dulia,* veneration given to saints.

(P. 195.) So the Roman Church has established Marian feasts, encouraged Marian devotions, held impressive series of Marian congresses, founded Mariological academies, gathered together Marian sources and literature in Marian libraries, and published scientific magazines devoted exclusively to Mariology.

While Carol presents all these phases of Mariology as official teaching of the Catholic Church, not all of it has yet been declared as dogmas that the faithful are required to believe under threat of penalties. But the Very Reverend John A. Flynn, president of St. John's University, in March of the Marian Year (1954), predicted that within the next hundred years at least three more Marian dogmas will be decreed by the pope: Mary as Co-Redemptrix of the human race, as Mediatrix of all graces, and as Queen participating with her Son in the power of ruling the world.

Carol's book, which was published with the blessing of the Roman Church, may properly be considered part of the conditioning of Roman Catholics to accept these future dogmas. When and if they are decreed, it is difficult to see how the papacy can any longer succeed in distinguishing between worship of Christ and worship of Mary. Even now millions of lay members of the Roman Church and a large share of its priests have all but substituted Mary for Christ as the source of those spiritual blessings which human beings seek from God. The very word " cult," used by Roman Catholics to describe the *hyperdulia* given to Mary, is foreboding. Technically it means " a system of worship of a diety, or the rites of a religion." Protestants look upon the cult with grave misgivings.

An evaluation of Mariology from the viewpoint of evangelical Christianity may be found in *The Virgin Mary: The Roman Catholic Marian Doctrine*,[9] a significant book by Giovanni Miegge, professor of church history in the Waldensian Faculty of Theology at Rome. Miegge explains fully, fairly, and accurately, all phases of Mariology, offers certain information not found in Carol's book, and indicates where the cult of Mary is headed.

. He shows that Roman Catholic teaching makes Mary a copy of

Christ. Analogies or parallels are drawn between the life, person, and work of Mary and the life, person, and work of Christ, at every point and at every step from her birth to her assumption into heaven. From the viewpoint of " richness of liturgical content, number of festivals, the exalted tone of devotion," the cult of Mary is the highest form of Catholic devotion. There are daily and weekly practices of devotion offered her. Three months of the year are consecrated to her. A number of annual feasts are celebrated in her honor. There are numerous orders, confraternities, and the like, in which she is perpetually worshiped. Miegge enumerates almost fifty titles given to her in one litany. (Pp. 181–182.) To those devoted to her cult many exceptional benefits are promised: for the individual in this life, in death, and after death; for the family, the church, and society. Devotion to her " is morally necessary for salvation." If anyone refuses to venerate her, " it is morally impossible that he be saved " (p. 182).

Moreover, attempts are now being made to " integrate Mary more completely in the Trinity." Her divine Maternity is declared to have procured " for the divine Persons a new and unique glory." Through it the " Father acquires a real authority over the Son "; . . . the Son is given a new life, " a temporal life "; and " the Holy Spirit . . . receives a fecundity in regard to the Son, contributing to give him a body." " In short, Mary completes the Trinity." (P. 189.)

From his study Miegge draws certain conclusions that reflect the judgment of evangelical Christians the world over. " By all the traditional canons," he declares, " this, to Protestants, is the essence of idolatry." Mary has been elevated to the status of a goddess. She is worshiped as the eternally feminine. For the salvation of people and for all their practical religious needs Mary is more important than Christ. If this cult develops much farther, someday it will be said " that within Catholicism, Christianity has given up the field to a different religion " (p. 191).

Protestants are unwilling to compromise with this Mariology. They deny it and reject it. They cannot and will not unite with a Roman Church that is rapidly changing Christianity into a form of religion radically different from the evangelical Christianity they find in the New Testament.

3. *The doctrine of the priesthood.* Our concern at this point is not with the total Catholic doctrine of the priesthood but with the teaching that the priest has authority to act as a substitute for God, to perform certain functions ordinarily reserved for God, to control and dispense God's power, and to act as a mediator between God and man. The Roman Church claims this authority for the priest primarily on three grounds: that the authority of the " keys of the kingdom," given by Jesus to Peter (Matt. 16:19) and to his successors, includes the power to forgive sins and in turn is delegated to the priest; that in the Mass the priest has power to transform the elements into the actual body and blood of Christ, so that when he handles the consecrated elements he handles and controls Christ; and that as a representative of God the priest has the power to bless people and objects.

Catholic publications are, therefore, fraught with such statements as these:

> The priest can not only make Christ present at the altar, confine him in the tabernacle, and take him therefrom again for the benefit of the faithful: he can offer him, the Son of God become man, as a sacrifice for the living and the dead. Christ . . . is at the disposal of the Catholic priest.[10] . . . [The priest's] most august function is . . . to call down the Almighty from heaven — to hold God in his consecrated hands. He receives power to bless, to bring God's benediction upon anyone or anything. . . . He, a man and a sinner, has the marvelous power of forgiving the sins of other men.[11] . . . The priest . . . is a middleman, . . . he brings God into the world and immolates him in the Consecration and Communion. This earth-shaking event happens at his word every day! He is the controller of divine life in the world.[12] . . . Each morning . . . in his hands he holds the creator of the universe, omnipotent God.[13]

The Protestant interpretation of Christ's words to Peter has already been discussed. We do not believe that those words, when properly interpreted, give the priest the divine powers the Roman Church claims for him. The passage in Matt., ch. 16, is sometimes supported in Catholic writings by the statement of Jesus to his disciples after his resurrection, " If you forgive the sins of any, they are forgiven; if you retain the sins of any, they are retained " (John 20:23). These words were addressed to all the disciples, not to an apostle or to any other official leader. They should be considered in connection with what Jesus said about the intimate relationship between men forgiving one another and God forgiving them. (Matt. 6:14.) When a Christian forgives a fellow man, or when a whole group of Christians, called the church, forgives a person — restores him to their fellowship and treats him as though he had never sinned — that godlike deed is ratified or sanctioned in heaven. Any divine Christlike deed on earth receives the support and blessing of God. That is all the passage in John means. It does not mean that Christ empowered his followers to exercise the divine authority to forgive sins.

The Roman doctrine of transubstantiation of the elements in the Lord's Supper and the manner in which it is interpreted to give the priest power to handle and control God in this world and to dispense for God his powers and favors, have been repudiated by all Reformed Christians since the beginning of the Reformation. That interpretation of the Supper, and the abuses associated with it, were among the main causes of the Reformation. Protestants consider this to be a form of magic, of superstition, of paganism.

The priest's supposed authority to pronounce a blessing upon people and things will be considered in the next section. Suffice it to say here that all Christians in one sense can be the instruments of God for blessing their fellow men. But the claim that the priests as a class have authority and ability to control God's blessings and transmit them to people and things by a particular type of ritual is considered by Protestants to be another form of magic.

To summarize, Protestants believe that God is at all times sovereign and free, and that he surrenders his divine prerogatives to no man, no group of men, no institution. Therefore, they repudiate the Roman Catholic claims to be able to substitute for God, to perform his prerogatives, to control his powers.

The Spiritual Worship of God

Protestants believe that the relationship between God and man is a personal or spiritual relationship, that it is essentially the meeting of Spirit with spirit, Mind with mind. Hence they believe that true worship is a spiritual approach to God, that "God is spirit, and those who worship him must worship in spirit and truth" (John 4:24). Wilhelm Pauck describes the nature of the religious experience as "inwardness, thought, spirit." [14] The individual person approaches God, the divine person, directly. He does not have to use "a complicated ecclesiastical apparatus" to get to him. A vital worship experience takes place within the mind, the conscience, the consciousness of the worshiper. (Cf. Eph. 4:23; Phil. 2:5; Rom. 12:1-2.) Worship, as Karl Heim insists, is a "transaction between God and my conscience . . . a clear spiritual act . . . accomplished in complete lucidity of mind." [15] It is what a thinking man does when he has fellowship with another thinking being called God.

Protestants, therefore, question the wisdom and the validity of the Roman Catholic doctrine of sacramentals. This doctrine has been officially stated, in Sullivan's *The Externals of the Catholic Church,* thus:

> Sacramentals are certain prayers, actions, and things which have been blessed by the church that we might obtain from God spiritual and temporal benefits by their devout use. They obtain these benefits for us through the faith we bring to their use, and through the prayers which the church offers for those who use them. The chief favors we obtain from the sacramentals are: actual grace, protection from evil spirits, aid to devotion, forgiveness of venial sins, the remission of temporal punishment due to sin, and certain temporal blessing, such as health of body. [16]

The sacramentals blessed by the church include: the sign of the cross, the cross and the crucifix, holy water, vestments, the stations of the cross, the holy oils, candles, the rosary, scapulars, the Agnus Dei, palm branches, incense, church bells, religious medals, ashes, Christian symbols.

Sullivan treats these sacramentals in a manner characteristic of Roman Catholic writers. He insists that Catholics do not think of them as superstitions or magic. Then he proceeds to explain them in such manner that the reader can only conclude that he is describing superstitions. He states that the Catholic, unlike the pagan, does not trust in these sacramentals because of some virtue or magical power he imagines them to possess. He trusts only in God. He declares at fairly regular intervals that the person using them must bring faith to their use, must have a right spirit in his heart, or otherwise they have no virtue. Immediately after making these statements, however, he promises a variety of blessings that one can gain from their use. This is precisely the way similar objects are used in pagan religions.

For example, we read: " When a priest is ordained his hands are anointed with holy oil to give them the power to confer blessings by the sign of the cross. . . . When holy water is blessed the sign of the cross is made over it twelve times. . . . Whenever [the faithful] make the sign of the cross, with the invocation of the Most Holy Trinity, they are granted an indulgence of one hundred days. When they make the same holy sign with blessed water, they may gain an indulgence of three hundred days." [17] Holy water is given to the faithful to be taken to their homes and used frequently for the blessing of persons and things. An indulgence of three hundred days is given for every time it is taken home.[18]

" The spiritual benefits of the rosary are very numerous," the faithful are told. These benefits " are attached directly to the beads themselves, and are gained by anyone properly using the beads " that have been properly blessed by the priest.[19] The scapular is usually a small cloth or metal model of the garment (scapular) worn as part of a monastic habit. It is worn under the clothing by a person who wishes to share in the merits and prayers of the members of a particular order. One of the best-known scapulars is that of " Our Lady of Mount Carmel." Those who wear it enjoy "the protection of the Mother of God " as well as " become the sharers in all the fruits of the good works of the great religious order of the Carmelites." [20] During the last war this scapular was given to Catholic servicemen in large numbers. I have in my possession one on which is found this statement: " Never be without the scapular which Our Lady now places in your hands! Do not risk dying without Mary's promise: WHOEVER DIES CLOTHED IN THIS SCAPULAR SHALL NOT SUFFER ETERNAL FIRE! " To receive these benefits, a scapular must be worn constantly. " If the wearing of it has been neglected for a long time, no indulgences are gained during that time. As soon as the scapular is resumed, the spiritual benefits begin again." [21]

Another favorite sacramental is the Agnus Dei, or Lamb of God, because it is blessed at stated seasons only by the pope. God is asked to give his blessing to it so " that the sight or touch of the lamb impressed on it may guard us against the spirits of evil, against sickness and pestilence, against tempest, fire, and flood; that it may strengthen us against temptations, and those who use it may be preserved from a sudden and unprovided death. Also in the prayers it is especially recommended to women who are expecting motherhood." [22]

Roman Catholics have other devotions, not strictly classified as sacramentals, that should also be mentioned. Among these some of the best known are the devotion to the Sacred Heart of Jesus, the invocations of the saints, the veneration of images, the veneration of relics, the forty hours' adoration, and pilgrimages to distant shrines.

The devotion to the Sacred Heart of Jesus originated with Marguerite Marie Alacoque, a nun who lived a life of prayer in one of the religious communities in France in the seventeenth century. She claimed that Jesus appeared to her on several occasions and " showed her his heart, pierced with a wound, en-

circled with a crown of thorns, surrounded by flames and sur-
mounted by a cross, and commanded her to practice and to teach
others the devotion to his Sacred Heart." Sullivan asserts that
the Roman Church does not pass on the truth or falsity of these
claims. It merely declares that the devotion is an excellent form
of worship and that it is not opposed to divine revelation, recom-
mends it to the faithful, urges them to use it, and grants spiritual
favors to all who do so.[23]

Prayers are made to saints, he tells us, because Catholics believe the saints can and do intercede to God for us. Images are
venerated only as a means of increasing homage toward the person they represent. Relics of saints and martyrs are venerated
because the virtues that these persons practice were virtues of
the whole person, both of the body and of the soul. Since their
bodies will rise again in the final resurrection, the Roman
Church pays homage to them, even to small fragments of them.
" Catholics believe that God is sometimes pleased to honor the
relics of saints by making them instruments of healing and other
miracles, and that he bestows grace and favors on those who keep
and venerate them." [24] For these and all other devotions, including the forty hours' devotion and the pilgrimages, the Roman
Church promises special blessings and indulgences.

Closely related to the Roman Catholic doctrine of sacramentals
— indeed an important aspect of it — is what is known as " liturgical piety." [24a] This is a form of piety that consists of re-enacting
" in, by, and for the Church " the liturgical acts that are found
primarily in the Mass, in the events of the Christian year, and in
the daily Divine Offices. Christ actually comes to the Christian
personally as he engages in the Roman Church's liturgy. By going
through the events of Christ's life from his birth to his ascension,
the individual lives " in a permanent state of communion with
sacred things." These liturgical acts, then, constitute in themselves a form of piety and a fountain of grace.

This area of Roman Catholic teaching is to be thought of as an
effort to materialize the spiritual, or to make the spiritual more
real through visible objects and actions.[24b] In certain areas of

Protestantism there has been developing rapidly in recent years a " neosacramentalism " in which this Roman doctrine of sacramentals, virtually in the form that has just been described, is being taught and practiced.

Precisely how far this can be done without ultimately leading to idolatry, magic, superstition, and to ritual holiness as a substitute for ethical holiness, it is not possible to say with certainty. Traditionally Protestants have made limited use of material objects and ritual actions to signify spiritual truths, to recall historical events, and to aid devotions. These may be thought of loosely as "Protestant sacramentals." But every effort has been made to prevent them from being regarded as objects of devotion, as sources of spiritual benefits, as magic wands by which to command and control divine power, as charms to protect from evil forces, as constituting in themselves a form of righteousness acceptable to God.

No one is in a position to say how many Roman Catholics can or cannot participate in the elaborate system of sacramentals erected by their church and think of them merely as *aids to* devotions instead of *objects of* devotion. But this can be said with some confidence. When the Roman Church not only permits but encourages the use of these sacramentals and offers special favors, grace, and rewards for their use, the door is opened widely for superstition, semi-idolatry, and erroneous notions of piety to enter. Protestants who are encouraging the restoration of sacramentals on a large scale are running a grave risk of transforming their predominantly spiritual worship into a form of quasi-material worship alien to the nature of New Testament Christianity.

Furthermore, it is a fundamental Protestant teaching that Christians do not commune with things but with a Person, and that neither things nor outward actions can in themselves be bearers of grace. Grace is the love of God, the assurance of the forgiveness of sin, freely given by God directly to the sinner, which issues in a new personal relationship between him and God. That grace does not need to be channeled through an object, an action, or another person. In short, the relationship between man and God is a spiritual or personal relationship.

The differences between Protestant and Roman Catholic systems of worship constitute another barrier between the two bodies. A well-educated Catholic priest with a doctor's degree, who became a Protestant a few years ago, recently told me that he did not have a sudden, spectacular conversion to Protestantism. One day he awoke to the realization that he no longer needed to rely upon the sacramentals as offered by his church. " At that moment," he declared, " I became a Protestant."

SALVATION BY FAITH ALONE

Salvation by faith alone (*sola fide*) has always been a central doctrine of evangelical Christians. This is usually spoken of as justification by faith. (Cf. Rom. 3:23-25; 5:1-2; 11:5-6; Gal. 2:16, 21; Eph. 2:8.)

Faith means a personal acceptance of the redeeming love of God in Christ, a commitment of our lives to him, trust in his gracious offer of forgiveness, belief in the sufficiency and efficacy of Christ's atoning death. Salvation is a spiritual transaction between God and the believer, a spiritual miracle that takes place in the heart. This makes unnecessary all mediators except Christ himself. The believer trusts solely in the merits of Christ. God's redemption cannot be won, merited, or purchased by anything we ourselves do. Karl Heim claims that this doctrine of salvation by faith alone " has done away with the earthly priest, with his power to absolve sin, his authority over conscience, and all his sacramental institutions for the salvation of men." [25]

Hence Protestants reject the Roman Catholic doctrine of salvation by good works. The Roman Catholic Church teaches that it has power and authority to forgive sins. It exercises this power through a declaration of absolution by the priest as a part of the sacrament of Penance. According to the official teaching of the Roman Church, the sacrament of Penance can remove only the guilt of mortal sin. This sacrament removes also the fear of eternal punishment. But there still remains a temporal penalty to be expiated before heaven can be attained. This penalty can be paid wholly or in part by " penances, mortifications, devotions, almsdeeds, and other good works," while a person is still living. But if any of the penalty is unpaid at death, the soul must stay in purgatory, or it may be " remitted by the Church through indulgences, and this removal may be accomplished while we are living in this world, or (through the charity of others) after we have been sentenced by divine justice to purgatorial pains." [26]

Indulgences are possible because the Roman Church claims to have access to " an infinite store of merit," called the " treasury of merit." The merits of Mary, who had no sins to atone for, were stored in heaven. For nearly two thousand years the multitudes of saints, known and unknown, in the Roman Church, who acquired more merit than was needed for their salvation, have been heaping up merits in the heavenly treasury. The Roman Church also has access to the infinite merits of Jesus Christ. This " great corporation," the Roman Church, controls these merits for the benefit of the faithful and dispenses them from the treasury — draws upon them — through indulgences. The sale of indulgences was one of the immediate provocations of the Reformation. Few Protestants are aware that their use is almost as common today as in the sixteenth century.

Are indulgences sold now as in the days of Martin Luther? " There is no doubt," declares Paul Blanshard, " that the ceremonial accompaniments of prayer and indulgences are paid for in cash at standard prices and sometimes at competitive prices." [26a] This fact is corroborated by Emmett McLoughlin, the former Roman Catholic priest, in his autobiography.[26b] He states bluntly that the Mass " has succumbed to the dollar." He is referring primarily to masses for the souls of the dead. Fees or " stipends " at fairly standard prices, he asserts, are received for these masses and for " remembrances " at them. These fees are " split," portions of them being retained in the parishes where they are originally received and portions sent to priests all over the world. Names to be remembered at masses accumulate on forms handed out to the faithful and, like the fees, are distributed widely to priests over the world. At masses in the month of November, priests place the lists of names on the altar and, nodding toward the bundle, ask God to "release from purgatory" those souls whose names they have not even read. (P. 80.)

One of the important publications of the Roman Church of our day is *The Raccolta: A Manual of Indulgences Prayers and Devotions Enriched with Indulgences* (Authorized by the Holy See. Official edition).[27] This is a book containing more than six hundred pages of prayers, hymns, and devotions, at the end of each of which indulgences are promised for its proper use. For example, after the first ejaculation from the Roman Breviary are these lines: "An indulgence of five hundred days. A plenary indulgence on the usual conditions if this ejaculation is recited devoutly every day for a month" (p. 3). Extra indulgences are promised if certain prayers are "recited in the presence of" or "before the blessed sacrament" (pp. 82, 98, 101). This means that the faithful get extra merits if they attend mass. Other extra indulgences are promised if the faithful pray before an image of Jesus Christ crucified (p. 135), if they take part in the solemn Eucharistic procession with which the Eucharistic Congress is usually closed, if they visit the Blessed Sacrament exposed for public adoration (p. 483), and if they kiss the rosary and at the same time recite the words of a certain prayer (p. 627).

Protestants reject this system of indulgences on several grounds.

1. They consider indulgences to be a form of spiritual bribery, a method of paying people to attend mass, to participate in certain festivals promoted by the church, and to go through certain acts of devotion.

2. They deny that there is any such thing as the treasury of merits to which the church has access, and that it is authorized to dispense the same for the remission of the penalties of sins of any type. They deny that any such merits are needed.

3. The whole doctrine of salvation by good works is contrary to the New Testament doctrine of salvation by faith alone.

The differences between the Roman Catholic and Protestant doctrines of salvation are antithetical and, therefore, irreconcilable.

THE RESPONSIBLE PERSON

The right of private judgment is usually listed among the basic doctrines of Protestantism. It *is* basic! But actually that doctrine is only one aspect of the much larger and more inclusive doctrine of the responsible person.

Protestants believe that every man is endowed by God with freedom and equipped with the ability to use it. They believe that God himself respects this freedom. He endows us with mental powers and trusts us to use them. He does not desire the abject obedience of his children or their credulous acceptance of his truth. He makes no attempt to command or coerce their wills. He wants them to attain to what Ernest F. Scott once called "moral autonomy," or independence of outward compulsion. God asks them to co-operate with his divine purpose on their own volition, from their free inner choices. Through the patient and gracious influence of his Spirit upon their moral judgments, consciences, and wills, God hopes his children will grow up into mature personalities who can be relied upon to be self-directing. His plan in Christ for building a spiritual Kingdom is predicated upon the dependability of such individuals.

Protestants believe this doctrine of the responsible person is an essential Biblical doctrine. The Bible teaches that God creates, preserves, and redeems men in order that they may become personalities with the moral qualities of his own nature. In the first chapter of Genesis we read that "God created man in his own image" (Gen. 1:27). Jesus told his disciples, "You, therefore, must be perfect, as your heavenly Father is perfect" (Matt. 5:48). The word "perfect" in the original Greek is *teleios,* which means literally "wanting nothing necessary to completeness." The word is used throughout the New Testament to indicate "full grown" persons. In the modern versions the word in its several forms is frequently translated "mature" and "maturity." (Cf. I Cor. 2:6;

14:20; Eph. 4:13; Col. 1:28; Heb. 6:1; James 1:4.) God wants us to become mature, fully grown, fully responsible moral persons.

When the New Testament uses the expression " sons of God " it means mature, responsible persons. (See I John.) In a momentous passage, Rom. 8:18-23, Paul expressed the daring thought that God's whole creative and redemptive purpose for the universe will be achieved when in Christ men at last become sons of God. He declares that " the creation waits with eager longing for the revealing of the sons of God " (v. 19), that " the whole creation has been groaning in travail together until now " (v. 22), and that creation will be set free from its agony when it obtains " the glorious liberty of the children of God " (v. 21).

One aspect of this liberty which is stressed in the New Testament, especially in the epistles of Paul, is freedom from Jewish legalism (cf. Rom., ch. 7) and ceremonialism (cf. Gal. 2:4-5; 4:9-10; 5:1; Col. 2:20-23). But the New Testament stresses a much larger freedom from which all other freedoms issue, namely, the freedom of the human spirit vouchsafed to us in Christ. In his letters to the Romans and Galatians, Paul deals with freedom from the law in the larger context of spiritual freedom. In both epistles he urges his readers to live and walk by the Spirit. (Cf. Rom. 8:2, 4; Gal. 5:13-26.) Living and walking by the Spirit is the New Testament way of saying what we have just been describing as living like free, responsible sons of God.

It is in the framework of that spiritual freedom that the Protestant doctrine of the right of private judgment is to be understood. Protestants have never taught that the individual has a right to interpret the Scriptures by his own unaided insight, or that he is free to conjure up all sorts of fanciful or whimsical religious beliefs solely from his own mind.

Every person who finds spiritual freedom in Christ is still subject to God. He is bound by the revelation of God in the Scriptures. He is still tied to his fellow men and expected to strive, in co-operation with them, to discover how to implement his Christian freedom in group living. He profits by the experience of his race. He makes use of the accumulated stores of human wisdom.

He seeks light from all the authorities available. But he accepts the judgment of no one unconditionally. He thinks for himself. He makes his own free investigations, tests his own opinions by the opinions of others, weighs the evidence for and against, revises his own judgment as he is in the process of forming it. He pushes aside whomsoever and whatsoever — priests, bishops, popes, councils, and churches — who presume to thrust themselves between him and God. In the end it is his own judgment that binds his conscience. To surrender his private judgment is to extinguish the light within him that makes it possible for him to know God, to hear him, and to apprehend his truth.

Much of the teaching of Jesus and of the New Testament church is devoted to the task of training people how to become responsible persons in the sector of the world in which they live and labor. To his trained disciples he entrusted the work of the Kingdom. (Cf. Matt. 5:13-14; 28:19-20.) Following their Master at this point, Protestants confidently entrust the complicated problems of the human-divine society to Christ-committed, Christ-guided, Christ-empowered men and women.

God created men to be free moral beings. Their rights to open-minded investigations, to free and fearless inquiry, to independent search for the truth, to discuss and debate, to assent and dissent, to question, to make mistakes and profit by them, to read and think and speak, to wrestle at firsthand with the problems of human living — all these rights are God-given and therefore inviolable and inalienable. They must be preserved at all costs. This doctrine of the responsible person is bound up with the nature of evangelical Christianity, essential to its existence, vital to its continuance.

The teaching and practice of the Roman Catholic Church are diametrically opposed to the Protestant doctrine of the responsible person. Rome believes in making and keeping individuals dependent upon the church. Rome teaches that the individual is free to accept what the church teaches, but not free to decide for himself whether that teaching is true or false, and not capable of doing so.

In his encyclical *Mirari vos* (1832), Pope Gregory XVI denounced "liberty of conscience" as an "absurd and erroneous opinion," the "product of delirium," and a "pestilent error." He labeled liberty of the press "that deadly freedom, never adequately to be execrated and detested." [28] Freedom of conscience and of opinion was one of the errors Pope Pius IX roundly denounced in his famous *Syllabus of Errors* (1864). In his encyclical *Immortale Dei* (1885), Pope Leo XIII quoted and approved Gregory's position and added on his own that "the unrestrained freedom of thinking and of openly making known one's thoughts is not inherent in the rights of citizens." [29] Early in the present century Pope Pius X declared that the church "is essentially an unequal society," composed of two categories of persons, the hierarchy and the faithful. The authority to guide, he said, resides solely in the hierarchy. The multitude of the faithful "has no other right than that of allowing itself to be led, and, as a docile flock, to follow the shepherds" (*Vehementer Nos*, 1906). [30]

The clearest recent statement of the Catholic teaching that the faithful are supposed to be *receptive subjects* of the hierarchy, is found in *The Role of the Laity in the Church*, by Gerard Philips. [31] He states that Christ himself instituted the Catholic order, which distinguishes between the clergy, who have the right to direct, and the laity, who have only the right to receive direction. In performing their function, the clergy are expected "to guard the faithful against the spirit of independence and dissent" (p. 25). It is "unthinkable for a Catholic" to make a "conscientious objection" to a "formal decision of authority" (p. 34). "Liberty of conscience" never won anything. "Obedience alone liberates, for it alone snaps the chains of obstinate individualism." (P. 35.) Christ himself apportions the work in his church and "demands that some should obey others" (p. 57).

The standard Catholic textbook on church and state, used in colleges and universities, *Catholic Principles of Politics*, by Ryan and Boland, [32] and the standard Catholic work for teachers, *Freedom Through Education*, by Redden and Ryan, [33] both are based on the official Catholic teaching about freedom as just outlined.

The incompatibility of this teaching with the Protestant doctrine of the responsible person will become clearer as we consider the ways in which the Catholic Church implements this teaching in the various aspects of its work.

1. *Roman Catholic censorship*. This censorship, designed to control what the faithful read, hear, see, and think, is carried on under two spearheads, one directed toward Catholics and the other toward both Catholics and non-Catholics. For its own members the Roman Church has a list of books, called the *Index librorum prohibitorum*, which they are forbidden to read. The Index was first published in 1559 and it has been published continuously ever since. The number of books in English now on the list consists of some five thousand titles. But books listed by name constitute only a fraction of those covered by the Index, because any book (the term " book " includes magazines, newspapers, and even pictures), magazine, or newspaper that comes under any one of the twelve categories, whether on the list or not, may be forbidden.[34]

Before a Catholic publishes a book, he must secure the *Nihil Obstat* (nothing objectionable) of the diocesan censor and the *Imprimatur* (let it be printed) of the diocesan bishop. Any Catholic publisher who prints a book without the *Imprimatur* faces excommunication and boycott. (Canon 2318.) Once a book has been put on the denounced list by the proper official, Catholic booksellers and reviewers, as well as publishers, are placed under restrictions in its use and threatened with penalties for nonobservance of the restrictions.[35] Catholics who co-operate in the production and distribution of both forbidden books and magazines are guilty of varying degrees of sinfulness. This includes those who are concerned with printing, publishing, editing, typesetting, proofreading, preparing and handling the paper, mixing the ink, servicing the presses, selling the ink, paper, and machinery, etc.[36] Catholics are forbidden not only to read books that are on the Index but to buy, or sell, own, borrow, or lend them, under penalty of mortal sin or even excommunication. In fact, Catholics are forbidden by Canon Law (Canons 1398 and 1399) to read anything that criticizes the Catholic Church or any of its fundamental doctrines or that makes light of any point of Catholic belief or practice.

Closely associated with the Index, possibly subsidiary to it, and certainly far more important and efficient, is a world-wide system of local censorship that the bishop of each diocese is directed and empowered to carry on. This censorship is designed to condemn, and, if possible, to prevent, all anti-Catholic statements in books, newspapers, magazines, plays, films, and on radio and television programs, and to protest against books objectionable to Catholics being placed in public libraries and, in some cases, being used as textbooks in public schools. This method of censorship was considered at length in another connection in Chapter I. Suffice it to say here that so effective have these campaigns of censorship been that, generally speaking, publishers, motion-picture producers, radio and television stations, will not produce anything, and newspapers and magazines will not permit anything to appear in their columns, that might expose them to the threat of a Catholic boycott.

By these means the Catholic hierarchy endeavors not only to control the media of communication for their own purposes, but also to exercise thought control over Catholics and non-Catholics alike, to suppress free discussion and open-minded debate of important public issues, and to repress facts they do not want their members to face.

2. *Catholic moral theology.* Whether so designed or not, the Catholic system of moral theology makes members of the Roman Church dependent upon the hierarchy. The system is so extensive and intricate that only the moral theologians themselves, after long reasoning and careful analyses, can determine the degree of right and wrong involved in certain types of behavior. This makes it necessary for the laity to consult their priests in order to discover what they are permitted or forbidden to do in specified practical situations.

One can discover how the system operates by examining *Medical Ethics for Nurses,* by Charles J. McFadden.[37] The author discusses eight kinds of conscience (pp. 20–26) and nine types of moral acts (pp. 27–31), defines each, differentiates it from the others, lays down rules governing its use, and illustrates how it applies to specific problems. " Since it is only our free human actions for which we can be held responsible," he affirms, " it is evident that any factor which lessens knowledge or freedom also decreases the moral guilt attached to an action " (p. 38). So he discusses and differentiates four kinds of " hindrances to accountability," each of which is broken down into subsidiary classes. Each of these is analyzed to determine when and to what degree the nurse can be held accountable for her action.

One of the problems the Catholic nurse faces is whether or not to assist at operations that the Roman Church considers to be immoral. This question is answered by the author with a long discussion of the nature of co-operation. He consumes fifteen pages differentiating between four kinds or degrees of co-operation and laying down rules to guide nurses in determining the degree of moral guilt, if any, she incurs in applying these rules to specific cases. In the same elaborate manner he discusses the ethics of birth control (several kinds), of sterilization, of abortions (several kinds), and of professional secrecy (several kinds).

Obviously, this so complicates the ethical problems faced by nurses that a conscientious nurse, who wishes to avoid committing sin, must consult her priest in advance to secure directions about what to do in a given situation. Otherwise, she must go to her priest after she has acted to discover whether she has committed a sin of some degree, which she must confess and for which she must seek forgiveness.

Francis J. Connell has written another book,[38] with the same general purposes as McFadden's book, but in less detail for each group considered. He writes for Catholic legislators, judges, soldiers and sailors, policemen, lawyers, doctors, nurses, schoolteachers, and social-service workers. He treats the problems that the members of each group face in their respective spheres, analyzes these in detail, and offers the answers worked out by the moral theologians. At intervals he advises the Catholic in public life to go to his priest or bishop for continuous moral and ethical advice. The priests are also instructed to keep their parishioners informed of the Roman Church's moral teaching and, if necessary, to admonish them in the confessional about the necessity of utilizing this teaching as a guide to daily living.

A compendium of Catholic moral theology devotes twenty-six pages [39] of fine print to the discussion of sexual sins of all forms and down to the minutest details. Sexual sins are described as "complete" and "incomplete," "natural" and "unnatural," "directly voluntary" and "indirectly voluntary," "internal" and "external." These are analyzed to determine whether they are mortal or venial sins. Kisses are described as "paternal," "fraternal," "customary," "affectionate," "ardent," "prolonged," and "soul," and the morality of each is passed upon. [40] Included in the list of sexual sins is the sin of using and manufacturing contraceptives. Jobbers, salesmen, manufacturers, druggists, and hired pharmacists, taxi drivers who convey people to houses of prostitution — all are included. Ribald songs are analyzed according to the "age and sensual propensity" of the listener. [41]

Long casuistic reasoning is required to settle the simplest practical questions. What, for example, do the moral theologians teach about fasting after midnight before going to mass? This involves a group of problems such as: What is and what is not classified as food? Can one wash one's teeth, gargle one's throat, smoke, dissolve a cough drop in one's mouth? Another series of problems arises when the Communion is given to a person who is seriously ill and finds it difficult to retain food in his stomach. The moral theologians give the official answers as to the length of time it takes for the sacred host to digest, what to do if the host is not retained long enough to be digested, how to dispose of it with the reverence due the sacred body of Christ, etc. [42]

Manifestly this system is not calculated to develop responsible persons who make their own moral decisions, but persons who will depend upon the Roman Church to make these decisions for them.

3. *Complete Catholic life.* The Catholic Church is trying to

segregate its members into distinctly Roman Catholic organizations covering every phase of practical living. It is trying to build up a self-sufficient Catholic culture, separated and insulated from, quarantined against, the larger culture of the society in which it exists. Catholic priests are taught that one of their main functions is to persuade and aid the faithful to live a " Catholic life." In his book on preaching, *Effective Preaching*,[43] Thomas V. Liske, professor of speech at a Catholic seminary in Chicago, stresses this as one of the primary purposes of Catholic preaching. He states over and over that Catholics must be given "inspiration to live a fully Catholic life," or persuaded to live " a more Catholic life " or " the completely Catholic life." (See pp. 10, 24, 33, 124, 198.) " Every Catholic would be a complete and perfect Catholic," he asserts, " if he was really convinced of the truth of all the wonderful things he knows to be the absolute truth." (P. 202.) By " absolute " truth he means " Catholic truth," an expression he also uses in the book. (P. 190.)

At present there is a Catholic organization of one sort, or under one name, or another, that parallels and in reality competes with, similar organizations representing every phase of our American culture as a whole. These are for all ages: children, youth, men and women. They are for all interest groups: educational, scientific, literary, economic, musical, legal, artistic, etc. All these organizations are knit together closely under the authority and watchful eye of the hierarchy and used for the Roman Church's purpose and advantage.

Furthermore, Catholics are forbidden to attend non-Catholic services of worship and non-Catholic schools. They are discouraged from associating with non-Catholics in ordinary business and social activities. By campaigns against the use of contraceptives and against intermarriages of Catholics and members of other religious groups, they hope to outbreed non-Catholics and make the United States a Catholic country. " We are going fast," one Catholic monsignor boasted. " The fact that the average Catholic family is larger than the non-Catholic, owing to the church's attitude on birth control, will in time make the United States a Catholic nation." [44] As yet the Catholic hierarchy has not deemed it wise to organize a Catholic political party in the United States, although there are Catholic blocs within both the Democratic and Republican parties, and in national and state legislative bodies.

There can be no doubt that if the Catholic policies succeed as intended, they will produce a culture within a culture, or a state within a state. If carried to their logical conclusions, they would substitute the church for, or equate it with, the Kingdom of God. In fact, Pope Leo XIII called the church the " perfect society " founded by Christ. From the history of countries that are predominantly Catholic we well know that a *complete Catholic society* would be something entirely different from the ideal society envisaged by Protestants.

Protestant churches also organize age groups and, occasionally, interest groups, along denominational lines. But this is not for the purpose of separating their people culturally from society as a whole. The purpose of organizing along denominational lines is to do a better job of *Christian* education. Protestants have no desire to see any church, not even their own, control all citizens for its own ends. They want only to develop Christians who, as responsible citizens of the larger social order, will operate the social machinery according to Christian principles and for Christian ends. They emphasize loyalty and obedience to Christ and his ideals, not loyalty and obedience to the church itself.[45]

Protestants therefore find it impossible to reconcile their doctrine of the free and responsible person with the Roman doctrine of the dependent and controlled person. To put them into a church in which Roman practices prevailed would be equivalent to strapping them in a mental, moral, and social strait jacket. In the story of his break away from the Catholic priesthood, Emmett McLoughlin [46] tells how he felt as though he had escaped from a dark dungeon into the clear sunlight, as a free man restored to his birthright. To the great masses of Protestants, uniting with a church that operates according to the Roman Catholic doctrine of controlled members would be like going from the free sunlight into a dark prison.

THE PROPHETIC MINISTRY

One of the early acts of all the Reformers was to substitute the New Testament idea of a prophetic ministry for the medieval idea of a priestly ministry. A detailed study of New Testament teaching concerning the nature of the ministry was made in Chapter II and needs only to be summarized briefly here.

The apostolic church made no distinction between clergymen and laymen, except as to function. Ordination was a method of recognizing that certain individuals possessed spiritual gifts that qualified them for special services, and of setting them aside for the performance of these services. It did not confer special powers and authorities. Among those who were set aside there was no such thing as a hierarchy of rank. All were of equal standing. The death of Christ for the redemption of mankind left no need of an earthly priesthood and no sacerdotal functions for a priesthood to perform. The Reformers restored this New Testament conception of the prophetic ministry. Karl Heim asserts that "Protestantism is the only form of religion in the history of the world which has passed beyond the need of priests." [47]

This Protestant doctrine of the ministry goes contrary to the main elements in the Roman doctrine of the priesthood, a number of aspects of which were discussed earlier in this chapter. Protestants repudiate the claims that clergymen are of a different order from laymen, that they possess priestly powers and authority, that certain acts are valid only when performed by ordained priests, and that priests have authority in the name and the place of God to forgive sins. To a host of Protestants there is no possibility of reconciling the differences between themselves and Roman Catholics at this point. One conception of the ministry must give way to the other before a union of the two bodies can ever take place.

A Democratic Church

The government of the New Testament church was also considered in Chapter II. The New Testament church was a self-governing fellowship. The authority to control rested in and belonged to the members as a whole, not to any individual or group. Authority possessed by an official was not inherent in his office, but delegated by the body that appointed him. To that body he was responsible for the exercise of his functions. Some form of representative democracy is, therefore, the form of polity most in harmony with the principles and practice of the New Testament church. When the Reformers found it necessary to organize separate churches, they were set up according to these New Testament principles. But it was not until after almost two centuries of experimenting that freedom in this area of the church's life was approximately attained. Indeed it has not been achieved to the same degree in all countries and in all Protestant denominations down to the present time.

From the Reformation to the present, Protestants have regarded the papacy as an absolute dictatorship without the warrant of either Scripture or reason and have denied that the pope possesses the divine rights he claims. The Roman Church is a form of imperialism that is out of harmony with the democratic processes that have been at work for the last three or four centuries. Protestants who have once become free men cannot be expected to bow again to a yoke of ecclesiastical bondage.

A Free Church in a Free State

A major doctrine of Protestantism that became a decisive factor in the formation of our American democracy was the doctrine of the separation of church and state, or as it is better expressed, the doctrine of a free church in a free state. This doctrine clashes with the Roman Catholic position that the ideal arrangement for the Catholic Church is for the state to be what is known as " a Catholic state." This problem of church and state is currently a critical issue in Protestant–Roman Catholic relations in our country. For this reason Chapter V will be devoted entirely to its consideration.

The eight doctrines just discussed do not exhaust the points where there is extreme divergence between Protestantism and Roman Catholicism. But they constitute the major differences and suffice to point out the obstacles to union between the two groups. In the light of the facts given, it is difficult to imagine any large number of Protestants being willing to agree to a union that, on the one hand, retains the Roman Catholic beliefs, and, on the other hand, does not safeguard the evangelical beliefs, just contrasted with them. Also it is highly improbable that the two sets of beliefs could exist side by side in the same church without serious internal dissensions. For the present the two sets of doctrines are irreconcilable and will be for a long time to come. No worth-while service would be rendered Christendom by trying to make them compatible. The time has come for these things to be said as openly and strongly by Protestants to their constituents as Roman Catholics say them to their constituents. If that frank step were taken, the way would be cleared for the two groups to carry on conversations designed to find a workable basis for peaceful coexistence and for mutual co-operation toward attainable common goals.

A PROTESTANT MAGNA CHARTA

Unfortunately too few Protestants are well enough informed either about their own faith or about the Roman Catholic faith to engage fruitfully as equals in conversations with Roman Catholics. Protestants have not had sufficient incentives to discover the things they actually hold in common. The many and varied divisions of Protestants have served to exaggerate their differences and have acted as a screen to conceal their agreements.

Each group has been so zealously stressing and developing its own distinctive emphases that it has not felt the need of giving much thought to what it shares with all the others. Even in the last few decades, during which Protestants have been drawing closer together in the ecumenical movement, many have spoken of a "unity in diversity" without undertaking to describe that unity in detailed and concrete terms. But this description cannot be deferred indefinitely. In fact, the growing demands of the Irenic Movement for more conversations between Protestants and Catholics, explained in Chapter I, are making such a description inevitable.

Protestants should not be deterred from this undertaking because they know beforehand that it would be impossible to produce a creed in the technical sense of a discriminating and precisely worded theological formulation that would be acceptable to all. But a large amount of *general* theological agreement could be reached about many, if not most, of the essential doctrines discussed in this chapter, as well as about policies and principles involved in the pressing social and political problems demanding the united approach of Protestants.

A group of the best minds representing the various denominations of Protestantism should gather together behind closed doors, detached for a period of months from the noise and confusion of the world, somewhat after the manner of the drafters of the Constitution of the United States, and draw up a Manifesto, or Magna Charta, of Protestant positions. Such an undertaking would face many difficulties but probably no more than the difficulties faced by our nation's founding fathers. But it would not be either impracticable or impossible. Given a keen awareness of the need of such a project and a strong desire to tackle it, there is no reason why it could not be accomplished.

A Protestant Manifesto of this kind would serve a number of useful purposes. Once drafted, it could be made available for study by Protestants in denominational and interdenominational gatherings. It could also be used in colloquies with Roman Catholics as common positions and beliefs that, in principle, Protestants cannot surrender. The existence and use of such a manifesto, representing Protestantism as a whole, would clear the religious atmosphere, bring out in the open many things that now rankle beneath the surface, establish a solid basis for an honest and uninhibited exchange of views with Roman Catholics, and aid in achieving the only feasible *rapprochement* between the two groups in our country.

Chapter V
Religion in Our American Society

There can be no doubt that tensions between Protestants and Roman Catholics in our country are mounting rapidly. This is not due, as some would have us believe, to the perversities of human nature, but to the fact that the conflicts between basic beliefs and principles of the two groups are becoming increasingly apparent and are being brought out into the open.

There has been a noticeable change in this regard in the last twelve months. The differences between Protestants and Roman Catholics are now being more frequently and frankly discussed than ever before on radio and television programs, in magazine articles, in news dispatches, in the weekly religious columns of daily newspapers, and in religious journals. Apparently, at long last the policy of disdainful name-calling and derogatory labeling is beginning to be replaced with the policy of open reporting and comparison of conflicting opinions, and of free expression of honest convictions. Let us hope that the time is drawing near when Protestants who express disagreement with a policy, program, practice, or belief of the Roman Catholic Church are not thereby regarded as defaming it or engaging in an anti-Catholic campaign. Actually they are pursuing the policy long ago followed by the apostle Paul. " By the open statement of the truth," Paul declared, " we would commend ourselves to every man's conscience in the sight of God." (II Cor. 4:2.) This policy is calculated, in time, to relieve the tensions somewhat. Certainly it is in line with the American way of publicly presenting the facts about issues over which there is wide disagreement.

Much of the tension between Protestantism and Roman Catholicism revolves around the problem of religion in our American democratic society. This chapter will be devoted to that aspect of the Protestant-Catholic problem. An effort will be made to indicate the precise points in this particular area at which the two groups differ and to discuss the possible ways in which differences can be resolved, tensions relieved, and principles of peaceful coexistence arrived at. Specifically, the purpose of the chapter is candidly to give reasons why Protestants express concern about and opposition to certain policies and positions of Roman Catholicism in the United States of America.

Before we enter upon this discussion, the reader should be reminded that Roman Catholics, not Protestants, have been responsible for initiating a public discussion of this problem. The Roman Catholic hierarchy have long been carefully planning a long-range campaign, upon which they have only recently embarked openly, to gain certain political objectives in the United States.

Chief among these objectives are: tax support for Roman Catholic parochial schools, the appointment of an American ambassador to the Vatican, the wider recognition of Catholic Canon Law by our civil courts, a closer tie between the Catholic Church and the state, and an increasing number of Roman Catholics in public office, including the presidency of the United States.

The aggressiveness of the Roman hierarchy at these points, especially through their extensive and capably operated news agencies, have provoked wide discussion of these subjects in the various media of communication in our society. This discussion in turn has stimulated secular opinion-forming organizations to conduct interfaith conferences on these religious-political subjects. Two of these organizations, the Fund for the Republic and the Extension Department of the University of California, were mentioned in the Preface to this book.

In order to prepare themselves to participate in this discussion intelligibly and fruitfully, Protestants, therefore, have found it necessary to restudy and restate the political implications and applications of their distinctive beliefs. This chapter will be devoted to that topic.

PROTESTANTISM AND THE AMERICAN DEMOCRACY

1. *The founding of the government.* In *Democracy and the Churches,* one of the significant books of the last decade, James Hastings Nichols has shown that modern democracy is not the child of the sixteenth-century Reformers, but of the Puritan revolution of seventeenth-century England. None of the sixteenth-century Reformers believed in religious liberty. Anabaptists, Quakers, and other Separatists were persecuted by Lutherans, Calvinists, and Romanists alike. Not until the Reformation was a century or so old did Protestants begin to realize the full democratic implications of their beliefs. Even then it was only the Puritan wing of the Reformation that came fully to this realization. Another century of toil and sacrifice passed before their views were incorporated in democratic governmental societies. Among these societies one of the most important was the United States of America.

Nichols says that Puritan Protestantism, as originally structured in the seventeenth century, became the common ancestor of the denominational groups who constituted the overwhelming majority of colonial Christians and were the most influential in the formative period of the American Government. By formative period is meant roughly the eighteenth century and the first half of the nineteenth century. These Puritan groups were the Congregationalists, Baptists, Presbyterians, Quakers, and the Puritan party within the Anglican Communion. To these were later added Methodists and, early in the nineteenth century, the Disciples. Roman Catholics were so few that they were a negligible factor, either as opponents or proponents, until after the end of this formative period. In 1770 there were 22,000 Roman Catholics out of 4,000,000 inhabitants, and 56 Roman Catholic churches out of a total of 3,228 churches, in the American colonies.

From time to time Roman Catholic writers claim that their church made a distinct contribution to religious liberty in

America. Evidence offered in support of this claim is of three kinds: (a) They call attention to the fact that toleration was practiced for the first time on American soil in the Catholic colony of Maryland. Several Protestant writers have shown that this toleration was due to the political exigencies of the time, not to any Catholic convictions about freedom.[1] (b) They allege that Thomas Jefferson derived some of the principles and exact wording of the Virginia Declaration of Rights and the Declaration of Independence from the writings of Cardinal Robert Bellarmine, a noted Jesuit theologian of the late sixteenth and early seventeenth centuries. This allegation is based upon a legend that appeared first in a paper, " Cardinal Bellarmine and the Virginia Bill of Rights," by Mr. Gaillard Hunt, in *The Catholic Historical Review,* October, 1917. Prof. David S. Schaff has proved conclusively that this claim is pure legend, unsupported by the facts.[2] Despite Schaff's decisive conclusions, the theory was incorporated in an important Roman Catholic college textbook as late as 1943.[3] (c) They credit Francis Suarez, S.J., one of the contemporaries of Bellarmine, with being an important source of American democratic ideals. After a careful study of the teaching of both Bellarmine and Suarez, Nichols declares that neither had any interest in democracy as such, but only in safeguarding the right of the pope to intervene in monarchical absolutism.[4] Neither of them believed in representation by the people, in religious toleration, or in separation of church and state. It cannot be said, therefore, that the writings of either of these Catholics provided any of the ideas that went into the making of our democracy. Any contribution the Roman Catholic Church has made to democracy in modern times, asserts Nichols, has been " only where it was in a religious minority, and there only to the extent of demanding a distinct sphere for its own clerical absolutism." [5]

So the determining influence in the formation of our Government was exerted by Puritan Protestants and others who shared the same fundamental democratic views.

2. *Freedom of the individual.* The first and most essential thing to be said about our Government for this study is that freedom

was written into its very structure. In the Declaration of Independence our fathers stated that they were assuming "the separate and equal station to which the Laws of Nature and of Nature's God entitle them," and also that "we hold these truths to be self-evident, that all men are created equal, that they are endowed by their Creator with certain unalienable Rights."

Blackstone, the great English jurist, whose book is sometimes referred to as the lawyers' Bible, declared: "The law of nature being coeval with mankind and dictated by God himself, is, of course, superior in obligation to any other. It is binding all over the globe in all countries and at all times; no human laws are of validity, if contrary to this." The word "inalienable" (unalienable) is defined in Webster's New International Dictionary thus: "Incapable of being alienated, surrendered, or transferred. . . . That is inalienable which one cannot give away or dispose of even if one wishes; . . . under the Constitution of the United States, personal liberty, freedom of speech, etc., are *inalienable* rights."

Evidence is abundant from their writings that the founders of our Government meant to say that freedom is "natural" and "inalienable" in the above meanings of those words; that is, in their thinking, freedom was something final, something ultimate. By this they did not mean that freedom itself is absolute, that it has no limitations. Rather, they meant that God deals with men, and that therefore men should always deal with one another, on the basis of freedom. Democratic *procedures,* or *processes,* are the divine and therefore the permanent principles of human relations. All efforts for the improvement of human society, if they accord with God's principles, must be made within the framework of freedom or by means of democratic processes.

In Chapter IV, when the doctrine of the responsible person was under consideration, it was shown that Protestants believe that freedom of the human spirit is an essential doctrine of New Testament Christianity. Freedom inheres in the nature of the world in which we live, in the nature of God and of God's dealings with men, in the nature of men and of men's dealings with one another. The rights God vouchsafed to men in Christ are inviolable and inalienable. God gave them, and no power on earth has the right to take them away. The men who set up our constitutional democracy drew their concepts of freedom, consciously or unconsciously, from a background of these evangelical Christian beliefs.

We often hear it said that the people of the United States have a constitutional right to change their Government into any form of their own choosing. Unquestionably that is their legal right, because the Constitution provides for its own amendment. In a decision concerning the constitutionality of the Smith Act, under which some communists were convicted of disloyalty, the Supreme Court in June, 1957, declared that the overthrow of the government is not forbidden by that Act " so long as the advocacy is not coupled with efforts to instigate revolutionary action." The *legal* right to overthrow our Government by constitutional procedures is written into the constitution itself. But a *legal* right is not necessarily a *natural* right.

Our founding fathers recognized the right of appeal to revolution. In the Declaration of Independence they declared that "whenever any Form of Government becomes destructive of these ends [i.e., of freedoms], it is the Right of the People to alter or to abolish it." The people have a right to alter and abolish *that form of government which is destructive of freedom*. The appeal to revolution, at least in our democracy, is a right to be exercised only if the Government is denying freedom. It is not an unlimited natural right to be exercised for the purpose of destroying freedom itself.

When the people of the American colonies ratified the Constitution, they entered into a solemn unwritten covenant to trust freedom, to make it the lasting basis of human relations. Ever since then, American citizenship has carried with it the obligation to subscribe to that same covenant. This means that we agree not to submit freedom itself to a plebiscite, not to use freedom of speech to destroy freedom of speech, not to use elections to abolish elections. In short, it means we will not use the facilities of liberty to destroy liberty. The acid test of a person's loyalty to the American way of life is whether or not he would deny to any person or group the rights vouchsafed under the American Constitution, even if he had the power to do so.

3. *Separation of church and state.* Strange to say, when the Constitution was finally adopted, it contained little reference to, and no list of, the rights to which they believed every person is entitled. This serious omission was somewhat quickly remedied by the adoption of the first ten amendments to the Constitution, which we now call The Bill of Rights. Article I of this Bill is the primary concern of this study. It states:

> Congress shall make no law respecting an establishment of religion, or prohibiting the free exercise thereof; or abridging the freedom of speech or of the press; or the right of the people peaceably to assemble, and to petition the Government for a redress of grievances.

Other rights are specified in succeeding articles. And in each instance it is implied that under no circumstances shall Congress pass a law abridging the rights indicated.

When the people adopted that amendment, they originated the distinctive American and Protestant doctrine of the separation of church and state. Light is thrown upon the meaning of the first two clauses of Article I for those who first ratified it, by two historical items. The first item is the following statement in a letter to the Danbury Baptists' Association by Thomas Jefferson:

> I contemplate with sovereign reverence that act of the whole American people which declared that their legislatures should " make no law respecting an establishment of religion, or prohibiting the free exercise thereof " thus building a wall of separation between church and state.[6]

The second item consists of two sections of the Constitution of the Presbyterian Church, which were published in their final form in 1788, while the colonies were still voting on the civil Constitution. One section declares that they do not want the state to aid any religious organization. The essential sentence in this declaration is:

> [Presbyterians] consider the rights of private judgment, in all matters that respect religion, as universal and unalienable: they do not even wish to see any religious constitution aided by the civil power, further than may be necessary for protection and security, and, at the same time, be equal and common to all others (Form of Government, Chapter I, Section 1).

The other section declares that the state may not assume any of the functions of a religious society. The main function of the state, so far as religious organizations is concerned, is

> to protect the church of our common Lord, without giving the preference to any denomination of Christians above the rest, in such a manner that all ecclesiastical persons whatever shall enjoy the full, free, and unquestioned liberty of discharging every part of their sacred functions, without violence or danger (Confession of Faith, Chapter XXIII).

These statements reflected the beliefs common to all Protestant groups in the colonies at the time. They give a clear explanation of what those who wrote Article I intended to say.

4. *Loyalty to the Constitution.* Throughout their history American Protestants, though in the overwhelming majority, have conformed consistently to our basic constitutional laws. They have refused to seek support of the state for their own churches, or to seek the police power of the state to suppress or in any way hamper the religious activities of minority groups such as Roman Catholics and Jews. Although conceivably they might have mobilized enough sentiment to repeal the first amendment in order to make Protestantism as over against Catholicism, or Christianity as over against Judaism, the established religion of the state, they have never attempted to do so. They have not sought support for their church programs from Government funds, but have supported all their enterprises by the voluntary and freewill gifts of their members. They have not desired the support of civil

laws for their ecclesiastical doctrines and disciplines, but have considered these to be purely moral and spiritual matters. They have believed that the civil status of no person should be dependent upon his ecclesiastical status, or, to state it the other way round, that one's ecclesiastical standing should have no civil effects.

Winfred E. Garrison well expressed for all American Protestants their doctrine of the separation of church and state when he said:

> As for us, say American Protestants, a free church and a free state (the political organization of society), existing side by side *in* a free nation, seems to be the system that is most consistent with the nature of the church, in so far as the New Testament describes it, with the character of Christianity, and with the divinely given natural right of man to make free choice in matters of religion.[7]

ROMAN CATHOLICISM AND THE AMERICAN DEMOCRACY

Let us now try to ascertain what is the official teaching of the Roman Catholic Church about democracy in general and about our American democracy in particular and its relationship to it. By *official* teaching is meant that teaching which is set forth, interpreted, and permitted by the Vatican's magisterium, not teaching that represents merely the opinions of individual Catholics. This teaching may be considered under the following seven headings.

1. *The freedom of the individual.* In Chapter IV facts were submitted to show that the Roman Catholic Church's policy is designed to make the individual a dependent person, not a free, responsible person in the sense in which that term is ordinarily used in America. The facts were of four kinds: quotations from papal encyclicals, a description of Catholic censorship, a brief exposition of the Catholic system of moral theology, and an explanation of the Church's effort to persuade its members to live a complete Catholic or church-directed life. The quotations submitted from

the encyclicals of Pope Gregory XVI (1832), of Pope Pius IX (1864), of Pope Leo XIII (1885), and of Pope Pius X (1906), denounced in one way or another liberty of conscience, freedom of the press, freedom of expressing one's thoughts, and the right to self-direction.

That treatment of the subject will suffice for the purposes of the topic under consideration just now, provided the reader reminds himself that everything said on the subject in Chapter IV is involved with the questions yet to be discussed in this chapter.

2. *Democracy as a form of government.* The chief modern sources for the official Roman Catholic teaching concerning political principles are the two papal documents already mentioned: *The Syllabus of Errors,* which accompanied the encyclical *Quanta Cura* of Pius IX (1864),[8] and Pope Leo XIII's encyclical *Immortale Dei* (1885).[9] The *Syllabus* sets forth Catholic teachings by stating eighty errors that the papacy denies or condemns. Someone has estimated that the first one fourth of these are theological, the last three fourths political, in nature. *Immortale Dei* also contains both types of teaching, but like the *Syllabus,* is predominantly political. Both documents will be referred to many times in the remaining portion of this chapter.

The Syllabus of Errors. This document lays down the basis on which the Roman Catholic hierarchy claims political authority over civil governments. In his covering letter Pius says of the errors in general:

> These false and perverse opinions are so much the more detestable, by as much as they have chiefly for their object to hinder and banish that salutary influence which the Catholic Church, by the institution and command of her divine author, ought freely to exercise, even to the consummation of the world, not only over individual men, but nations, peoples, and sovereigns, and to abolish that mutual co-operation and agreement of counsels between the priesthood and governments, which has always been propitious and conducive to the welfare both of church and state.[10]

The *Syllabus* was intended to be an official refutation of the position of Charles Montalembert, the noted French historian and most distinguished spokesman for liberal Catholicism in his day. At an international congress of liberal Catholics held at Malines in 1863, Montalembert declared himself in favor of "the principle of the ecclesiastical neutrality of the state, the reciprocal independence of church and state, the suppression of all religious privileges and constraints, the principle, in short, of religious liberty, liberty of conscience, and liberty of worship."[11] The next year Pope Pius delivered his encyclical to the bishops for the express purpose of contradicting Montalembert's positions. Primarily, then, the *Syllabus* is a document setting forth the official position of the Roman Church on the question of church and state. This aspect of the document will be taken up in the next section.

Nevertheless, he dealt, though briefly, with the Roman Church's attitude toward democracy itself. Possibly this brevity can be accounted for by the fact that once the Roman Church's basic theory of the supremacy of the hierarchy over the state is accepted by any government, its own freedom of action is secondary. But even so, first and last the pope says enough to make quite clear what the Vatican thinks of political democracy. The *Syllabus* as a whole has been described by Nichols as the "most elaborate and uncompromising repudiation of any reconciliation between the principles and practices of Roman Catholicism and those of liberal democracy."[12] In item 80 the pope repudiates the idea that "the Roman pontiff can, and ought to, reconcile himself, and come to terms with progress, liberalism, and modern civilization."[13] This statement is clearly a wholesale condemnation of all aspects of the modern movement toward a free society.

In the *Syllabus* he condemns the rule of the majority (item 60: denies that "authority is nothing else but numbers"), and the appeal to revolution (item 63: denies that "it is lawful to refuse obedience to legitimate princes, and even to rebel against them").[14] Speaking to a delegation of French pilgrims some ten years later, Pius called universal suffrage a "universal delusion," a " frightful disease." [15] When his theory of church and state has been explained in the next section, it will become crystal-clear that he is uncompromisingly opposed to the idea of a free, democratic state.

Immortale Dei. This document, like the *Syllabus,* is primarily concerned with the relation of church and state. But in two or three places the pope deals specifically with the Roman Church's theory of government. He speaks of

> the harmful and lamentable rage for innovation which rose to a climax in the sixteenth century, threw first of all into confusion the Christian religion [this refers to the Protestant Reformation], and next, by natural sequence, invaded the precincts of philosophy, whence it spread amongst all classes of society. From this source, as from a fountainhead, burst forth all those later tenets of unbridled license which, in the midst of the terrible upheavals of the last century [this refers to the democratic movements of the eighteenth and nineteenth centuries], were wildly conceived and boldly proclaimed as the principles and foundation of that new jurisprudence which was not merely previously unknown, but was at variance on many points with not only the Christian, but even with the natural law.[16]

Among the several principles underlying the popular democratic societies that he rejects is the principle that "no man has any right to rule over other men." He also rejects the kind of government based upon that dangerous and false maxim. "In a society grounded upon such maxims," he asserts, " all government is nothing more or less than the will of the people, and the people, being under the power of itself alone, is alone its own ruler." [17] As he proceeds he denounces these ideas: that the sovereignty of the people resides in the multitude; that the people have the right to think for themselves, to publish their own views, to form their own personal judgments about religion, to exercise the right of private judgment, and to follow their own consciences as the sole and sufficient guide. He agrees with Pope Gregory XVI that all these are shameless liberties.[18] This language obviously refers to popular democracies both ecclesiastical and civil.

The pope states that "every civilized community must have a ruling authority," and that the source of that authority is God. So "whoever holds the right to govern holds it from one sole and single source, namely, God." Then he adds a statement that has often been quoted by American Catholics to justify their claim that they can be loyal Catholics and loyal Americans at the same time. The statement is: "The right to rule is not *necessarily,* however, bound up with any special mode of government. It may take this or that form, provided only that it be of a nature to ensure the *general welfare.*" [19] (Italics supplied.) The italicized words are the key to that statement. The Roman Church always reserves the right to decide when a government ensures the general welfare. And it always decides that no form of government is good for the general welfare that does not admit that God has given it sole charge over all the spiritual affairs of the human race, and permit it to exercise its full power and authority unhindered.[19a] Precisely what power and authority it demands as wholly its own in all civil societies will become clear in the next section.

In an extended commentary on Leo's position, Ryan and Boland express the belief that, when properly interpreted, his teaching permits Catholics to support the American democracy. But they explain that it may also permit them to support several kinds of undemocratic governments, such as a one-man rulership over a semicivilized tribal community (pp. 85–86); the intervention of a civilized power in the affairs of a savage or semisavage community to set up a stable government for their own welfare (pp. 86–87); and a fascist government that "promotes the common good to a reasonable degree" (pp. 120–121). Officially, then, the Catholic Church supports in principle no form of civil government. Whether it supports one civil government or another depends on political exigency and the degree to which it is given a free rein to pursue its own purposes.

Not one pope in the last two centuries has said anything that could be interpreted to mean that the Catholic Church *in prin-*

ciple ever sanctions democracy, or *in principle* ever opposes monarchy in any of its forms. As a matter of temporary expedience and for the interests of the Roman Church, qualified endorsement has been given to democracy, and qualified opposition declared to fascism. But the Vatican has consistently opposed every genuine democratic movement since the Reformation.

Nichols made an exhaustive, thoroughly documented study of the relationship between the churches and the democratic movements in modern times. His study shows that the Roman Catholic Church has been allied with political absolutism in the five democratic upsurges in the last one hundred and fifty years: the French Revolution, the Revolution of 1830, the Revolution of 1848, the wave of Catholic democracy that began about 1890, and the wave of Catholic democracy between the two world wars.

Pope Leo XIII gave some encouragement to democracy in the 1890's in order to " break the ruinous identification of French Catholicism with monarchism and disloyalty to the Republic, and to cultivate the new laboring classes before they should fall completely into the hands of the Marxists." [20] But his successor, Pius X, " brutally purged away " this effort from 1900 to 1912. Speaking of the period between the two world wars, Nichols says:

The Catholic alliance with Fascist counterrevolution in this last generation pointed up again the purely external and opportunistic basis on which Roman Catholicism had come to terms here and there with democracy. There was no intrinsic kinship between Roman Catholicism and liberal democracy. Unlike Protestantism, the Roman Church had never fought for democracy when democracy was weak. The Roman Church had accommodated itself to democracy when democracy, supported by other systems of thought, had proved itself a power to be reckoned with. And . . . to those democratic liberties by which the Roman Church itself could profit. . . . [Any contributions the Roman Church made], however im-

portant, were only accidentally democratic, and were used by
the hierarchy as steppingstones for its further undemocratic
program.[21]

Further information about Roman Catholic political machina-
tions and maneuverings against democracies and in favor of au-
tocracies since the close of the First World War is given in Avro
Manhattan's *The Vatican in World Politics* (Gaer Associates,
Inc., 1949).

3. *Church and state.* The Roman Catholic Church believes in
the union, not the separation, of church and state.

a. *Official teaching.* As already indicated, the official Catholic
teaching on this subject is found in the two documents referred
to above.

The Syllabus of Errors. Pope Pius lays down the principle of
clerical supremacy in politics, namely, that when the church and
the civil power conflict, the state must yield to the jurisdiction of
the church (item 42). He devotes the first eighteen items of the
Syllabus primarily to a condemnation of " naturalism " and " ra-
tionalism " and recurs to this again in several other places (e.g.,
items 50, 56, 57). Specifically, he condemns the " moral " and
" civil " laws that operate independent of " ecclesiastical authority "; that is, he rejects the theory of natural law upon which the
American democracy is based.

He affirms that it is an error to say, " The church ought to be
separated from the state, and the state from the church " (item
55), or to say, " Civil laws may and ought to keep aloof from
divine and ecclesiastical authority " (item 57). He describes the
Roman Catholic Church as a " true and perfect society " (item
19), and claims that it has the right to exercise its authority without the permission of the civil authority (item 20), that it possesses
power to use force " direct and indirect " (item 24), and that the
sacred ministers of the church and the Roman pontiff may not be
excluded from exercising " charge and dominion over temporal
affairs " (item 27).

When the claim of the Roman Church to be the "perfect society" is spelled out, it means this:

A society that possesses the right to all organs and functions necessary to its welfare, economic, judicial, military, political. The Roman court has the right to political rule directly as a state, with all functionaries from diplomats and soldiers down to secret police and executioners, to use force where necessary, and also indirectly, by using its spiritual disciplines over Catholic citizens, to break laws, to coerce or overthrow governments. . . . Even in liberal and democratic societies, consequently, a Roman Catholic police officer may be required to take orders from the bishop.[22]

Immortale Dei. The basic proposition, on which everything else political in this document rests, is that the individual is obligated to obey legitimate authority. (Rom. 13:1-2.) Jesus Christ established the one true society, the church, and handed over to it his exalted and divine office that he received from God. God, therefore, sets rulers over the multitude of peoples on earth. He divided "the charge of the human race between two powers, the ecclesiastical and the civil, the one being set over divine, the other over human things."[23]

He insists, as do Protestants, that the church should be free. The authority of the church is "the most exalted of all authority," he declares; "nor can it be looked upon as inferior to the civil power, or in any manner dependent upon it."[24] The church, not the state, he avers, "is to be man's guide to Heaven. It is to the Church that God has assigned the charge of seeing to, and legislating for, all that concerns religion; of teaching all nations; of spreading the Christian faith as widely as possible; in short, of administering freely and without hindrance, in accordance with her own judgment, all matters that fall within its competence."[25]

But he does not admit that the state also should be free. Among the rulers God has appointed over human beings, one ruler should be "the head of all,"[26] Peter and his successors, the popes.

God provided the church " with a *civil sovereignty* as the surest safeguard of her independence." [27] (Italics mine.) " There must, accordingly, exist, between these two powers [church and state], a certain orderly connection, which may be compared to the union of the soul and body in man." [28] People cry out that matters affecting the church must be separated from that of the state. This is an " unrightful " position for the church,[29] he declares. " To exclude the Church, founded by God Himself, from the business of life, from the power of making laws, from the training of youth, from domestic society, is a grave and fatal error." [30]

Furthermore, the state has a positive obligation to the church. The state has a duty to God of " public profession of religion." [31] It is " a sin in the State not to have care for religion," [32] meaning not to care for the true or Catholic religion. One of the chief duties of all who rule " must be to favor religion, to protect it, to shield it under the credit and sanction of the laws, and neither to organize nor enact any measure that may compromise its safety." [33] He goes on to explain that he means by those words: " The Church, indeed, deems it unlawful to place the various forms of divine worship on the same footing as the true religion." [34]

Looking back with nostalgic feelings to medieval days, he said, there was a time when " the religion instituted by Jesus Christ . . . flourished everywhere, by the favor of princes and the legitimate protection of magistrates; and Church and State were happily united in concord and friendly interchange of good offices." [35] He quotes a letter written to Pope Paschal II: " ' When kingdom and priesthood are at one, in complete accord, the world is well ruled, and the Church flourishes, and brings forth abundant fruit. But when they are at variance, not only smaller interests prosper not, but even things of greatest moment fall into deplorable decay.' " [36]

The reader should not suppose that this teaching is outmoded. It is the official doctrine of the Roman Church as taught at the present time. This encyclical is quoted in full, commented on item by item, and used as the basis of the doctrine of church and state in Ryan and Boland's textbook. This same teaching is put out in the form of catechisms for use in their schools.[37]

b. *Diplomatic relations with civil governments.* Because the Roman Catholic Church, as has been shown, claims the right to both temporal and spiritual powers and maintains that the latter is superior to the former, it does not hesitate, as an ecclesiastical body, to engage in political negotiations and understandings with civil governments. Pope Leo XIII asserted:

> It cannot be called in question that in the making of treaties, in the transaction of business matters, in sending and receiving Ambassadors, and in the interchange of other kinds of official dealings, they [rulers] have been wont to treat with the Church as with a supreme and legitimate power.[38]

That is to say, the Roman Church claims, as one of its prerogatives, the right to be consulted in the political affairs of nations.

In his *Syllabus,* Pius IX denied that " the secular power has authority to rescind, declare and render null, solemn conventions, commonly called concordats . . . without the consent of the Apostolic See " (item 43). The dictionary defines a " concordat " as " an agreement made between the pope and a sovereign government for the regulation of ecclesiastical matters." Item 43, then, seems to mean that " concordats are papal concessions to states, binding on the latter, but changeable at the pope's pleasure." [39] In another item of the *Syllabus* (item 62), he denied that the " principle of nonintervention . . . ought to be proclaimed and observed." This refers to the customary agreement by modern states not to interfere in the internal affairs of one another. The denial of the validity of this principle by the pope is equivalent to declaring it to be his privilege to intervene, and persuade nations to intervene, in the affairs of governments when he considers the welfare of the Roman Church to be at stake.

Throughout our history sporadic attempts have been made to persuade our Government to establish full diplomatic relations with the Vatican, but up to now the attempts have not been successful. The most recent effort along this line began with Franklin D. Roosevelt's appointment of Myron C. Taylor as his "personal representative" to the Vatican in 1939. The Vatican itself regarded Mr. Taylor as the actual ambassador from the United States and treated him as such. This provoked so much opposition that when Mr. Taylor resigned in 1950, the House of Representatives specified in an appropriation bill that governmental funds could not be used for the support of this type of mission without the express sanction of Congress. In 1951, President Truman nominated General Mark W. Clark as a full ambassador to the Vatican. Public sentiment was expressed so strongly against this that General Clark withdrew his name before Congress could pass upon his nomination. The matter has not been brought up again, although from time to time rumors are heard that the Roman Catholics are waiting for a propitious moment to do so.

c. *Double citizenship of American Roman Catholics.* Over the years Roman Catholics have reacted in several different ways when Protestants called attention to the fact that the official teaching of the Roman Catholic Church on church and state not only contradicts the official American policy on church and state, but makes Roman Catholics citizens of two countries at the same time. Until recently the most common reaction of Catholics has been to deny that the Vatican is a state. That also has generally been the position of the United States Government. Repeated efforts by Protestants to get an official ruling from the Attorney General or from the Department of State concerning the particular category in which the Vatican is classified, have usually resulted only in evasive or unclear replies.

Another reaction of Catholics has been to depreciate, or even to deny the validity of, the American doctrine of church and state. For example, Father John Courtney Murray once spoke of it as "that negative, ill-defined, basically un-American formula, with all its overtones of religious prejudice." [40] This type of attitude is now being manifested in the attempt to secure new and more liberal interpretations of the Constitution from the Supreme Court that will weaken, nullify, or erase this traditional doctrine. More will be said of this a little later.

Currently some Roman Catholics are openly admitting that the Vatican is both a state and a church, but insisting that Roman Catholics can hold citizenship in both the United States of America and the Vatican without any conflict between the two. Two recent occurrences will serve to make this plain.

In order to prevent its public officials from becoming indebted in any way to a foreign Government, our forefathers wrote into the Constitution this provision:

> No person holding any Office of Profit or Trust under them [the United States], shall, without the Consent of the Congress, accept of any present, Emolument, Office, or Title, of any kind whatever, from any King, Prince, or foreign State. (Article I, Section 9.)

In 1957, Congressmen John W. McCormack and John J. Rooney, both Roman Catholics, were given the papal decoration of the Order of St. Gregory the Great. The National Catholic Almanac of 1957 described the decoration as a " civil and military award to the subjects of the Papal States." Both these Congressmen deposited the decorations with the Department of State until Congress passed a bill, which the President signed, permitting them to accept the decorations. Although there was some discussion at the time whether this meant that Congress regarded the Vatican as a " foreign State," at least one Catholic publication frankly so interpreted the action. *The New World,* the official organ of the Roman Catholic Archdiocese of Chicago, said, in its issue of July 26, 1957:

> By signing the bill the President recognized His Holiness, Pope Pius XII, as the head of a sovereign state. And so he is. Not only is he the spiritual ruler of 400,000,000 Catholics; he is the temporal ruler of the sovereign state of the Vatican. The two positions can be separated, as the President admitted by signing the bill.

In reply to a letter of inquiry about the decorations, the State Department said that " the State of Vatican City, by all leading authorities on international law, is recognized as a sovereign state which became a formal member of the family of nations by virtue of the Lateran Treaty of 1929." But the statement went on to say that "the United States has never extended formal recognition to the State of Vatican City or to its Government." [41]

With the same general purpose in view as Article I, Section 9, of the Constitution, Congress passed the McCarran Immigration and Nationality Act in 1952, which embodied similar provisions of a 1940 law. This Act, among other things, provides that a citizen "shall lose his nationality by . . . voting in a political election in a foreign state or participating in an election or plebiscite to determine the sovereignty over foreign territory." This law has been enforced against a number of American citizens, including Father Bruno Durigon of the Franciscan Order. He voted in the Italian elections in 1946 and 1948 and sought to regain his citizenship in the courts in Detroit in 1957. But it was not enforced against Archbishop Gerald P. O'Hara, an American citizen, who served for several years as papal nuncio, or Ambassador of the Vatican, to Ireland, although the attention of the Government was called to the fact that his acceptance of such a position was a violation of the McCarran Act. Nor has it been enforced against Archbishop Aloysius Muench, of North Dakota, an American citizen, who is now serving as papal nuncio to Germany. The State Department took the position in the case of Archbishop O'Hara that the law was not intended to apply to such officials.

At the time some Catholic spokesmen argued that the Vatican's diplomatic corps is attached not to the Vatican City State but to the religious body, the Holy See. But the Roman Catholic writer, Bernard Wall, in his recent study of the Vatican, declared quite frankly that these and all other papal nuncios of whatever nationality are regarded as citizens of the Vatican when they are on their missions. He also further asserted that the question of the ultimate political loyalties of these nuncios is still unsettled in America. [41a]

While preparations were being made at the Vatican for the

Cardinals to select a successor to Pope Pius XII in October, 1958, Glenn L. Archer, executive secretary of Protestants and Other Americans United for Separation of Church and State, urged Secretary of State John Foster Dulles to apply the law referred to above to the three American Cardinals who were in Rome to vote for the "sovereignty over foreign territory."[42] Ten days later the State Department ruled that the American Cardinals could vote in the election without endangering their American citizenship. The ruling declared: "It is only incidental that by virtue of his office as head of the Catholic Church the Pope is also the head of the State of Vatican City. Accordingly, the Department is of the view that the papal election is not a ' political election ' within the meaning of the above cited statute."[43]

Although the wording of the law is plain, the State Department has decided, arbitrarily in the judgment of many, that the law does not apply to the foreign state called the Vatican. This decision seems to be based upon two positions: (1) the Vatican is not a large enough state to qualify under the law; (2) the Vatican can be separated into two entities. At one time it may be regarded as a state and at another time as an ecclesiastical body, according to the definition of its particular acts at the moment. So our Department of State declares upon one occasion that the Vatican is a sovereign state, and at another time that it is in reality only a religious society.

This, of course, is the position the Vatican wants every government to take: namely, the Vatican is both a state and an ecclesiastical body; as head of the Vatican the pope is free, and Catholics are privileged, to declare that he is acting in either capacity or in both capacities at once, as best suits his pleasure and purpose at the moment; and his function in one area never conflicts with his function in the other area. This is an anomalous and confusing situation. It enables Roman Catholics to engage in what appears to others to be double-dealing and subterfuge to gain their ends. That is, they play both ends against the middle. More and more Americans are insisting that Rome cannot have it both ways. Sooner or later the American Government and its people must change this intolerable political-ecclesiastical ambiguity. The growing sentiment on this point augurs ill for the internal peace of our country.

This situation provokes a number of questions. Is it possible for a person to be loyal to two sovereign states at the same time without any possibility of a conflict's arising between the two? Or to state it another way, can a person serve two political masters with perfectly balanced loyalty to each? Can our American democracy legally or prudently permit any large block of its citizens to maintain a double political allegiance of any kind? The American people as a whole have never come to grips with these questions simply because hitherto they have not felt it was necessary to do so. But they cannot much longer defer doing so squarely and decisively.

The Roman Catholic Church as a foreign state cannot be compared to any other foreign state, because no other state claims to be also an ecclesiastical society with canon laws that control its subjects and that must be superior to the civil laws of the country in which those subjects maintain their citizenship. Hence, recognizing the Roman Catholic Church as a legitimate sovereign power and establishing diplomatic relations with it are unlike similar arrangements with other sovereign powers. To admit that any group of American citizens may give allegiance to a foreign state of any kind is to weaken the foundation of our democracy. To admit that the Roman Catholic clergy and laity in the United States are free to give their allegiance to the foreign church-state with its headquarters in Rome, is to invite and encourage Roman Catholics to make our country a Roman Catholic state. Just what is meant by a *Roman Catholic state* will be explained shortly.

4. *Religious liberty.* In the *Syllabus,* Pius IX denied that men are free to profess any religion they choose (item 15); that they may find salvation in "the observance of any religion whatever" (item 16); that there is "good hope" for the salvation of "all those who are not at all in the true Church of Christ" (item 17, meaning, of course, the Roman Catholic Church); and that Protestantism is "another form of the same true Christian reli-

gion, in which form it is given to please God equally as in the Catholic Church " (item 18). Furthermore, he claimed that the Roman Church has the power " of defining dogmatically that the religion of the Catholic Church is the only true religion " (item 21); that the Catholic religion should be " held as the only religion of the state, to the exclusion of all other forms of worship " (item 77); that laws " in some Catholic countries, that persons coming to reside therein shall enjoy the public exercise of their own peculiar worship," are to be condemned (item 78); and that the " civil liberty of every form of worship, and the full power, given to all, of overtly and publicly manifesting any opinions whatsoever and thoughts, conduce more easily to corrupt the morals and minds of the people, and to propagate the pest of indifferentism " (item 79).

Does all this teaching apply to the United States of America? The official answer to that question is: " Not for the present. As a matter of temporary expedience, or as a *modus vivendi* awaiting a more ideal arrangement, Catholics in America should abide by the democratic position of equal freedom for all religious bodies."

Two quotations from Connell's book, referred to previously, will make this clear. He informs Catholic legislators that:

Catholics of the United States seek no special governmental favor for their church. They accept unequivocally the American plan of granting equal rights to all religious organizations. Of course, Catholics are not so illogical as to believe that, *as far as God's law is concerned,* any religion has a real right to exist except the one true religion established by the Son of God for all mankind. But *as far as civil legislation in the United States is concerned,* Catholics agree that the most practical system is complete freedom for all denominations.[44]

He advises the schoolteacher that:

She may, indeed, explain and uphold the American system granting equal rights to all religions, but in lauding this system she should make it clear that she is limiting her praise to our own country, because of particular conditions prevailing here, and that she has no intention of condemning other lands in which a different procedure prevails. She must not speak in such wise as to give the impression that all forms of religious belief possess a natural right to exist and to propagate. Only the true religion possesses such a natural right.[45]

This same position is set forth at length by Ryan and Boland,[46] and will now be summarized. The state must not only care for religion " but recognize the *true* religion." For " no individual, no group of individuals, no society, no State is justified in supporting error or in according to error the same recognition as to truth." (Pp. 313–314.) This principle, of course, has complete application only to Catholic states. Pope Leo XIII (encyclical on *Catholicity in the United States*) praised the attitude of our Government and laws toward religion. But he went on to say: " 'It would be very erroneous to draw the conclusion that in America is to be sought the type of the most desirable status of the Church, or that it would be universally lawful or expedient for State and Church, to be, as in America, dissevered and divorced ' " (p. 315). The desirable relationship from the Catholic viewpoint is a union of church and state in which " the State should officially recognize the Catholic religion as the religion of the commonwealth " (p. 316).

Would such recognition imply that " no other religion should be tolerated "? Others would be permitted to worship " within the family, or in such an inconspicuous manner as to be an occasion neither of scandal nor of perversion to the faithful." But they would not be permitted to propagate their false beliefs among Catholics. (P. 317.) Does this sound intolerant? It is intolerant, but it is not " therefore unreasonable. Error has not the same rights as truth " (p. 318). But cannot this argument be turned against Catholics by a non-Catholic state? No, for several reasons. A Protestant state could not logically take such an attitude because, on Protestant principles, Catholics have a right to hold their religious convictions without molestation. Furthermore, provision is made in the constitutions of Protestant countries for religious freedom. And it is a basic principle of the Roman Church that in such countries — that is, when Catholics have not the power to establish a " completely Catholic State " — Catholics are sworn to abide by the constitutional provisions for religious liberty. (Pp. 319–320.)

But suppose the Constitution is changed by the votes of Catholics who have become the majority, and the country becomes a Catholic state, what will the Catholic state do? " Apparently, the latter State could logically tolerate only such religious activities as were confined to the members of the dissenting group. It could not permit them to carry on general propaganda nor accord their organization certain privileges that had formerly been extended to all religious corporations, for example, exemption from taxation." (P. 320.)

At this point the reader should be reminded of two important facts: (1) Roman Catholic youth are indoctrinated with precisely this same point of view in other textbooks widely used in parochial schools. This can be ascertained by examining two books in their educational series, published by William H. Sadlier (New York, 1945), entitled *Living Our Faith,* by Anthony J. Flynn, Sister Vincent Loretto, and Mother Mary Simeon; and *Christian Principles and National Problems,* by Anthony L. Ostheimer and John P. Delaney. (2) The Vatican has concluded concordats with many nations in which Roman Catholics are in the majority. In all these concordats, as Bernard Wall has clearly shown, the church demands freedom for itself but not " freedom in itself." " There can hardly be any doubt," he states, " that in its concordats with Catholic countries the Vatican does not normally trouble to safeguard the rights claimed by Protestants, Jews, and Freethinkers." [46a]

In all such countries, to one degree or another, depending upon the extent to which a particular country may be regarded as a Catholic state, the Roman Catholic Church has been given the special privileges and favors indicated in Ryan and Boland's book, and the freedom of minority religious groups have been re-stricted in the ways suggested in that same book. There can be no doubt, then, that the same arrangement would be sought in whole or in part in America should they gain the ascendancy here. The very existence of the Roman Catholic doctrine of church and state is a potential threat to religious liberty.

But to return specifically to the concluding remarks of Ryan and Boland on this subject. Realizing that their utterances are likely to be most disturbing to Protestants, the authors endeavor to allay these fears with a statement that can be summarized briefly as follows:

The possibility of these things being realized in any country of the world is " so remote in time and in probability that no prac-tical man will let it disturb his equanimity or affect his attitude toward those who differ from him in religious faith." Of course, " some zealots and bigots will continue to attack the Church " because they are afraid that " some five thousand years hence the United States may become overwhelmingly Catholic and may then restrict the freedom of non-Catholic denominations. Never-theless, we [Catholics] cannot yield up . . . [our convictions] to avoid the enmity of such unreasonable persons." So we propose to go on professing our beliefs about church and state, " confident that the great majority of our fellow citizens will be sufficiently honorable to respect our devotion to truth, and sufficiently realis-tic to see that the danger of religious intolerance toward non-Catholics in the United States is so improbable and so far in the future that it should not occupy their time or attention." (Pp. 320–321.)

This is a bold application to America of Louis Veuillot's fa-mous proposition about religious liberty: " Where we Catholics are in the minority, we demand freedom in the name of your principles; where we are in the majority, we deny it in the name of our principles." [47] Here we are officially informed by Roman Catholic professors that their church is taking advantage of the tolerance and freedom afforded them in our American-Protestant tradition to deprive Protestants of their freedom if and when they become powerful enough to do so. At the same time they are urging Protestants to take the indifferent attitude, "It can't happen here," while they proceed to make it happen here. And all who oppose their procedures and positions, or discuss publicly the problem of church and state involved in them, are classified as "zealots," "bigots," and "unreasonable persons."

Not all American Catholics agree with Ryan and Boland that American constitutional laws are binding on American Catholics only as a matter of *expediency,* or until it becomes possible to change the laws. At present a group of Roman Catholic leaders in the United States is engaged in a concerted effort to prove that Roman Catholics may support *permanently* the American Constitution and the religious pluralism it implies, and still remain loyal Catholics. This will be brought up again later in the next chapter.

5. *Roman Catholic educational policy.* The principles upon which this policy is based were stated by Pius IX in three items of the *Syllabus.* If the statements are changed from denials to assertions, their meaning becomes clearer. He asserts: (*a*) that Catholics may not "approve of the system of educating youth unconnected with the Catholic faith and the power of the Church, and which regards the knowledge of merely natural things, and only, or at least primarily, the ends of earthly social life" (item 48); (*b*) that the civil state does not have authority to operate its public schools free "from all ecclesiastical . . . control and interference" (item 47); or (*c*) in such a manner as to deny the right of the church "to interfere in the discipline of the schools, the arrangement of the studies, the conferring of degrees, in the choice or approval of the teachers" (item 45).

Obviously, these principles cannot be applied in the same way in Catholic and non-Catholic states. In a Catholic state the church and state execute a concordat that specifies the ways in which ecclesiastical authority may be exercised in educational policies and procedures. In non-Catholic states, which reject all ecclesiastical interferences in education, Catholics operate under the motto stated by Pius XI, in his encyclical letter, "Christian Education of Youth " (1929), namely, " Catholic education in Catholic schools for all the Catholic youth." [48]

To implement this policy the hierarchy undertakes three things: (a) To establish a system of parochial schools for the training of Catholic youth. (b) To prevent Roman Catholic youth from attending public schools. Canon 1374, in *Code of Canon Law* (1918), provides that " Catholic children must not attend non-Catholic, neutral, or mixed schools." But it further provides that " it is for the bishop of the place alone to decide, according to the instructions of the Apostolic See, in what circumstances and with what precautions attendance at such schools may be tolerated without danger of perversion to the pupils." (c) To secure support for Catholic schools from the state. Pius XI declared: " It is the duty of the state to help the church maintain its religious schools by aid from public funds and equally the duty of all Catholics as an act of religion to demand that the state perform the duty." [49]

Although this has been the policy of the Roman Catholic hierarchy throughout the history of our country, the hierarchy has not engaged openly in a national campaign to secure public funds for the support of their schools until recent years. That campaign, beginning in a modest way, has been steadily increasing in intensity and effectiveness until it has become a full-scale effort to modify the traditional interpretations of the Constitution by the Supreme Court so as to secure legal support of their schools out of both Federal and state funds.

For many years the Roman hierarchy has been assuring the American people that its church is not asking for funds directly for the support of its school system, but only for certain marginal services, such as free transportation, free lunches, free textbooks, and free health programs, which they regard as the constitutional right of every American child. They claim that this right is vouchsafed by the U. S. Supreme Court's decision in the Everson case (1947), which authorized local school districts to pay transportation expenses of school children. This payment, the court declared, did not aid any particular religious organization but aided only the child. On November 15, 1952, the daily newspapers carried a news item about "Secularism and Schools," a document issued by Roman Catholic bishops, in which they made use of this decision in the following manner:

> The state . . . has the duty to help parents fulfill their task of religious instruction and training. When the state fails in this help, when it makes the task more difficult, and even penalizes parents who try to fulfill this duty according to conscience, by depriving their children of their right under our Federal Constitution to auxiliary services, this can only be regarded as an utterly unfair and shortsighted policy.

For twenty-five years, more or less, the hierarchy has been working quietly in Washington, and with some success, to block Federal aid to public education until aid is also provided for parochial schools. As early as 1943 the director of the Department of Education of the National Catholic Welfare Conference stated, "The Catholic position is one of opposition to any measure for Federal aid to education that would: (a) interfere with local control of the purposes and processes of education, and (b) fail to make mandatory the inclusion of Catholic schools in its benefits." This statement appeared in the *Congressional Record,* Senate, October 12, 1942 (p. 96). But knowledge of this policy of demanding proportionately the same aid for parochial schools as that given to public schools did not become widely known until recently.

In 1956 Cardinal James Francis McIntyre, of Los Angeles, announced at the dedication of the University of Dallas, a Catholic institution, that he was in favor of a national educational plan for youth that would provide scholarships for American youth in somewhat the same way that Congress provided scholarships for the members of the Armed Forces in World War II and the Korean War. This statement was broadcast over the country through the American secular and religious press.

In its issue of October 25, 1957 (pp. 169 ff.), the *U. S. News & World Report* printed the digest of an article by Father Virgil C.

Blum, of Marquette University, a prominent Jesuit, calling for Government subsidy for the Roman Catholic educational program at the elementary and high school levels. The subsidy, he said, could be either a tax credit for parents of nonpublic school children, or a direct subsidization of the individual child, similar to that given by the Federal Government for the education of Korean War veterans. He favored the latter plan. This article also soon became national news.

By a strange reversal of logic Father Blum argued that Roman Catholics are making this fight for subsidy in order to preserve the freedom of religion vouchsafed in Article I of the Bill of Rights. He claims that Article gives all children equal right to an education. Not to support children who attend nonpublic schools is to penalize the parents because of their religious beliefs. It is forcibly to deny the children opportunity to attend a religious school of their free choice. Such an attitude, he insists, is equivalent to enforced uniformity, which is a characteristic of a totalitarian society, not of a democratic society like ours. He also argues that Government support of the Roman Catholic schools would be society's way of paying for the benefits it derives from such schools, that it would *restore* free enterprise in education, and that it would help preserve our other American liberties.[50] Someone has roughly estimated that if this plan were to be put into operation, it would cost the American taxpayers no less than one billion dollars a year.

On January 5, 1958, the daily newspapers carried an Associated Press dispatch that said: "A group of leading Jesuit educators took the position today that Roman Catholic schools should not be barred from any Federal aid Congress votes to spur education in America. . . . The Jesuits' views were given by the Reverend Edward B. Rooney, S.J., president of the Jesuit Education Association, during a two-day meeting of the presidents of the twenty-eight Jesuit colleges and universities of America." The article went on to quote Father Rooney as saying that Federal aid should " be made available on an across-the-board basis for all students and all institutions," and that the Catholic Church " has taken a definite stand against the Supreme Court's interpretation of the separation of church and state, and particularly against the denial of public money to sectarian schools."

In a number of communities in 1958, candidates for office openly pledged to Catholic voters that they would work for support of parochial schools from public funds. In Fall River, Massachusetts, Joseph V. Aguiar, Jr., a candidate for Representative, told the voters in a political advertisement, "If elected, I will introduce a constitutional amendment to force the state to pay 50 per cent of the cost of all new parochial schools." In Stamford, Connecticut, Martin F. Armstrong, Jr., a candidate for mayor, promised that, if elected, he would secure free transportation for children attending parochial schools. In Central Falls, Rhode Island, Raymond J. Morissette, a candidate for councilman, promised he would try to secure an annual appropriation out of city funds for the maintenance of parochial schools in the city.[51]

At long last, then, the Catholics' campaign for tax support for parochial schools is being openly aired before the whole nation. Their purpose is to try to get sectarian schools put on a par with public schools and to secure for their schools a proportionate share of all funds and services made available by the units of government for educational purposes.

The opposition of the Catholic Church to the decisions of the Supreme Court, which make illegal the use of public money for sectarian schools, has developed into a campaign to secure new interpretations of the Constitution that will make this procedure legal. An up-to-date report on the present status of this campaign and the future strategy of those engaged in it may be found in a pamphlet, *Religion and the Free Society,* published by the Fund for the Republic.[52] Four out of five chapters in this symposium deal primarily with that subject.

The pamphlet describes three methods that are being used in the campaign. One method is to impugn the historic interpretation, established by decisions of the Supreme Court, that the First Amendment to the Constitution erects a "wall of separation between church and state." For example, William Clancy, a Roman

Catholic layman, insists that this amendment was intended to ensure to individuals the free exercise of religion, not to forbid aid to religion. So he asserts that " To the extent that the ' absolute wall ' theory is supported in the courts, to that same extent a doctrine about which the Constitution itself knows nothing has been imposed on American life " (p. 29).

Another method is to argue that the cases in which the Supreme Court has permitted auxiliary benefits to children in parochial schools *might* become the basis of a future decision of the court that would validate *nonpreferential* aid to religious schools. By nonpreferential aid is meant aid to all schools, or to all religious schools, alike. No case as yet has been before the Court in which the validity of such aid has had to be faced squarely. But the Catholics are hopefully anticipating the time when this will happen.

Still another method is to make use of the fact that in recent years the First Amendment has, by some legal minds, been read into the Fourteenth Amendment. The First Amendment states, " Congress shall make no law respecting an establishment of religion, or prohibiting the free exercise thereof. . . ." The Fourteenth Amendment states, ". . . No State shall make or enforce any law which shall abridge the privileges or immunities of citizens of the United States; nor shall any State deprive any person of life, liberty, or property without due process of law, nor deny to any person within its jurisdiction the equal protection of the laws." Some legal minds raise this question: Precisely what restraints does the Fourteenth Amendment impose on the states? It does not contain the word " religion " as does the First Amendment. Does it, then, prohibit the states from making any " law respecting an establishment of religion, or prohibiting the free exercise thereof," or does it prohibit only those laws which affect the religious or other constitutional liberties of individuals? Some argue that it prohibits the latter only. So they are looking forward to the possibility that at some future date the Supreme Court *might* interpret these two amendments and their relations to each other so as to make it possible for the *states* legally to give aid to religious institutions, a thing that it is not possible for the *Federal* Government to do.

The several phases of this campaign to secure more liberal interpretations of the Constitution from the Supreme Court involve a number of lengthy and technical legal studies that cannot be considered here. But this brief explanation will indicate the several lines along which the campaign is moving.

An increasing number of facts, indicating how successfully Roman Catholics are attaining their educational objectives mostly without the express approval of the courts, has been accumulating in the last few years. A few — and only a few — of these facts which have emerged in the last two years will now be listed.

As the result of a complaint by the Northern California–Nevada Council of Churches to the Board of Education of San Francisco, the legal adviser to the Board admitted that public-school attendance officers have for many years been used on parochial school cases. The New York State Educational Commissioner admitted that training programs for Roman Catholic nuns-teachers were being financed out of state funds, although, as he explained, the "original intention had been to limit refresher courses to teachers in the state's public schools." Representatives of five parochial school districts in Lackawanna, New York, asked the city to appropriate funds to employ recreational supervisors in their parishes, despite a provision in the New York State Constitution which specifically forbids this use of public funds.

The citizens of Dobbs Ferry, New York, were asked to vote in an election to authorize the Board of Education to issue bonds to acquire twelve acres for school purposes. Catholics, urged to do so by the local priest, who was supported by Cardinal Spellman, voted in large enough numbers to defeat the bond issue. Previous to election day it was revealed that the Roman Catholic Sisters of Mercy had a secretly executed contract to purchase the entire site of sixty-three acres, on which they proposed to build a college and parochial school.

In 1958, the daily papers of San Francisco reported that, at the request of the Reverend John F. X. Connelly, S.J., president of the University of San Francisco, the mayor of the city had asked the Board of Education to declare as surplus a fifteen-acre school site so it could be sold to the parochial high school operated by the University. The superintendent of public schools immediately protested the contemplated sale because it would jeopardize the future development of the public-school system in a city in which land for school purposes is strictly limited by the geographical bounds of the city. In Providence, Rhode Island, it was revealed that a sale for one dollar of a public school for use as a parochial school and the sale of another public school for a similar purpose were pending, and that the renting of another public school for parochial use had been completed without the rental rate being made public.

The *Pittsburgh Press* reported that the Pittsburgh Board of Public Education had agreed to sell a ten-acre plot of school property in Brookline, quietly and without public bidding, to a Roman Catholic Church for a parochial school. A three-year effort in the courts to prevent the City of New York from using its right of eminent domain and $3,500,000 of tax funds to help Fordham University, a Jesuit institution, to secure an enlarged campus, failed in 1958. Shortly thereafter, and encouraged by the New York case, the mayor and city council of Providence, Rhode Island, began steps to provide land to one of the Roman Catholic churches of the city by a similar method, and the officials of St. Louis University, a Jesuit institution, announced plans to acquire land for an enlarged campus in St. Louis without competitive bidding.

Another series of facts could be assembled to show how, in the last ten years, in many states of the Union, Roman Catholics have elected majorities, or all members, of public-school boards and have then proceeded to turn those schools into parochial schools, or to sell or lease them to parochial schools, or to employ Roman Catholic nuns and brothers as teachers, or to close them if this was to the advantage of the parochial schools in the community. The schools to which these things have happened are variously referred to as "hybrid schools," or "semipublic schools," or "captive public schools." One Catholic professor, the Very Reverend John Doyle, labeled them the "so-called Catholic public schools." There are now literally hundreds of such schools in New England, New Mexico, Ohio, Kentucky, Indiana, Michigan, Illinois, Kansas, Missouri, and the Dakotas, to name only the states that have been mentioned in news items in recent years. In 1946, the superintendent of education of the State of Michigan discovered that parochial schools had been operated illegally for as many as twenty-five years in some nineteen public-school districts.

Many legal battles have been fought in the courts over these schools, a few of which have attracted national attention. The best known of these battles were over schools in North College Hill, Ohio, a suburb of Cincinnati (1947), in Dixon, New Mexico (1947–1948), and in Bradfordsville, Kentucky (1956). The full report of all instances where a violation of the principle of separation of church and state has been uncovered in the United States since 1948 may be found in the complete files of the monthly publication, *Church and State.*[53]

What attitude should Protestants take toward this problem? Has the situation become serious enough to endanger the very bases of our American democracy and to threaten our national unity? Many Protestants and other non-Catholics think so. Parochial schools exist primarily to propagate religious beliefs. They are avowedly sectarian. This was made clear by *The St. Louis Lutheran,* February 9, 1947, when it defined the function of these schools thus:

> What is a parochial school? It is an instrument by which a religious body establishes, confirms, and propagates its religious beliefs. It is not the primary purpose of a church school to serve the public good, but to serve its own purposes, i.e., the perpetuation of its own beliefs, religious, social, scientific, economic, for it is no longer a religious education principle that geography or mathematics may be divorced from religion. All

subjects taught in a parochial school are properly religious teaching. . . . Parochial schools . . . are special interest schools.[54]

How long can our democratic society stand if public officials secretly show favoritism or set aside the laws of the land at will simply to please Roman Catholics who are continuously bringing behind-the-scenes-pressure for special advantages to their sectarian school system as over against the public-school system? Can Americans wisely support with their tax money two competing schools systems, one public and dedicated to a democratic society, the other religious and backed by a church that is operated on essentially antidemocratic principles, and whose openly acknowledged purpose is to make this a church-state? Our system of public schools, in which young people of all religious faiths learn in their formative years how to live and work together for common purposes, is essential for national unity. To weaken that system by pouring a large share of our resources into a second system, and that a religiously and culturally segregated system, is to ensure an America divided against itself. How long can such an America stand? Furthermore, to permit Roman Catholic education to compete with our public schools for our tax money is to encourage the development here of that form of clericalism which has been such a divisive, disturbing, and obstructive force, and a danger to freedom in practically all countries where Roman Catholics have been the dominant force.

The Constitution of the United States puts no restrictions whatever upon the religious beliefs of its citizens. It does not deny any child the opportunity to attend a religious school of his or his parents' choice. But it does forbid Congress to pass any legislation " respecting an establishment of religion," or that prohibits " the free exercise " of religion. Any religious denomination — Protestant, Jewish, or Catholic — is free to set up its own system of parochial schools and support it with its own funds. Any individual member of a church that sets up such schools is perfectly free to attend them. But no religious society has a right to ask or expect members of other religious societies to be taxed for the support of its sectarian religious institutions. Nor does the Government have any right to use its funds to support any religious society, not even to support all religious societies equally. That would be a violation of the Constitution — or so the great majority of American citizens have always believed.

If the great majority of Americans are wrong, if the clear intent of the Bill of Rights in our Constitution can be invalidated, nullified, or circumvented for the advantage of any one religious group, then America is not the kind of democracy we have always supposed it to be, and we have no way of ensuring the permanency of our cherished freedoms. Because of the widespread indifference to the significance of the First Amendment for our basic freedoms, someone asserted recently that if we did not already have that amendment in the Federal Constitution, it could not now be passed. So long as Roman Catholics continue their efforts to break down the wall of separation between church and state, just so long is it going to be difficult, if not impossible, for Catholics and non-Catholics to live and labor together in peace in our American society.

6. *Canon law and civil law.* The word "canon" means rule. The term "canon law" refers now almost exclusively to ecclesiastical rules concerning doctrine and discipline. For many centuries preceding the Reformation, canon law was a legally recognized division of public law throughout Europe. The church and the state divided the responsibility for disciplining citizens. The church handled all cases of discipline of a strictly moral or spiritual nature, and was also given jurisdiction over its members in certain other matters, such as the handling of wills, marriages, and burials. The state had jurisdiction in cases more distinctly civil or social in nature. Both civil and canon law were of equal validity in the land. That dual arrangement still obtains to a large extent in England, where the Anglican Church is the established church.[55]

Under our American plan of separation of church and state, churches no longer have jurisdiction in cases of a strictly civil nature. Churches of all faiths, however, are allowed, each in its own way, to discipline their ministers and members. All religious bodies, therefore, have some type of canon law. They have written or unwritten creeds to which ministers, officers, and members are expected to subscribe, systems of government to which all are supposed to conform, and moral standards that they hold up as ideals to be attained. They have some form of court — congrega- tion, official board, diocese, conference, convention, presbytery, synod, or what not — by which their laws are judged and applied. But these laws and the machinery for their application operate strictly within the bounds of the particular ecclesiastical organiza- tion that sets them up. The maximum penalties such courts can inflict are to take away a minister's or an official's credentials and to excommunicate members from their fellowship. This arrange- ment is legal so far as the state is concerned, but the actions of a church court have no civil effect, no legal standing, no validity outside that church's own fellowship.

Churches may appeal to civil courts to enforce their judgments. This is often necessary where property is involved. Individuals may appeal to civil courts to determine whether ecclesiastical penalties should be inflicted upon them. But in both types of ap- peal the state decides only two things: whether a church court is acting strictly within its own jurisdiction and whether it has vio- lated a civil right that the state is expected to safeguard equally for individuals of all faiths. Nor does the judgment of ecclesiasti- cal courts in the least affect the right of the state to bring its own charges against ministers, officers, and members of religious so- cieties. Finally, no religious society can appeal to the civil courts to apply its canon laws to members of other religious societies.

This American arrangement is designed to safeguard the rights of churches as well as of other institutions, the rights of church members as well as of other people. Churches as social institutions and church members as citizens are under the jurisdiction of civil government. The powers of state are not to be used for the bene- fit of one religious society as over against other religious societies, or to support the beliefs and practice of one in preference to another. In short, all groups and individuals are to be given equal treatment by the state.

Protestants agreed to this arrangement at the beginning. In fact, they helped devise it. They have operated under it without any feeling of restraint ever since. Each Protestant denomination has developed its own canon laws to suit itself and has been content to apply them within its own jurisdiction, leaving other religious groups to do likewise. Thus they have respected the rights of others, safeguarded their own rights, and preserved freedom for all.

The Roman Catholic Church has never given its official consent nor its wholehearted support to this arrangement in the United States. It claims the right to govern its " subjects " wherever they are found. And when there is a direct contradiction between its canon law and civil law, so that a choice must be made between the jurisdiction of the church and that of the state, the jurisdiction of the church takes precedence. *The Catholic Encyclopedia* states this matter thus:

> In cases of direct contradiction [between church and state], making it impossible for both jurisdictions to be exercised, the jurisdiction of the church prevails, and that of the state is excluded.[56]

The Roman Church claims exclusive jurisdiction over such matters as marriages and divorces of its members, the ownership and control of property, and the education of its youth.

Emmett McLoughlin, the well-known Roman Catholic priest of Phoenix, Arizona, who left the church some years ago, said that when he became a priest:

> The Constitution of my country and the laws of its states dimmed into trivialities in comparison with the all-powerful code of Canon Law of the Roman Catholic Church. I became in truth a citizen of the church living — by accident — in the United States.[57]

Roman Catholics in strategic positions are informed of the Roman canon law and are directed to abide by it. Catholic legislators are admonished not to support bills that make it legal for information to be given about the use of contraceptives, or that legalize abortion, sterilization, and euthanasia. If such bills pass, Roman Catholic judges are admonished not to hand down decisions permitting them to be put into effect.[58] If necessary, Catholic judges may be ordered by Roman Catholic authorities to dismiss civil suits brought against a Catholic clergyman, or to obey canon law in cases involving divorces [59] and church property,[60] even though he violates his oath of office in so doing. The Roman Catholic Church is able to exercise so much influence on prosecuting attorneys and judges that a suit in a civil court against Catholic clergymen and sisters is seldom heard of in our country. The November, 1958, edition of *Church and State* reports that a Catholic priest, Father Raymond Rucki, of Hatley, Wisconsin, was convicted and fined $100 for disobeying laws against gambling and $250 for operating a bar without a hard-liquor license at a picnic sponsored by his church in that community.

Here are a few items gleaned from two or three monthly issues of *Church and State* (1958) that show how Roman Catholics view civil law when it conflicts with canon law. Roman Catholic attorneys in Sante Fe, New Mexico, received a directive not to secure divorces for Roman Catholics without permission from the archbishop, Edwin V. Byrne. In the diocese of Pittsburgh, Roman Catholic lawyers were reminded that the law of their church requires them to clear every divorce case involving a Roman Catholic with Bishop John F. Dearden, before they may bring it into court. John J. Rafferty, of New Brunswick, New Jersey, who officially represented the Roman Catholic Church, attacked the law enforcement program of the New Jersey Bingo-Raffles Commission because it interfered with bingo and raffle games in Roman Catholic parishes. Under the very law the Commission was set up to enforce, these games were illegal. Eight Roman Catholic priests in Bloomfield, New Jersey, ordered Roman Catholic children in public schools to walk out of classes on two days in defiance of teachers, principals, and school boards who refused to submit to the wishes of the church by violating a state law governing religious holidays.

7. *The welfare of the church is supreme.* Another fact that bears directly upon the attitude of the Roman Catholic Church to our American democracy is that the church permits and encourages its members to engage in unethical practices when those practices advance the cause of the church. That is, the welfare of the church is supreme. When the welfare of the church is involved the " end justifies the means."

A few examples of these practices will suffice to explain the principle. When the state imposes a limit on the amount of tax-free property the church can hold, Catholics are informed that, by virtue of the fact that canon law denies the right of the state so to legislate, their consciences are released to use " subterfuges and evasions of laws on mortmain or taxation." [61] Catholic lawyers " out of loyalty to the church" are bound by canon law to discourage clients from trying to invalidate a will in favor of the church, even though the will does not conform fully to the law.[62] In order to secure a position to teach in a public school a Catholic may be asked to sign an agreement not to impose Catholic tenets on the class. But a Catholic teacher is told he does not violate this agreement when he teaches Catholic doctrines in his classes, because " he is a delegate of the parents rather than of the government." [63] Catholic nurses are advised to baptize a dying child of non-Catholic parents without their knowledge if the parents will not give their consent.[64]

Catholic nurses are instructed how to use a specially prepared card, employed by " The Apostolate to Assist Dying Non-Catholics," to secure a confession of the Catholic faith surreptitiously. McFadden, who explains the card and its use, admits that this method savors of deceit. But he asks, " Why should anyone question the method or the means so long as they are legitimate and attain the end? " [65] The Roman Catholic Church takes the liberty of mistranslating a phrase in the Oath of Hippocrates taken by physicians, to make it conform to their modern interpretation of the use of contraceptives as an abortion. The promise not to give a woman "an instrument to procure abortion" is changed to a promise not to give her "a pessary (diaphragm) to cause abortion." [66]

The Roman Catholic claims of the primacy of Peter are not supported by the known facts of history. But Catholic historians have "strained the resources of Roman apologetics almost to the breaking point," and used the most "extraordinary subtlety" to explain away the facts inconsistent with their claims.[67] Competent historians agree that the growing centralization of power in the hands of medieval popes was "facilitated by the production and unsuspecting acceptance of an extraordinary series of forged documents." Yet the church has never repudiated them.[68]

In the Vatican Decrees of 1870, which declared the infallibility of the pope, "at least five times the testimonies adduced from ancient authorities are vitiated by insolent tampering with the documents or gross misrepresentations of the sources appealed to." [69] The action of the Vatican at that time was vigorously opposed and condemned by Lord Acton, a noted Roman Catholic and Regius Professor of History, at Cambridge. In a debate a few years later he asserted, "The passage from the Catholicism of the fathers to that of the modern popes was accomplished by willful falsehood; and the whole structure of traditions, laws, and doctrines that support the theory of infallibility and the practical despotism of popes, stands on the basis of fraud." [70] He also declared that Rome "inculcates untruthfulness, distinct mendacity, and deceitfulness. In certain cases it is made a duty to lie." But he went on to say that those who teach this doctrine "do not become habitual liars in other things." [71] Precisely so! Rome encourages unethical practices when they promote the power and honor of the church. One is exempt from the obligation to be truthful when he is furthering the success of the church.

Kerr analyzes the pope's encyclical *Lux Veritatis* (1931).[72] He submits facts to prove that the letter contains "unfounded assumptions" and "perversions of the evidence," and abounds in the "grossest errors" and "misrepresentations" and even "mistranslations." He also tells of G. G. Coulton's exposures of misstatements in the works of Cardinal Casquet on English monasteries. When his attention was called to these errors, the Cardinal not only offered no apology, but repeated the same errors unaltered five years later in a new edition of his work. This provoked Coulton to say, "After a good deal of reading I have no hesitation in saying that it is impossible to trust a Romanist book as one naturally trusts other books by educated men." [73]

Any discriminating reader of large numbers of Roman Catholic books that have been published in the last twenty or thirty years will readily agree with Coulton's statement. In reading such books one finds it necessary to watch for incoherences, devious arguments, contradictory statements left unreconciled, withholding of facts, half-truths, double talk in the use of terms, and even the rewriting of history to put the church in the best possible light before the general public and before Catholics themselves. Similarly, all public utterances, articles in newspapers, magazines, pamphlets and leaflets, by Catholics and advertisements of the Knights of Columbus — all have to be carefully scrutinized for accuracy. [74]

The facts given in this chapter explain why Protestants have long questioned whether Roman Catholics can wisely and safely be entrusted with the responsibilities of high offices in our American Government. That question is now being freely discussed in the newspapers, in magazines, and on the air because of the current campaign, well organized and apparently well financed, to nominate a Roman Catholic as a candidate for the presidency of the United States in 1960. That problem will be considered in the next chapter.

Chapter VI
Roman Catholics in Public Office

Protestants, facing all the facts about Roman Catholicism given in this book, are justifiably perplexed and concerned when Roman Catholics are given places of public responsibility in the Government. They cannot but ask such questions as these: Are they wholeheartedly dedicated to our American system of separation of church and state, or would they work from the inside to make this a Catholic state? Would they labor constantly to secure equal privileges for all churches, or would they seek special favors for their own church? If they had the power to do so, would they deprive other religious groups of their freedom to hold, teach, and propagate their faith, or would they restrict them on the grounds that only the Catholic Church has the truth and that error has not the same right as the truth? When the canon law of their church conflicts with the civil laws of the land, will they keep their oath to support the civil laws or will they choose to obey the laws of their church? When an important issue arises in which their consciences lead them to take a position contrary to the demands and perhaps threats of excommunication by their bishops, will they follow their consciences or yield to the pressures of their clergymen?

CATHOLIC NEO-AMERICANISM

Roman Catholics react in different ways to these questions raised by Protestants. Those in charge of the Catholic action and publicity media of the Roman hierarchy usually brand them as the expressions of bigoted and prejudiced persons and try to prevent both Roman Catholics and others from paying any attention to them. But other groups of American Catholic clergymen and laymen have been striving in all sincerity for more than half a century to allay these fears by trying to convince themselves and their Protestant brethren that it is possible for Catholics to be at the same time loyal members of their church and loyal citizens of America.

One of the first major efforts along these lines was made in the 1890's. That effort came to be known as Catholic *Americanism*. This movement grew out of the work and teaching of Father Hecker, the founder of the Paulist order. He held that Catholicism *alone* was consistent with the American love of freedom, but that it must be a new or rejuvenated Catholicism. After his death a group of noted Catholic prelates — Cardinal Gibbons, Archbishops Ireland, Keane, and Kain, and Monsignor O'Connell — undertook to infuse American Catholicism with the American spirit, to bring it more nearly into harmony with American ideas. Among other things these liberal Catholics fraternized with non-Catholics and claimed that there is no irreconcilable conflict between American democracy and the Roman Church.

In time, differences of opinions among the leaders of the movement developed. Pope Leo XIII finally wrote two letters, one to the apostolic delegate to the United States, and another to Cardinal Gibbons (1899), condemning this " Americanism." After that no voice was raised in defense of the views condemned by the pope. This particular wave of Catholic Americanism had spent its force.

For the last twenty or thirty years another Catholic Americanism movement has been steadily gaining momentum. A few years before his untimely death Thomas A. Sugrue, the well-known Catholic writer, who was highly critical of his church at some points, reported optimistically of the dreams some American Catholics have of controlling the Vatican and adapting it to American democratic ways. In fact, he said, the opinion is general that " the deed is already accomplished." He even predicted that before long there " may be an American pope." [1]

Among the outstanding proponents of this Catholic neo-Americanism is Father John Courtney Murray, professor of theology at Woodstock College, who is one of the ablest of Roman apologists in America today. He is a vigorous proponent of the point of view that Roman Catholics are loyal Americans and can safely be trusted to preserve our democratic institutions and traditions.

Murray has written extensively to justify American religious pluralism, or freedom of religion, on the basis of Roman Catholic teaching. A brief summary and critique of his point of view may be found in an article by Edwin R. Spann in *Religion in Life,* Spring, 1956 (pp. 205 ff.). Murray does not favor the position of Ryan and Boland that was described in the last chapter, namely, that Roman Catholics accept the American Constitution on the principle of temporary expedience, and that as soon as a Catholic government is set up, it is then obligated on Catholic principles to limit the rights of all other religious groups. Rather, he believes that the Roman Catholic Church has sufficient reasons on historical, theological, and prudential grounds, for permanently supporting Article I of the Bill of Rights. By this means he endeavors to show that non-Catholics in the United States have no reason to be apprehensive about Roman Catholics endangering religious freedom in America.

Spann clearly shows that despite Murray's professed disagreement with Ryan and Boland, and his lengthy arguments to establish a different American Catholic position, he actually comes out at the same place. That is, he does not prove that, as a matter of principle, the Roman Catholic Church will not suppress Protestantism in America. Rather, he leaves the pope free to declare, as a matter of expedience, that the restriction of Protestantism is necessary.

Another incisive critique of Murray's position may be found in an article in *Theology Today* (January, 1959) entitled "Catholic Controversy on Church and State," by Antonio Márquez. The controversy with which he deals is between Father Murray, the representative of the liberal American Catholics who claim that the official doctrine of Rome on church and state has changed in recent years, and Cardinal Ottaviani, who insists that the official teaching of the Roman magisterium on this subject has not changed. After analyzing and comparing the writings of these two leading Catholics, the author says:

> The last word is not for Murray and his colleagues, but against them. The Roman Catholic doctrine in the light of the teaching of the church has not changed. . . . Any contrary line of reasoning may appear excellent, but is not Roman. Murray's articles are the expression of a Roman Catholic theologian working with non-Roman Catholic presuppositions. His study is, therefore, irrelevant from the point of view of Roman Catholic principles and life. His doctrine cannot be taken as the doctrine of the church but as a doctrine of his own and, consequently, as a sectarian doctrine. (P. 541.)

Paul Blanshard gives documented evidence to show that Murray has been taken to task by the Vatican, the American bishops, and the American diocesan press for " daring to apply to the unchanging teachings of the pope the ' pendulum ' theory of interpreting church law, under which a narrow papal mandate may mean one thing to the Catholics of one age, and another thing to the present-day Catholics of the West." In an exchange of letters between the Vatican and *The New York Times* in 1953, it was revealed that the church opposes the views of Father Murray and other " liberal Catholics " in the United States, and regards their positions as a " departure from the true Catholic theological path." [2]

Stanley I. Stuber, a prominent Protestant churchman who attended the first seminar on Religion in a Free Society, held in May, 1958, under the auspices of the Fund for the Republic, and participated in by religious leaders of all faiths, described the feelings of frustration which increased among non-Catholics as the conversations proceeded. The Roman Catholic delegation consisted of professors and editors, not of members of the hierarchy. Chief among the delegates was Prof. John Courtney Murray, S.J. Stuber reports that these Catholics " would not accept responsibility for many of the expressed doctrines and dogmas of the Roman Catholic Church which are now causing all the fears and concerns among Protestants." They claimed that non-Catholics misunderstood and misrepresented the doctrines and in some cases put such a " liberal interpretation on particular doctrines that the Protestant Reformation, with its basic issues, seemed for the moment rather superfluous." But by their refusal to accept responsibility for their interpretations they implied that they were speaking only for themselves, not for the Vatican's magisterium. Still again, as Stuber states, it is clear that when the " showdown comes and the issue is finally drawn, the Roman hierarchy always has the final, authoritative word." [3]

To Protestants the question of authority is crucial in the whole problem of ultimate Catholic loyalty to the United States. John Cogley, former executive editor of the liberal Catholic journal, *The Commonweal,* and now officially responsible for arranging the seminars on Religion in a Free Society for the Fund for the Republic, is one of the few leaders of contemporary Catholic Americanism who has publicly recognized this. Sometime ago he undertook to allay the fears of non-Catholics who keep asking questions about the long-range purposes and intentions of the Roman Church with reference to the United States. With brutal frankness he stated:

> I sympathize with the questioners, but wonder if what some of them are asking for is not so much a statement of intention as a repudiation of the theological doctrines that provide the logical framework for the " Catholic State " thesis. If the latter be it, Catholics will never be able to give them that answer.[4]

A few pages farther on he made another significant statement:

> In the Catholic scheme spiritual authority is all-important and the popular will has little or no effect on the government of the church.[5]

We are indebted to Mr. Cogley for those honest admissions. They substantiate two things that Protestants have been saying for many years. These are: First, that American Catholics cannot repudiate the official doctrine of the Roman Catholic magisterium concerning the " Catholic State " and remain good Catholics. Secondly, that the official Roman purpose to make all countries, including the United States, Catholic states is not affected by the will or wish or public utterances of American Catholics. The official doctrine of the church, not the utterances of American Catholics, *is* the concern of Protestants. So long as that doctrine remains unchanged Protestants can never completely trust the assurances of Catholics, however sincerely given, that they expect always to be loyal to the United States. For Protestants cannot be sure when a showdown comes whether Catholics will or will not bow to the authority of their church.

Thus far the popes have allowed these recent exponents of Catholic neo-Americanism to advocate their point of view openly and freely. But should a pope at any time condemn this Americanism, as Leo XIII condemned the Americanism of the 1890's, what would those Catholics do? Would they yield, as did Cardinal Gibbons and his colleagues, or would they defend our American democracy? If they are loyal Catholics, there would be but one thing to do: yield to the supreme authority of the pope. What then would become of their assurances that the American democracy is safe in Catholic hands? Until authority is taken from the pope and placed in the hands of the people, there can be no guarantee by American Catholics that, if they were in the majority, religious freedom would be preserved in our country. American Catholics can give no trustworthy assurances that the pope and his court have been permeated by the spirit of American Catholicism, or that Catholic canon law and teaching have been modified in the least by what American Catholics speak or write.

A ROMAN CATHOLIC PRESIDENT

One critical problem that grows out of current Catholic Americanism is the effort to elect a Catholic president of the United States. As stated earlier, this effort at present is being widely publicized in the American media of communication and discussed in current interfaith conferences. The first attempt to elect a Catholic to the presidency was made in 1928, when Alfred Smith, governor of New York and a Roman Catholic, was the Democratic candidate for the presidency. In 1956, Senator John Kennedy, of Massachusetts, a young Catholic of parts, came within one or two votes of being chosen the Democratic candidate for Vice-President. Recently a political campaign of some proportions to nominate Mr. Kennedy as the Democratic candidate for the presidency in 1960 has been booming. At this writing another campaign is developing to promote the candidacy of Pat Brown, a Roman Catholic who was elected governor of California by an overwhelming popular majority in 1958. In 1928 and in 1956 anyone who raised the question of a Catholic's fitness for office on the ground of his religion was labeled a prejudiced person or a religious bigot by Catholics and by some Protestants. The same thing will be done with increasing frequency and force from now until the general election in 1960.

The label of bigotry would be justified if a Roman Catholic were to be disqualified for holding office because of his *mere religious beliefs*. Moreover, this would be a violation of a provision of Article VI of the Constitution, which specifies that " no religious Test shall ever be required as a Qualificaton to any Office or public Trust under the United States." But much more is involved than religious beliefs. Other factors of grave import for the safety of our Government are involved, as the facts submitted in this study indicate. Unfortunately, the full implication of these facts has not yet been faced squarely by the American people as a whole.

A member of the Roman Catholic Church is not a member of a mere religious society. He is a subject (that is the Roman Church's own term) of an autocratic government. The pope is an absolute monarch. He claims to rule the earth by divine right. He also claims that he has been divinely authorized to exercise the power and authority of God himself over the souls of men in this world and in the next. Catholics are under obligations to obey his orders under penalty of eternal damnation (mortal sin). These orders are transmitted through prelates who are directly responsible to him and to his court. Catholics holding offices of public trust in our American Government are in honor bound to serve the interests of the Catholic Church and obey its laws, even if this should mean going contrary to the interests and laws of the unit of civil government they are supposed to represent. Knowing these things, Protestants are rightfully apprehensive when Catholics are chosen for high positions in our American civil society. It allays our apprehensions very little to be told that many Catholics do not obey orders from the pope. What Catholics, and in what positions?

If a Roman Catholic candidate for the presidency has been well trained and properly counseled by his father-confessor, he knows very little of what has been written in this book about his church; for he has been carefully shielded from this kind of information. When Al Smith was a candidate for the presidency he was asked in an open letter, published in the *Atlantic Monthly* (March, 1927), to explain, among other things, how he reconciled the Constitution and *The Syllabus of Errors*. In reply he disclaimed any knowledge of that document or any responsibility to it. Without a doubt, that was an honest statement.

Roman Catholic moral theology teaches that one is morally accountable for his acts only when he is consciously rebelling against the laws of his church; that is, if he is in ignorance of those laws when he commits an act, he does not sin. Under circumstances involving minor wrongs a confessor is supposed to be cautious about informing an ignorant penitent of the wrongness of his actions, especially if he is convinced the penitent will prove too weak to discontinue his actions, lest he himself become guilty of provoking the person to sin. But when a person's ignorance runs the risk of leading to some major evil, or of sacrificing some major good, such as injuring or neglecting the welfare of the church, then the confessor is obligated to instruct that person concerning his duty, regardless of the consequences.

So it comes about that in a liberal democracy the Catholic

Church, operating on the above principle, gives her members minimal information about their obligations to the Vatican's principles of politics " until they are in sight of the power to put them into effect." [6] Should a Catholic be elected President of the United States, it would then become the duty of his confessor to inform him what his church expects of him in that important capacity. The question for which Protestants seek an answer is, What would a Catholic president do then?

A Catholic president would have many opportunities to exercise power and influence in behalf of his church. A president's authority to appoint men to positions within the Government at home, to appoint them to represent America abroad, to set national policies, to suggest legislation, and his opportunity to influence the members of all departments of the Government, are extensive. We know all too well how much influence the Roman Catholic Church has been exercising in the departments of our Government under Protestant presidents through the years.

The results of Roman Catholic pressures in Washington in recent years are portentous. Some of these results have already been given in other connections in this study. Others will now be mentioned. Since 1946, Representative John McCormack (D., Mass.), a Roman Catholic, has personally been responsible for so-called " sneak through " gifts of Federal funds to Roman Catholic causes amounting to $36,390,000. These gifts are: $30,000,000, paid or in process of payment, for war claims and war damages to Catholic churches in the Philippines (this sum includes the $8,000,000 now known as Philippine " Grab " bill, passed by the 84th Congress, $30,000 of which was for Protestant claims); $1,000,000 for the pope's summer palace; $4,000,000 for Providence Hospital in Washington, D.C.; and $1,590,000 in two bills for Georgetown Hospital in Washington.[7]

In the 83d Congress, 71 separate bills were introduced for the " relief " of about 150 Roman Catholic nuns, all of whom came to the United States between 1947 and 1951 on six-month visitor's permits.[8] These nuns came to our country to relieve the shortage of teachers in Catholic parochial schools. In 1957, President Eisenhower asked Congress to pass legislation that would permit clergymen and members of religious orders to enter our country without regard to quotas or other restrictions of our immigration laws. This was also designed to relieve the shortage of teachers in Roman Catholic schools.[9] A treaty with the Catholic Republic of Haiti, prepared by the State Department and signed by Vice-President Nixon when he was in that country in 1955, left out the clauses guaranteeing religious liberty that are standard in our treaties with other countries. This was a concession to Roman Catholic pressure. Only the watchful eye of some Protestants prevented the treaty from being recommended by the Senate's Foreign Relations Committee.[10]

For many years the State Department of the Government has had on its staff a disproportionate number of Roman Catholics. In the international crises between the two world wars, Roman Catholic pressures on American foreign policy caused the State Department consistently to throw its influence in favor of fascist or antidemocratic nations, often to the amazement and disappointment of freedom-loving peoples of earth. Roman Catholics held a near monopoly of crucial diplomatic posts in all major countries following the Second World War.[11]

These pressures would increase by leaps and bounds if a Roman Catholic were president. Not in modern times has a Catholic been elected president of a democratic country that remotely approaches the United States in importance. With free access to the president, at least through his confessor, the staff of the Roman Church, already efficiently in operation and well equipped and disciplined, would have opportunity to press for preferential treatment in ways not hitherto opened to it. Should a Roman Catholic president hesitate to use the powers and privileges of his office to do something requested by his church that he believed to be contrary to his oath of office, the church would have authority to command him to do it. If he refused to obey, it could declare him guilty of mortal sin or excommunicate him from the church — two forms of punishment feared by all Catholics. Should he refuse to yield, he would cease to be a Catholic. If he should yield, he would do only what he has been taught to do, and what he has promised to do, namely, to obey the commands of his church at all times. At that moment, and at that moment only, would it be determined whether a Roman Catholic president is a free man or whether he is a subject of his church.

THE VALIDITY OF PROTESTANT APPREHENSIONS

What has been said in this connection should not be regarded as a wholesale charge that all Roman Catholics are unfitted for public office. Such a charge would be false and grossly unfair. The loyalty of many Roman Catholics in public office is unquestionable, and their conduct of the affairs of their offices is beyond reproach.

From the Protestant viewpoint the crux of the problem is found in the claims and purposes of the Roman Catholic hierarchy and in the system of theology upon which these are based. Always in the background there stand the unalterable purpose of the hierarchy to make the United States of America a Catholic state and the demand of complete obedience to their commands from every faithful Roman Catholic subject. The very existence of that system is potentially a subtle and dangerous political influence in the life of any Roman Catholic officeholder. Whether that influence becomes real or not depends in part upon the importance for the purposes that the hierarchy attaches to the office held, and in part upon the independence and courage of the officer himself.

Protestants therefore claim the right, inherent in our American free elections, publicly to do three things: (1) to question each Roman Catholic candidate about his individual attitudes toward political matters in which his church is interested and involved; (2) to discuss freely the political plans of the Roman Catholic hierarchy that conflict with our American democracy; and (3) to do both these things without being charged with religious prejudice and bigotry and without being classified as hatemongers.

The facts in this study explain precisely why Protestants question whether Roman Catholics can wisely be entrusted with the responsibilities of high offices in America. Those who raise this question are not conjuring up imaginary fears. They are not fanatics. They are not prejudiced. A prejudiced person prejudges a case, forms his opinions before he has sufficient knowledge. Protestants are apprehensive for the simple reason that they *have* sufficient knowledge about the teaching and practices of the church to which Catholics belong and to which they have sworn obedience and allegiance. For the good health of our society and of our relations with one another, the sincerity and reality of these apprehensions should be recognized, both by our fellow Protestants and our Catholic brethren, and dealt with accordingly. Nothing is gained by decrying the facts or by scoffing at those who insist on disclosing and discussing the facts. The problem involved is too serious to be dealt with in such fashion. A full, frank, honest airing of the facts can provide the only suitable atmosphere in which to establish and sustain cordial relations.

The *fears* of American Protestants can be allayed only by the *deeds* of American Catholics. Let the Roman Catholic hierarchy desist from their efforts to make this a Catholic state and to gain preferential position and treatment for their church and its institutions. Let them accept and adjust to our American system of separation of church and state. Let them be content to exercise the religious freedom accorded them under the Constitution without seeking ultimately to deprive others of their religious freedom. Let them co-operate wholeheartedly and unreservedly with American free institutions. When they do these things, and only then, will Protestants have the trustworthy evidence they require concerning the genuineness of the Americanism of Roman Catholics.

Religious conflict and distrust will not vanish from the American scene until every religious group has a mystical and trustworthy feeling of belonging to a brotherhood, all members of which are so genuinely devoted to freedom that they can be depended upon to support it and preserve it for themselves and for all other citizens.

Chapter VII
Some Proposals for Protestant Action

What should Protestants do about the facts and problems dealt with in this study? A number of possible answers to that question have been suggested as the study proceeded, and need not be repeated. Here, at the close, my concern is that the Protestant reader shall feel: (1) that the facts should be taken seriously, faced frankly, and discussed openly; (2) that Protestants are equipped and qualified to make a constructive contribution to the solution of the problems involved; and (3) that the time has come for Protestants to take the initiative in doing something about them. A few things that Protestants need to do if they expect to exercise in the present acute situation the productive leadership for which they are eminently qualified, will now be briefly discussed.

Overcome Complacency

Long and fairly satisfactory living together under the American Constitution has produced a perilous complacency among Protestants. When the Government of the United States was in process of formation, the American society consisted of a complexity of religious minorities, most of whom were Protestants of one type or another. As a matter of both conviction and necessity, therefore, the colonists deliberately rejected the idea of an established or state church and instead " established " a system of religious pluralism. Under this system a large number of Protestant groups have lived and labored together in relative peace for almost two hundred years. Despite their debates, divisions, and jealousies, they have developed among themselves an amazing number and variety of unitive and co-operative movements. So it may rightly be claimed that American Protestants have become experienced in maintaining a successful pluralistic religious society.

This success can be attributed largely to the fact that all have been loyal to the American system and to the constitutional principles upon which it is based. They have implicitly trusted one another to respect freedom as a permanent principle of group relations. At the same time, they have taken it for granted that citizens of all other religious faiths would do the same thing. That is, the average American Protestant more or less takes religious freedom for granted. He assumes that religious tolerance is universally respected and effective throughout the land. It rarely occurs to him that it could ever be otherwise. He is so self-satisfied about American religious freedom that he is unwilling to admit that it is in any peril or needs any defense.

Furthermore, the average Protestant has a keen, almost innate, sense of fair play. He instinctively resents any criticism of the other person's religion, although he is quick to criticize his own. Up to a point this sense of good sportsmanship is commendable. Without doubt it has been conducive to good relations. But to the extent that it has not been balanced up with alertness to the unfairness of other groups and to the threats that an irenic spirit may bring to freedom itself, it has issued in a false security.

Generally speaking, therefore, it has been difficult to get Protestants to face the kind of facts about Roman Catholicism that have been presented in this study. Sporadic attempts have been made by some Protestants to convince their fellow Americans that some of the policies of the Catholic hierarchy are a potential threat to religious freedom. While these attempts have created a stir, they have usually been of comparatively short duration or limited in influence. This has not been due to the fact that these attempts were made by leaders who were imprudent and immoderate, although some leaders have been of this character. Rather, it has been due to the fact that many Protestants are intolerant of or indifferent to any reference to Catholic policies. In fact, as many writers have observed recently, there is an unwritten taboo among many Protestants not only against discussing " the Catholic problem," but against admitting that such a problem exists. As long as that taboo prevails, freedom is going progressively to be in graver danger.

When Roman Catholics were limited in number and influence, this general indifference to the facts seemed of no great consequence. But now that they have increased in numbers and in power and have become more aggressive and more vocal about their intentions, this indifference is becoming serious. Our American system of religious pluralism, and of separation of church and state, which guarantees freedom for all groups, is so vigorously challenged by the Roman hierarchy that a forceful countereffort by those who believe in the wisdom and validity of our system is called for. By experience and conviction Protestants are — or ought to be — prepared to give wise and effective leadership in this effort. But that leadership cannot be properly and fully exercised until they eliminate their prejudices against making, or listening to others who make, a critical study and just appraisal of Roman Catholic beliefs and practices and of their social and political implications.

Awake to Realities

The disturbing amount of reluctance among Protestants to acquaint themselves with the facts about Roman Catholicism and of unwillingness to assimilate those facts once they are presented, is not the only problem. Many Protestants who are realistic about most other matters live in a sort of dream world when they think about Catholicism. Apparently they imagine Catholicism to be something they wish it to be instead of trying to discover what it actually is. I offer no explanation, psychological or otherwise, for this attitude, but state it as a fact and record the conviction that Protestants should awake to the realities of the existing situation.

To begin with, they need to face the facts about the nature of the Roman Catholic Church and the way it operates. They seem to judge that church by their knowledge of Protestant churches. That is, they assume that the experiences of Catholics in their church are similar to the experiences of a Protestant in his church. To be sure, there are a number of parallels between the two bodies and between the problems their members face. But there are many crucial differences between the two.

There is nothing in Protestantism comparable to the dual nature of Catholicism as a church and a state and the dual allegiance of its members, the absolute power and infallibility of the pope, the authoritarian government of which he is the head, the intolerance and extravagant claims of Rome, the dependence of its members upon the priests through the confessional, the Catholic system of moral theology and the control of the church over its members from birth to death and in the next world. Protestants who make a study of the organization, theological teaching, and inside operations of the Catholic Church find themselves in another world. The differences between the way in which the Roman Church and the Protestant churches are set up and operate are the constituent elements, the hard core, of what we call the *Roman Catholic problem*. There is no such thing as a *Protestant problem* in that same sense.

For example, professional people and public officials who are Protestants face no such problems with their church as do the same groups who are Catholics. Protestant lawyers, doctors and nurses, schoolteachers, judges, legislators, policemen, publishers, etc., are not placed under the direct supervision and oversight of clergymen who can not only demand that they obey the canon law and moral theological codes of their church but who can also threaten them with excommunication and damnation (mortal sin) if they do not obey orders. Those problems are unique with Catholics.

No one is qualified to deal constructively with the question of Protestant–Roman Catholic relations in our country who does not appreciate these fundamental differences between the two groups. The failure to deal with these differences candidly and realistically is to handle the question superficially.

Again, Protestants need to be realistic about the distinction between Roman Catholics and the papacy. That distinction is also a significant factor in understanding the nature of the religious problems in America. Many Roman Catholic clergymen and laymen would like to see papal policies changed to conform to the requirements of the American system. There is nothing they would like to see more than an Americanized Catholic Church, a church adjusted permanently to the Constitution of the United States and to the pluralistic religious system guaranteed by it. But Catholic laymen and clergymen, singly and in groups, cannot speak for or influence or change the policies of the papacy. This fact is often as frustrating to liberal Catholics as it is misleading to Protestants. Liberal movements arise among Catholics. Leaders of these movements grow enthusiastic about the possibility of modernizing the Vatican. They dream of this, hope for it, work for it, only to find their efforts finally obstructed, nullified, or perhaps forbidden by a papal directive they are commanded, or know themselves obligated, to obey. The official position of the church is what the pope says, not what Roman Catholics wish he would say. Until Protestants assimilate this fact into their thinking, they are not in a position to understand the Roman Catholic problem, to engage with discrimination in colloquies with representative Catholics, to read and evaluate Catholic publications, and to search for common ground on which to stand with them.

INITIATE ANOTHER GREAT DEBATE ON REFORMED BELIEFS

As Protestantism was forced at the time of the Reformation to engage in a prolonged debate to win a proper place in Christendom for the evangelical doctrines of Christianity, so it must now engage in another great debate to ensure the survival of those doctrines. The issues revolve not only around the doctrines as such but also around their political and social implications and applications. The freedoms — all freedoms — of our American liberal democracy are at stake. In the long run, all those freedoms hold together. No freedom can be preserved unless religious freedom is preserved. The debate will be long. It will be hard. It will require all the knowledge, the wisdom, the courage, the self-discipline, the Christian graces, the divine determination and holy zeal we can muster. But Protestants need not shun the debate or fear the outcome. They are in a strategic position to take the lead in a national discussion of the issues involved. They stand solidly upon the basic principles upon which, and only upon which, men of diverse religious beliefs can succeed in living together peaceably and working together harmoniously in a pluralistic society.

Earlier it was stated that secular organizations, such as the Fund for the Republic and the Extension Department of the University of California, are now promoting conferences on the religious problem in the United States. Also it was predicted that the number of such conferences, on both the national and the local level, will undoubtedly increase in the years ahead. The time has come for the Protestant churches to promote their own conferences along these lines and to embark upon a long-range plan to train their ministers and laymen for participating in these conferences and to equip them with the resources to do so intelligently and constructively.

An open and unabashed announcement by Protestants, through the National Council of Churches and other interdenominational organizations, and through the facilities of the several denominations, of their intention to engage in such a debate through all means of communication and throughout the whole country, would perform a wholesome national service. If the issues between Protestants and Roman Catholics were brought out into the open, instead of being permitted to rankle and fester beneath the surface, it would make for a healthier society. Such a move would give heart and hope to, and would unquestionably receive the support of, large groups of Americans of all religious faiths and of no religious faith, and of all organizations dedicated to the preservation of human liberties.

ENTER THE POLITICAL ARENA

Protestants believe that the unique American system is a significant attempt to implement in the political order certain principles of our evangelical faith. That system is not now and will never be a perfect implementation of those principles. But it contains the democratic means for its own improvement while it safeguards the principles for future generations. As explained in this study, the Roman Catholic hierarchy is continuously and assiduously at work to make the United States, as it is at work to make all countries in which it exists, a Catholic state. So long as it pursues these purposes in our democratic society, Protestants and other Americans who believe in free churches in a free state have no honorable and prudent choice but to oppose them. This means that Protestants must engage in political action in a way and to a degree they have not heretofore done.

Whether we like it or not, religion at the present time is mixed up with politics in our country. It is a debatable question whether religion and politics can or should ever be kept separated. Certainly religion always involves political implications. Wherever and whenever those implications become actual issues in our political elections, they should be discussed with all the freedom that other issues are discussed. Religion is an important, probably the most important, area of our national life. Any major segment of our corporate life is a legitimate subject for public discussion in a free society. Under prevailing conditions in America, political education and action on the part of Protestants is essential and unavoidable.

That such action portends unfortunate and unpleasant religious controversy in our country cannot be denied. But the Roman Catholic Church has made this inevitable by the political campaign in which it is engaged to change the constitutions of the Federal and state governments, and to gain the political power in Congress and the state legislatures and in our political parties, necessary to make America a Catholic state. Throughout their history most American Protestants *on principle* have opposed bringing sectarian religion into politics. Throughout their history American Catholics *on principle* have brought sectarian religion into politics directly and indirectly. At the present time, Catholics are engaged openly in the most vigorous political campaign of our American history to secure special privileges and benefits from the Government for their sectarian purposes. This campaign has many ramifications. Protestants have no other recourse than to expose and oppose their efforts at every point by the social and political means provided for in our free society.

WILLINGNESS TO BE PROTESTANTS

The current expression, " Let the church be the church," could well be modified to read, " Let Protestants be Protestants." Protestants quite properly take pride in their freedom to criticize and change their church, their broadmindedness, their tolerance of, and willingness to fraternize and co-operate with, people of other faiths. But these worthy attitudes have been carried to such extremes in our times that Protestants are lamentably uninformed about their own distinctive Biblical, historical, and theological beliefs and lacking in a proper understanding of the social significance of those beliefs. Hence many of them are easily attracted by certain beliefs and practices of Roman Catholicism that, in actual fact, are in open conflict with the Reformed faith.

In the course of this study attention has been called to the deplorable drift backward toward Rome in much Protestant thinking about the church, the ministry, church government, and worship. The best some of our Protestant thinkers have to offer is a neomedievalism, a neo-Catholicism. Markus Barth, son of Karl Barth, called attention to this backward trend in a recent study of the New Testament doctrine of the church in *Interpretation*.[1] He says:

It seems, whether consciously or not, that much current Protestant thinking knows nothing better than to lead and pave the way to Rome. While it is obvious that every church has to rethink, to recover, to rephrase, and even to criticize her own tradition and her heritage — even if it be the heritage of Luther and Calvin! — it is still doubtful whether only moves backward, toward a static conception of the church, toward a mysterylike sacrament, toward a collective security apparatus, toward different kinds of priesthood, will help toward the unity we seek. (Pp. 155-156.)

He questions the wisdom of Protestants trying to compete with some of the popular appeals, the dramatic doctrines, and the extravagant practices of Rome. Our contribution to the ecumenical church, he declares, is in other fields:

The humble service of preaching, teaching, curing souls, gathering the dispersed and lost, which the Reformers taught us to respect, and the hard service of facing the political, military, social, and economic problems — a service which the modern age not unjustly expects from the church or which it attempts to quench out — cannot be done by a church which desires to be "high." (P. 155.)

He is particularly concerned about the young Christian churches in Africa and India, the churches in the slums and suburbs of our cities, the empty churches in Europe, the free churches, the worried churches who need something better, both in doctrine and in organization, than "*a Protestant counter-Rome*" (p. 156).

Protestantism is unwisely neglecting and risking the loss of many of the things that it is well prepared to offer to the disillusioned millions on earth and that the modern age desires and expects in the Christian church. It is not done for. We have not reached the end of the Protestant era, as some would have us believe. Protestantism is still, as it has long been, God's best hope for a free human race and a free human society. To imitate or to envy Rome is to betray our great heritage. A resurgence of the basic tenets of Protestantism and their implementation into the complexities of our modern world are an imperative, a divine obligation. The problems of our age cannot be solved by a revival of the doctrines that were challenged, or changed, or discarded by the Protestant Reformers, but by a revival of, and better understanding of, the evangelical doctrines they recovered. We should not be hoping and working for a Romanized Protestantism, but for an " evangelicalized " world. Let Protestants dare to be Protestants!

Notes

CHAPTER I

1. A pamphlet, *Religion and the Free Society,* was published by the Fund in 1958 and may be secured upon request to the Fund, 60 East 42d Street, New York 17, New York.

2. *Presbyterian Life,* July 23, 1955.

3. Daniel Jenkins, *The Strangeness of the Church,* pp. 114, 115. Doubleday & Co., Inc., 1955.

4. Walter M. Horton, *Christian Theology: An Ecumenical Approach,* pp. 202–203. Harper & Brothers, 1955.

5. Robert McAfee Brown, *The Significance of the Church,* footnote p. 57. The Westminster Press, 1956.

6. See *Harper's Magazine,* August, 1958, p. 80.

7. Charles Boyer, *One Shepherd: The Problem of Christian Reunion,* pp. 37 f. and 83. P. J. Kenedy & Sons, 1952. Quotations from this book are used by permission.

8. *Ibid.,* p. 40.

9. Ernest B. Koenker, *The Liturgical Renaissance in the Roman Catholic Church.* University of Chicago Press, 1954.

10. John Knox, *The Early Church and the Coming Great Church.* Abingdon Press, 1955.

11. Geddes MacGregor, *The Vatican Revolution.* The Beacon Press, Inc., 1957. Quotations from this book are used by permission.

12. Karl Adam, *One and Holy.* Sheed & Ward, Inc., 1951. Copyright, 1951. Quotations from this book are used by permission.

13. W. H. Van de Pol, *The Christian Dilemma.* Philosophical Library, Inc., 1952.

14. Boyer, *op. cit.*

15. George H. Tavard, *The Catholic Approach to Protestantism*. Harper & Brothers, 1955. Quotations from this book are used by permission.

16. Winfred E. Garrison, *The Quest and Character of a United Church*. Abingdon Press, 1957. Quotations from this book are used by permission.

17. Albert C. Outler, *The Christian Tradition and the Unity We Seek*. Oxford University Press, 1957.

18. Garrison, *The Quest and Character of a United Church*.

19. See documented report of this in " The Book They Couldn't Ban," by Clarence W. Hall, in *The Christian Herald*, July, 1950.

20. See *The Pulpit*, September, 1957, p. 3.

21. See *Theology Today*, April, 1957, pp. 55–56.

22. See *Life*, April 28, 1958, p. 16, for comments on some of the 350 protests received up to that time.

23. Cf. Paul Blanshard, *The Right to Read*, The Beacon Press, Inc., 1955; and Richard McKeon and others, *The Freedom to Read*, R. R. Bowker Company, 1957.

24. H. H. Remmers and D. H. Redler, editors. The Bobbs-Merrill Company, Inc., 1957.

25. E.g., George Seldes, *The Vatican: Yesterday, Today, Tomorrow* (Harper & Brothers, 1934); William Shaw Kerr, *A Handbook on the Papacy* (Philosophical Library, Inc., 1951); Hector Burn-Murdoch, *The Development of the Papacy* (Frederick A. Praeger, Inc., 1954).

Chapter II

1. Knox, *op. cit.*, p. 76.

2. The reader interested in a concise explanation of this type of criticism is referred to *Form Criticism*, edited and translated by Frederick C. Grant, Willett, Clark & Company, 1934; and *Origins of the Gospels*, by Floyd V. Filson, Ch. IV, Abingdon Press, 1938.

3. Quoted in *The Ministry in Historical Perspectives*, by H. Richard Niebuhr and Daniel D. Williams, editors, p. 18. Harper & Brothers, 1956.

4. Knox, *op. cit.*, p. 142.

5. *Ibid.*, p. 143.

6. See MacGregor, *op. cit.*

7. See Garrison, *The Quest and Character of a United Church*, p. 79.

8. H. H. Rowley, *The Unity of the Bible*, pp. 98–100. The Westminster Press, 1955.

9. Gregory Dix, *Jew and Greek: A Study in the Primitive Church*, p. 56. The Dacre Press, A. & C. Black, Ltd., London, 1953.

10. Winfred E. Garrison, *A Protestant Manifesto*, p. 95. Abingdon Press, 1952.

11. Hans Lietzmann, *The Founding of the Church Universal*, p. 51. Charles Scribner's Sons, 1950.

12. This is the conclusion of Prof. Markus Barth, of the Federated Theological Faculty of the University of Chicago, in a recent study of I Corinthians entitled " A Chapter on the Church — the Body of Christ," in *Interpretation*, April, 1958.

13. The first quotation is from an article by John Knox in *Religion in Life*, Winter, 1957–1958, p. 54; the second is from Knox, *op. cit.*, p. 148.

14. *The Christian Century*, April 27, 1947, p. 525.

15. *Interpretation*, July, 1949, p. 278.

16. William Neil, *The Rediscovery of the Bible*, p. 114. Harper & Brothers, 1954.

17. Claude Welch, *The Reality of the Church*, p. 165. Charles Scribner's Sons, 1958.

18. Revised edition. The Bethany Press, 1955.

19. Karl Adam, *op. cit.*, pp. 84–85, 92.

20. This has been amply and ably proved by Floyd V. Filson in his book *Which Books Belong in the Bible?* The Westminster Press, 1957.

21. Charles Boyer, *op. cit.*

22. Knox, *op. cit.*, pp. 42, 43.

Chapter III

1. See: Hans Lietzmann, *op. cit.*, and *The Beginnings of the Christian Church*, Lutterworth Press, London, revised, 1949; Edgar J. Goodspeed, *A History of Early Christian Literature*, University of Chicago Press, 1942; Cyril C. Richardson, editor, *Early Christian Fathers* (Library of Christian Classics, Vol. I),The Westminster Press, 1953; Jean Danielou, *The Bible and the Liturgy*, University of Notre Dame Press, 1956.

2. Philip Schaff, *The History of the Christian Church,* Vol. II, p. 121. Charles Scribner's Sons, 1883. Quotations from this book are used by permission.

3. Niebuhr and Williams, *op. cit.*

4. See Ignatius' letters to *The Ephesians,* ch. 5; to *The Magnesians,* chs. 6 and 7; to *The Philadelphians,* ch. 7; and to *The Smyrnaeans,* ch. 9.

5. Philip Schaff, *op. cit.,* p. 161.

6. Andrew C. Zenos, *Compendium of Church History,* p. 61. Presbyterian Board of Publication and Sabbath-School Work, 1896.

7. See Niebuhr and Williams, *op. cit.,* Ch. III, p. 66.

8. *Ibid.,* Ch. II, p. 37.

9. Cf. James Hastings Nichols, *Primer for Protestants,* pp. 28 ff. Association Press, 1947.

10. See William D. Maxwell, *An Outline of Christian Worship.* Oxford University Press, London and New York, revised, 1945.

11. Oscar Cullmann, *Early Christian Worship,* p. 8. Henry Regnery Company, 1953.

12. *Ibid.,* p. 16.

13. Knox, *op. cit.,* p. 16.

14. Schaff, *op. cit.,* pp. 426–427.

15. Garrison, *The Quest and Character of a United Church,* p. 112.

16. Schaff, *op. cit.,* p. 173.

17. Niebuhr and Williams, *op. cit.,* pp. 75–76.

18. Danielou, *op. cit.*

CHAPTER IV

1. David Schaff, *The Creeds of Christendom.* Sixth edition. Vol. I, p. 204. Harper & Brothers, 1931.

2. Cf. *A Protestant Manifesto,* by Winfred E. Garrison, who gives a significant interpretation of Protestantism by considering beliefs (1) common to all great religions, (2) common to all Christians, (3) distinctively Protestant, (4) alien to the Protestant spirit, and (5) denied by Protestants.

3. Cited by James Hastings Nichols in *Primer for Protestants,* p. 65.

4. Juniper B. Carol, *Fundamentals of Mariology,* p. 5. Benziger Brothers, 1956. Quotations from this book are used by permission.

5. An English translation of these Decrees is given in Appendix I,

pp. 165 ff., of *The Vatican Revolution,* by Geddes MacGregor. The quotation that follows immediately is from that book. A translation may also be found in Winthrop S. Hudson's *Understanding Roman Catholicism,* Ch. II (The Westminster Press, 1959).

6. Cited by Kerr, *op. cit.,* pp. 20–21.

7. Gerard Philips, *The Role of the Laity in the Church,* p. 173. Fides Publishers, 1956.

8. Carol, *op. cit.*

9. Giovanni Miegge, *The Virgin Mary; The Roman Catholic Marian Doctrine.* The Westminster Press, 1956.

10. Statement of an archbishop, quoted by Karl Heim, *Spirit and Truth,* p. 148. Lutterworth Press, London, 1935.

11. John F. Sullivan, *The Externals of the Catholic Church,* p. 79. P. J. Kenedy & Sons, 1951. Quotations from this book are used by permission.

12. Thomas V. Liske, *Effective Preaching,* p. 197. The Macmillan Company, 1951.

13. Thomas Dubay, *The Seminary Rule,* p. 11. The Newman Press, 1954.

14. Wilhelm Pauck, *The Heritage of the Reformation,* p. 120. The Beacon Press, Inc., 1950.

15. Karl Heim, *op. cit.,* pp. 99, 101.

16. Sullivan, *op. cit.,* p. 217.

17. *Ibid.,* p. 219.

18. *Ibid.,* pp. 229, 231.

19. *Ibid.,* pp. 85–86, 92.

20. *Ibid.,* p. 268.

21. *Ibid.,* p. 269.

22. *Ibid.,* p. 274.

23. *Ibid.,* pp. 324–325.

24. *Ibid.,* p. 344.

24a. See Louis Bouyer, *Liturgical Piety.* University of Notre Dame Press, 1955.

24b. Garrison, in *A Protestant Manifesto* (pp. 62 ff., 136 ff., and 161 ff.), evaluates this subject from the viewpoint of Protestant beliefs.

25. Karl Heim, *op. cit.,* p. 134.

26. Sullivan, *op. cit.,* p. 376.

26a. Paul Blanshard, *American Freedom and Catholic Power,* p. 49. The Beacon Press, Inc., revised, 1958.

26b. Emmett McLoughlin, *People's Padre*, pp. 77–80. The Beacon Press, Inc., 1954.

27. Benziger Brothers, 1952.

28. Quoted by James Hastings Nichols in *Democracy and the Churches*, p. 57. The Westminster Press, 1951.

29. John A. Ryan and Francis J. Boland, *Catholic Principles of Politics*, p. 300. The Macmillan Company. Copyright, 1922, 1940, by the National Catholic Welfare Conference. Quotations from this book are used by permission of The Macmillan Company.

30. Quoted by Pauck, *op. cit.*, p. 193.

31. Philips, *op. cit.*

32. Ryan and Boland, *op. cit.*

33. Redden and Ryan, *Freedom Through Education*. Bruce Publishing Co., 1944.

34. See Henry Davis, *Moral and Pastoral Theology*, pp. 130 ff., Sheed & Ward, Inc., 1952; and Heribert Jone and Urban Adelman, *Moral Theology*, pp. 272–273, The Newman Press, 1955.

35. Jone and Adelman, *ibid.*, p. 89.

36. *Ibid.*

37. Charles J. McFadden, *Medical Ethics for Nurses*. F. A. Davis, 1946.

38. Francis J. Connell, *Morals in Politics and Professions: A Guide for Catholics in Public Life*. The Newman Press, 1946. Quotations from this book are used by permission.

39. Jone and Adelman, *op. cit.*, pp. 145–161; 238–239; 534–542.

40. *Ibid.*, p. 158.

41. *Ibid.*, p. 157.

42. See *At Your Ease in the Catholic Church*, by Mary Perkins, pp. 11–14, Sheed & Ward, Inc., 1938; and McFadden, *op. cit.*, pp. 314–315.

43. Liske, *op. cit.*

44. Cited by McLoughlin, *op. cit.*, pp. 257–258.

45. See Nichols, *Democracy and the Churches*, pp. 112 ff., 131 ff., 158 ff., for comparison of the motivations behind Protestant and Roman Catholic churches in organizing church societies of various kinds.

46. McLoughlin, *op. cit.*

47. Heim, *op. cit.*, p. 151.

Chapter V

1. Winfred E. Garrison, *Catholicism and the American Mind,* pp. 159 ff., Willett, Clark & Company, 1928; Nichols, *Primer for Protestants,* p. 70, footnote; and Nichols, *Democracy and the Churches,* p. 31, footnote.

2. See "The Bellarmine-Jefferson Legend," in *Papers of the American Society of Church History,* Second Series, Vol. VIII, 1928. An excellent summary of David S. Schaff's paper may be found in Garrison, *Catholicism and the American Mind,* pp. 167 ff.

3. Ryan and Boland, *op. cit.,* p. 84.

4. Nichols, *Democracy and the Churches,* p. 26.

5. *Ibid.,* p. 28.

6. Leo Pfeffer, *Church, State and Freedom,* p. 119. The Beacon Press, Inc., 1953.

7. Garrison, *A Protestant Manifesto,* p. 198.

8. For an English translation of the encyclical and *Syllabus,* see Anne Fremantle, editor, *The Papal Encyclicals,* A Mentor Book, 1956, pp. 135–152. The *Syllabus* is summarized and analyzed by Nichols in *Democracy and the Churches,* pp. 94–100.

9. The English title of this encyclical is *The Christian Constitution of States.* The English translation of it may be found in Ryan and Boland, *op. cit.,* Ch. XXII; and in Winthrop S. Hudson, *Understanding Roman Catholicism,* Ch. III.

10. Anne Fremantle, *op. cit.,* pp. 136–137.

11. Nichols, *Democracy and the Churches,* p. 92.

12. *Ibid.,* p. 95.

13. Fremantle, *op. cit.,* p. 152.

14. *Ibid.,* p. 150.

15. Nichols, *Democracy and the Churches,* p. 100.

16. Ryan and Boland, *op. cit.,* p. 294.

17. *Ibid.,* pp. 294–295.

18. *Ibid.,* p. 299.

19. *Ibid.,* p. 285.

19a. The definition of what is meant by the " general welfare " or the " common good " is one main thing that distinguishes the Roman Catholic view from the Protestant view of religious liberty. For an explanation of this crucial point as it emerges in such Roman Catholic writers as Jacques Maritain, J. Courtney Murray, and John A.

Ryan, see "Religion and Civil Liberty in the Roman Catholic Tradition," by Winfred E. Garrison in *Church History*, Vol. XV, No. 3, October, 1946.

20. Nichols, *Democracy and the Churches*, p. 276.

21. *Ibid.*, pp. 276–277, 278.

22. *Ibid.*, pp. 96–97.

23. Ryan and Boland, *op. cit.*, p. 289.

24. *Ibid.*, p. 288.

25. *Ibid.*

26. *Ibid.*

27. *Ibid.*, p. 289.

28. *Ibid.*, p. 290.

29. *Ibid.*, pp. 299, 300

30. *Ibid.*, p. 298.

31. *Ibid.*, p. 286.

32. *Ibid.*

33. *Ibid.*

34. *Ibid.*, p. 300.

35. *Ibid.*, p. 293.

36. *Ibid.*, p. 294.

37. See Garrison, *Catholicism and the American Mind*, pp. 190–191.

38. Ryan and Boland, *op. cit.*, p. 289.

39. Nichols, *Democracy and the Churches*, p. 97.

40. Quoted by Blanshard, *American Freedom and Catholic Power*, 1958 edition, p. 59.

41. *Church and State*, October, 1957, p. 5.

41a. Bernard Wall, *The Vatican Story*, p. 131. Harper & Brothers, 1956.

42. *San Francisco Chronicle*, October 15, 1958.

43. *San Francisco Chronicle*, October 25, 1958. See also the article "The Papal Election and American Law," by Paul Blanshard in *The Christian Century*, November 19, 1958, pp. 1331 ff., for a full discussion of this aspect of the problem.

44. Francis J. Connell, *op. cit.*, pp. 12–13.

45. *Ibid.*, p. 156.

46. Ryan and Boland, *op. cit.*, Ch. XXIII.

46a. Bernard Wall, *op. cit.*, pp. 138, 139.

47. Quoted by Nichols in *Democracy and the Churches,* pp. 87–88.

48. Liberal quotations from this encyclical and other details concerning Catholic educational policies may be found in Stanley I. Stuber's *Primer on Roman Catholicism for Protestants,* Ch. 19. Association Press, 1953.

49. Quoted by J. M. Dawson, *Separate Church and State Now,* p. 60. Richard R. Smith, 1948.

50. The full-length original article appeared in *The Homiletic and Pastoral Review* of October, 1957.

51. *Church and State,* November, 1958, p. 4.

52. The address of the Fund for the Republic is 60 East 42d Street, New York 17, New York.

53. The organ of Protestants and Other Americans United for Separation of Church and State (POAU), 1633 Massachusetts Avenue, N. W., Washington 6, D. C. A careful study of the whole subject of Roman Catholic and public schools, including the phase of the subject just concluded, may also be found in Blanshard, *American Freedom and Catholic Power,* Ch. 5.

54. Cited by Dawson, *op. cit.,* p. 42.

55. See R. C. Mortimer, *Western Canon Law,* University of California Press, 1953.

56. *The Catholic Encyclopedia,* Vol. XIV, p. 251, c, d.

57. McLoughlin, *op. cit.,* pp. 12–13.

58. Connell, *op. cit.,* pp. 17, 33.

59. Items 67, 68, 69, 70, 73, 74 of *The Syllabus of Errors* declare that ecclesiastical courts, and not civil courts, have jurisdiction over marriages and divorce.

60. According to the *Syllabus,* the church has an " innate and legitimate right of acquiring and possessing property " (item 26) and civil governments may not suppress religious orders or take over the control of their property and revenues (item 53).

61. Nichols, *Democracy and the Churches,* p. 98.

62. Connell, *op. cit.,* pp. 109–110.

63. *Ibid.,* pp. 151, 153.

64. McFadden, *op. cit.,* p. 203.

65. *Ibid.,* p. 339.

66. *Ibid.,* p. 348.

67. Cecil John Cadoux, *Catholicism and Christianity,* pp. 453–454.

Dial Press, Inc., 1929. The documented facts submitted to substantiate this statement may be found on pp. 431 ff. See also Kerr, *op. cit.,* pp. 67–207.

68. Cadoux, *op. cit.,* pp. 482 ff. See also R. C. Mortimer, *op. cit.* He describes these forgeries and shows that they had an enormous influence upon the development of the Catholic canon law.

69. Kerr, *op. cit.,* pp. 271 ff., where supporting data for this statement are found. See also Cadoux, *op. cit.,* pp. 483 ff.

70. Cited by Cadoux, *op. cit.,* p. 482.

71. *Ibid.,* p. 508.

72. Kerr, *op. cit.,* pp. 301 ff.

73. *Ibid.,* pp. 10–11.

74. For documented facts about misstatements in the advertisements of the Knights of Columbus, which they refused to correct, see *The Christian Century,* August 10, 1955, p. 926; an instance of a mangled quotation; *Church and State,* July and September, 1955; and Paul Blanshard, *American Freedom and Catholic Power,* pp. 296 ff.

For facts showing how Roman Catholics rewrite history for their own ends, see Garrison, *Catholicism and the American Mind,* Ch. VIII; Nichols, *Primer for Protestants,* p. 70; and Paul Blanshard, *American Freedom and Catholic Power,* pp. 239 ff.

For facts showing how the Vatican manages truth for its own ends and engages in double talk, see Blanshard, *Communism, Democracy and Catholic Power,* Ch. X, The Beacon Press, Inc., 1951.

For facts about Roman Catholic intrigues, subtlety, etc., in world politics, see George P. Howard, *Religious Liberty in Latin America,* The Westminster Press, 1944; Avro Manhattan, *The Vatican in World Politics,* Gaer Associates, Inc., 1949; and Nichols, *Democracy and the Churches,* Chs. VI and VII.

CHAPTER VI

1. Thomas Sugrue, *A Catholic Speaks His Mind on America's Religious Conflict,* pp. 31, 32. Harper & Brothers, 1952.

2. Blanshard, *American Freedom and Catholic Power,* Revised.

3. *The Christian Century,* July 9, 1958, p. 807.

4. Article reprinted in *Catholicism in America,* p. 83. Harcourt, Brace and Company, Inc., 1953.

5. *Ibid.,* p. 89.

6. Nichols, *Democracy and the Churches,* p. 103. The authorities

quoted by Nichols are: Liguori, *Praxis confessarii,* Capit. primum, paragraph II, circa medici officium, 8, 9; Koch-Preuss, *Handbook of Moral Theology* (B. Herder Book Company, 1919–1925), Vol. II, pp. 164, 165; and McHugh and Callan, *Moral Theology* (Joseph F. Wagner, Inc., 1929–1930), Vol. II, p. 703.

7. *Church and State,* October, 1958, p. 1.

8. *The Christian Century,* April 14, 1954, p. 461.

9. *Ibid.,* February 13, 1957, pp. 189–190.

10. *Ibid.,* July 27, 1955, pp. 863 ff.

11. See Nichols, *Democracy and the Churches,* pp. 255–266.

CHAPTER VII

1. *Interpretation,* April, 1958, " A Chapter on the Church — the Body of Christ," pp. 131 ff.

Selected Bibliography

I. On Protestantism

Anderson, William K., editor, *Protestantism: A Symposium.* The Commission on Ministerial Training, The Methodist Church, 1944.

Arndt, Elmer J. F., editor, *The Heritage of Protestantism.* Richard R. Smith, Inc., 1950.

Bach, Marcus, *Report to Protestants.* The Bobbs-Merrill Company, Inc., 1948.

Bainton, Roland H., *The Reformation of the Sixteenth Century.* The Beacon Press, Inc., 1952.

Batten, J. Minton, *Protestant Background in History.* Abingdon Press, 1951.

Bouyer, Louis, *The Spirit and Forms of Protestantism.* The Newman Press, 1957. (Author is a Roman Catholic.)

Brauer, Jerald C., *Protestantism in America.* The Westminster Press, 1953.

Crapullo, George A., *The Protestant Faith* (pamphlet). Abingdon Press, 1957.

Dale, R. W., *Protestantism: Its Ultimate Principle.* Milton Publishing League, London, 1877.

Dillenberger, John, and Welch, Claude, *Protestant Christianity.* Charles Scribner's Sons, 1954.

Ferm, Virgilius, *A Protestant Dictionary.* Philosophical Library, Inc., 1951.

Ferm, Virgilius, editor, *The Protestant Credo.* Philosophical Library, Inc., 1953.

Flew, R. Newton, and others, *The Catholicity of Protestantism.* Lutterworth Press, London, 1951.

Garrison, Winfred E., *A Protestant Manifesto*. Abingdon Press, 1952.

Hall, Clarence W., and Holisher, Desider, *Protestant Panorama*. Farrar, Straus & Young, Inc., 1951.

Hamilton, Kenneth, *The Protestant Way*. Essential Books, 1956.

Hardon, John A., *The Protestant Churches of America*. The Newman Press, 1957. (Author is a Roman Catholic.)

Heim, Karl, *Spirit and Truth*. Lutterworth Press, London, 1935.

Jenney, Ray Freeman, *I Am a Protestant*. The Bobbs-Merrill Company, Inc., 1951.

Kerr, Hugh T., Jr., *Positive Protestantism*. The Westminster Press, 1950.

Long, E. L., *Conscience and Compromise: An Approach to Protestant Casuistry*. The Westminster Press, 1954.

Moehlman, Conrad H., *Protestantism's Challenge*. Harper & Brothers, 1939.

Morrison, Charles Clayton, *Can Protestantism Win America?* Harper & Brothers, 1948.

Munro, Harry C., *Be Glad You Are a Protestant*. The Bethany Press, 1948.

Munro, Harry C., *Protestant Nurture*. Prentice-Hall, Inc., 1956.

Nichols, James Hastings, *Primer for Protestants*. Association Press, 1947.

Parker, T. V., *American Protestantism: An Appraisal*. Philosophical Library, Inc., 1956.

Pauck, Wilhelm, *The Heritage of the Reformation*. The Beacon Press, Inc., 1950.

Reynolds, Arthur G., *What's the Difference in Protestant and Roman Catholic Belief?* (booklet). Abingdon Press, 1954.

Roy, Ralph L., *Apostles of Discord*. The Beacon Press, Inc., 1953.

Schaff, David S., *Our Fathers' Faith and Ours*. G. P. Putnam's Sons, 1928.

Sweet, William Warren, *American Culture and Religion*. Southern Methodist University Press, 1951.

Tillich, Paul, *The Protestant Era*. University of Chicago Press, 1948.

Underwood, Kenneth Wilson, *Protestant and Catholic: Religious and Social Interaction in an Industrial Community*. The Beacon Press, Inc., 1957.

Union Theological Seminary (Richmond) faculty, *Our Protestant Heritage* (a symposium). John Knox Press, 1948.

Whale, J. S., *The Protestant Tradition*. Cambridge University Press, Cambridge, 1948.

Wilburn, Ralph G., *The Prophetic Voice in Protestant Christianity*. The Bethany Press, 1956.

Wright, C. H. H., and Neil, C., editors, *The Protestant Dictionary*. The Harrison Trust, London, 1933.

II. On Religious Freedom

Allred, Vincent C., *The Legal Status of the Ante-Nuptial Promise Before Marriage*. The National Catholic Welfare Conference, 1952. (Presents the Roman Catholic viewpoint.)

Bainton, Roland H., *The Travail of Religious Liberty*. The Westminster Press, 1951.

Bates, M. Searles, *Religious Liberty: An Inquiry*. International Missionary Council, 1945.

Blanshard, Paul, *The Right to Read*. The Beacon Press, Inc., 1955.

Bready, J. Wesley, *This Freedom: Whence?* American Tract Society, 1942.

Cuninggim, Merrimon, *Freedom's Holy Light*. Harper & Brothers, 1955.

Davies, Alfred Mervyn, *Foundations of American Freedom*. Abingdon Press, 1955.

Davis, Elmer H., *But We Were Born Free!* The Bobbs-Merrill Company, Inc., 1954.

Howard, George P., *Religious Liberty in Latin America*. The Westminster Press, 1944.

McKeon, Richard, and others, *The Freedom to Read*. R. R. Bowker Company, 1957.

Miegge, Giovanni, *Religious Liberty*. Association Press, 1957.

Nichols, James Hastings, *Democracy and the Churches*. The Westminster Press, 1951.

Northcott, Cecil, *Religious Liberty*. The Macmillan Company, 1949.

Ruffini, Francisco, *Religious Liberty*. G. P. Putnam's Sons, 1912.

Trueblood, Elton, *Declaration of Freedom*. Harper & Brothers, 1955.

III. On Church and State

Bennett, John C., *The Christian as Citizen*. Association Press, 1955.

Bodo, John R., *The Protestant Clergy and Public Issues, 1912–1948*. Princeton University Press, 1954.

Butts, R. Freeman, *The American Tradition in Religion and Education*. The Beacon Press, Inc., 1950.

Cullmann, Oscar, *The State in the New Testament*. Charles Scribner's Sons, 1956.

Dawson, James M., *Separate Church and State Now*. Richard R. Smith, Inc., 1948.

Ehler, Sidney Z., and others, *Church and State Through the Centuries*. The Newman Press, 1954. (Presents the Roman Catholic viewpoint.)

Garbett, Cyril, *Church and State in England*. The Macmillan Company, 1950.

Greene, Evarts B., *Church and State*. National Foundation Press, 1947.

Gsovski, Vladimir, editor, *Church and State Behind the Iron Curtain (in Satellite Europe)*. Frederick A. Praeger, Inc., 1955.

Hudson, W. S., *The Great Tradition of the American Churches*. Harper & Brothers, 1953.

Johnson, Alvin W., and Yost, Frank H., *Separation of Church and State*. University of Minnesota Press, 1948.

Mochlman, Conrad H., *The Wall of Separation Between Church and State*. The Beacon Press, Inc., 1951.

Mortimer, R. C., *Western Canon Law*. University of California Press, 1953.

Muehl, William, *Politics for Christians*. Association Press, 1956.

Nelson, Claude D., *Church and State* (booklet). National Council of Churches of Christ in the U.S.A., 1953.

O'Neill, James M., *Religion and Education Under the Constitution*. Harper & Brothers, 1949. (Presents the Roman Catholic viewpoint.)

Parker, T. M., *Christianity and the State in the Light of History*. Harper & Brothers, 1955.

Persons, Stow, *Free Religion: An American Faith*. Yale University Press, 1947.

Pfeffer, Leo, *Church, State and Freedom*. The Beacon Press, Inc., 1953.

Ruff, G. Elson, *The Dilemma of Church and State*. Muhlenberg Press, 1954.

Schaff, Philip, *Church and State in the United States*. Charles Scribner's Sons, 1888.

Stokes, Anson Phelps, *Church and State in the United States,* 3 vols. Harper & Brothers, 1950.

Torpey, William George, *Judicial Doctrines of Religious Rights in America.* University of North Carolina Press, 1948.

Van Dusen, Henry P., and others, *Church and State in the Modern World* (a symposium). Harper & Brothers, 1937.

IV. On Roman Catholicism

A. By Non-Catholic Writers

Bartoli, Giorgio, *The Primitive Church and the Primacy of Rome.* Hodder & Stoughton, Ltd., London, 1909.

Bernhart, Joseph, *The Vatican as a World Power.* Longman's, Green & Co., Inc., 1939.

Blanshard, Paul, *American Freedom and Catholic Power.* The Beacon Press, Inc., 1949. Revised, 1958.

Blanshard, Paul, *Communism, Democracy and Catholic Power.* The Beacon Press, Inc., 1951.

Blanshard, Paul, *The Irish and Catholic Power.* The Beacon Press, Inc., 1953.

Burn-Murdoch, Hector, *The Development of the Papacy.* Frederick A. Praeger, Inc., 1954.

Cadoux, C. J., *Catholicism and Christianity.* Dial Press, Inc., 1929.

Cadoux, C. J., *Roman Catholicism and Freedom.* Independent Press, Ltd., London, 1936.

Delpech, James, *The Oppression of Protestants in Spain.* The Beacon Press, Inc., 1955.

Domenica, Angela di, *A Protestant Primer on Roman Catholicism* (booklet). The Author, 1949.

Dostoevsky, Fyodor, *The Grand Inquisitor.* Association Press, 1948.

Elderkin, George W., *The Roman Catholic Problem.* Vantage Press, Inc., 1954.

Fey, Harold E., *Can Catholicism Win America?* (pamphlet containing eight articles from *The Christian Century,* 1944–1945). The Christian Century.

Garrison, Winfred E., *Catholicism and the American Mind.* Willett, Clark & Company, 1928.

Gohdes, C. B. *Does the Modern Papacy Require a New Evaluation?* Lutheran Literary Board, 1940.

Herberg, Will, *Protestant, Catholic, Jew*. Doubleday & Co., Inc., 1955.

Infallible Fallacies: An Anglican Reply to Roman Catholic Arguments (pamphlet). Morehouse-Gorham Co., Inc., 1953.

Johnson, Frederick A., *Christ and Catholicism*. Vantage Press, Inc., 1954. (Presents a layman's viewpoint.)

Kerr, William Shaw, *A Handbook on the Papacy*. Philosophical Library, Inc., 1951.

Koenker, Ernest B., *The Liturgical Renaissance in the Roman Catholic Church*. University of Chicago Press, 1954.

MacGregor, Geddes, *The Vatican Revolution*. The Beacon Press, Inc., 1957.

Manhattan, Avro, *The Catholic Church Against the 20th Century*. A. Watts & Co., Ltd., London, 1947.

Manhattan, Avro, *The Vatican in World Politics*. Gaer Associates, Inc., 1949.

McKnight, John P., *The Papacy*. Rinehart and Company, Inc., 1952.

McLoughlin, Emmett, *People's Padre*. The Beacon Press, Inc., 1954. (This book was written by an ex-priest.)

Miegge, Giovanni, *The Virgin Mary: The Roman Catholic Marian Doctrine*. The Westminster Press, 1956.

Ranke, Leopold, *The Ecclesiastical and Political History of the Popes*, 3 vols. John Murray, Ltd., London, 1841.

Scott, C. Anderson, *Romanism and the Gospel*. The Westminster Press, 1946.

Seldes, George, *The Catholic Crisis*. Julian Messner, Inc., 1939.

Seldes, George, *The Vatican: Yesterday, Today, Tomorrow*. Harper & Brothers, 1934.

Skydsgaard, K. E., *One in Christ*. Muhlenberg Press, 1957.

Stuber, Stanley I., *Primer on Roman Catholicism for Protestants*. Association Press, 1953.

Winch, Raymond, and Bennett, Victor, *The Assumption of Our Lady and Catholic Theology*. Society for Promoting Christian Knowledge, London, 1950.

B. By Roman Catholic Writers

Adam, Karl, *One and Holy*. Sheed & Ward, Inc., 1951.

Adam, Karl, *The Spirit of Catholicism*. An Image Book (Doubleday & Co., Inc.), 1954.

Bouyer, Louis, *Liturgical Piety*. University of Notre Dame Press, 1955.

Boyer, Charles, *One Shepherd: The Problem of Christian Reunion*. P. J. Kenedy & Sons, 1952.

Brunini, John G., *Whereon to Stand*. Harper & Brothers, 1946.

Carol, Juniper B., *Fundamentals of Mariology*. Benziger Brothers, 1956.

Catholicism in America (articles from The Commonweal). Harcourt, Brace and Company, Inc., 1953.

Christopher, J. P., editor, *The Raccolta: A Manual of Indulgences Prayers and Devotions Enriched with Indulgences,* official edition. Benziger Brothers, 1952.

Connell, Francis J., *Freedom of Worship: The Catholic Position*. The Newman Press, 1946.

Connell, Francis J., *Morals in Politics and Professions*. The Newman Press, 1946.

Danielou, Jean, *The Bible and the Liturgy*. University of Notre Dame Press, 1956.

Davis, Henry, *Summary of Moral and Pastoral Theology*. Sheed & Ward, Inc., 1952.

Dubay, Thomas, *The Seminary Rule*. The Newman Press, 1954.

Ellard, Gerald, *Christian Life and Worship*. Bruce Publishing Co., 1956.

Ellis, John Tracy, *American Catholicism*. University of Chicago Press, 1955.

Graham, Aelred, *Catholicism and the World Today*. David McKay Company, Inc., 1952.

Gurian, Walderman, and Fitzsimons, M. A., editors, *The Catholic Church in World Affairs*. University of Notre Dame Press, 1954.

Harrison, Martin, *Credo: A Practical Guide to the Catholic Life*. Henry Regnery Company, 1954.

Healy, Edwin F., *Medical Ethics*. Loyola University Press, 1956.

Jone, Heribert, and Adelman, Urban, *Moral Theology*. The Newman Press, 1955.

Journet, Charles, *The Primacy of Peter* (reply to Cullmann's book on Peter). The Newman Press, 1954.

Kane, John J., *Catholic-Protestant Conflicts in America*. Henry Regnery Company, 1955.

Kelly, Virgil A., *The Truth About Catholics*. Dial Press, Inc., 1954.

La Farge, John, *A Report on American Jesuits*. Farrar, Straus & Cudahy, Inc., 1956.

Lynskey, Elizabeth, *The Government of the Catholic Church*. P. J. Kenedy & Sons, 1952.

Manual of Prayers for Use of Catholic Laity, A, new edition. John Murphy Company, 1930.

Masure, Eugene, *Parish Priest*. Fides Publishers, 1955.

Maynard, Theodore, *The Catholic Church and the American Idea*. Appleton-Century-Crofts, Inc., 1953.

Maynard, Theodore, *The Catholic Way*. Appleton-Century-Crofts, Inc., 1952.

Maynard, Theodore, *St. Ignatius and the Jesuits*. P. J. Kenedy & Sons, 1956.

McFadden, Charles J., *Medical Ethics for Nurses*. F. A. Davis Company, 1947.

Neuvecelle, Jean, *The Vatican*. Criterion Books, 1955.

O'Brien, John A., *Winning Converts*. P. J. Kenedy & Sons, 1948.

O'Neill, James M., *Catholicism and American Freedom* (Roman Catholic reply to Paul Blanshard). Harper & Brothers, 1952.

Perkins, Mary, *At Your Ease in the Catholic Church*. Sheed & Ward, Inc., 1938.

Philips, Gerard, *The Role of the Laity in the Church*. Fides Publishers, 1956.

Putz, Louis J., editor, *The Catholic Church in the U.S.A.* Fides Publishers, 1956.

Redden, John D., and Ryan, Francis A., *Freedom Through Education*. Bruce Publishing Co., 1944.

Ryan, John A., *The Catholic Church and the Citizen*. The Macmillan Company, 1928.

Ryan, John A., and Boland, Francis J., *Catholic Principles of Politics*. The Macmillan Company, 1940.

Schroeder, H. J., *Disciplinary Decrees of the General Councils*. B. Herder Book Company, 1937.

Smith, George D., *The Teaching of the Catholic Church*, 2 vols. The Macmillan Company, 1949.

Sugrue, Thomas, *A Catholic Speaks His Mind on America's Religious Conflict*. Harper & Brothers, 1952.

Sullivan, J. F., *The Externals of the Catholic Church*, revised by John C. O'Leary. P. J. Kenedy & Sons, 1951.

Tavard, George Henry, *The Catholic Approach to Protestantism*. Harper & Brothers, 1955.

Van de Pol, W. H., *The Christian Dilemma*. Philosophical Library, Inc., 1952.

Wall, Bernard, *The Vatican Story*. Harper & Brothers, 1956.

White, Victor, *God the Unknown*. Harper & Brothers, 1956.

Williams, Michael, *The Catholic Church in Action*. The Macmillan Company, 1934.

Woywood, Stanislaus, *A Practical Commentary on the Code of Canon Law*, revised by Callistus Smith. Joseph F. Wagner, Inc., 1952.

V. On Papal Encyclicals and Documents

Cheney, C. R., and Semple, W. H., *Selected Letters of Pope Innocent IV*. Thomas Nelson & Sons, 1953.

Fremantle, Anne, editor, *The Papal Encyclicals*. The New American Library of World Literature, 1956.

Gilson, Étienne, editor, *The Church Speaks to the Modern World: The Social Teaching of Leo XIII*. An Image Book (Doubleday & Co., Inc.), 1954.

Hudson, Winthrop S., *Understanding Roman Catholicism: A Guide to Papal Teaching for Protestants*. The Westminster Press, 1959.

Husslein, Joseph, editor, *Social Wellsprings*, Vols. I and II. Bruce Publishing Co., 1940 and 1942. Volume I is entitled *Fourteen Epochal Documents by Pope Leo XIII;* Volume II is entitled *Eighteen Encyclicals of Social Reconstruction by Pope Pius XI*.

Miller, Raymond J., *Forty Years After: Pius XI and the Social Order*. Radio Replies Press, 1947.

Moody, J. N., *Church and Society: Catholic Social and Political Thought and Movements*. Arts, Inc., 1953.

O'Connor, Daniel A., *Catholic Social Doctrine*. The Newman Press, 1956.

The Pope Speaks: The Words of Pius XII. Harcourt, Brace and Company, Inc., 1940.

Treacy, Gerald C., *Five Great Encyclicals*. The Paulist Press, 1939.

Williams, Melvin J., *Catholic Social Thought*. The Ronald Press Company, 1950.

Woods, Ralph L., editor, *A Treasury of Catholic Thinking*. The Thomas Y. Crowell Co., 1953.

Wynne, John J., *The Great Encyclical Letters of Pope Leo XIII.* Benziger Brothers, 1903.

Yzermans, Vincent A., *Valiant Heralds of Truth: Pius XII and the Arts of Communication.* The Newman Press, 1958.

Yzermans, Vincent A., editor, *All Things in Christ: Encyclicals and Selected Documents of Pius X.* The Newman Press, 1954.

Date Due